THE BOOK OF MARGERY KEMPE

so þat sche schulde callyn hem non abhomynacyon þis & suyt thus
faythfully þe lord in þe schip cordyng & castyng ful benstellyd
& conntentryd sche þey alders muchyng myst helpyn hem &
do what sche wolde and specyally þe woman of london had
most of þ passyon & þ infirmite to whom þo wrttys thus
most besy to helpyn & wforyn for oþ lord loue & be ch-
rite joy wolde had sche non so yet seyyd for th tol yn wmy
at douresy þa sche on of þ cũpany gut hym felaschep to gon
wt yf hym lth & safe sche only for sche myth geton no fe-
talbe to his ese sy for sche toke hir woy to Cantirbury & wold
be hir self alone sory & heuy in mand þ sche had no felaschip
sne þ sche knelb not ye wey woche was up be tymys in ye
morwenyng & cam to a polly manys howle knokkyng at
þ dosty good polly man hogehyd in hys clothyo on sperd &
on botemys cam to þ doy to wetyn hir wille woche pryd
hym yf he had any hors þ he wolde helpyn hir to Cant-
bury & sche wulde qwte hys labour & sche desiryng to do hys
plefaunce in alhy lords name & fulfyllyd hir mtent ledyng
hir to Cantirbury woche had gret joy in allhp lord þ sent
hir helpe & sowlyn in euy nede & thankyd hym w many
a deuout teer w meche sobbyng & wepyng my heud m
euy place þ sche cam in so far al þ it be not wretyn as wel
on zen half ye see as on þo halfe, ow þ wat as on þ lond
blyssyd mote god ben :;

No yeno sate went to london & clad in a cloth of
Canuas yt wey a sekkyn gellep as sche had gon
be sondyn þ se & had sche was comyn in to london
mech pepil knelb hir wel a nobbyn as mech as sche was not
clad as sche wold a bend for defaulte of mony sche desyry
to a gon on knobbynyn to þ tyme þ sche myth a mede so
cheffy albns þar a terche be for hir face, nor wtsondyng
sche dede so sou dissolute psony o supposyng it was a w-
kenue of hymne seydyn þ sche myth esly heryn yn wordyo
m to repref. & þ fals flesch þey zaue no good mete wyn

(See Page 304)

THE BOOK OF
MARGERY KEMPE

1436

A MODERN VERSION BY
W. BUTLER-BOWDON

With an Introduction by
R. W. CHAMBERS
*Quain Professor of English
in University College, London*

JONATHAN CAPE
THIRTY BEDFORD SQUARE
LONDON

FIRST PUBLISHED 1936

JONATHAN CAPE LTD.   30 BEDFORD SQUARE, LONDON
AND 91 WELLINGTON STREET WEST, TORONTO

PRINTED IN GREAT BRITAIN IN THE CITY OF OXFORD
AT THE ALDEN PRESS
PAPER MADE BY JOHN DICKINSON & CO. LTD.
BOUND BY A. W. BAIN & CO. LTD.

CONTENTS

The Chapters shewn in italics are given in the Appendix.

CONTENTS

vi

CONTENTS

CONTENTS

CONTENTS

ix

CONTENTS

CONTENTS

CONTENTS

CONTENTS

INTRODUCTION

The discovery of *The Book of Margery Kempe* is of the very greatest importance for the history of English Literature. The book is a biography, or autobiography, written when kings of the House of Lancaster were on the throne, and we shall find nothing with which we can compare it, even remotely, till, some four generations later, we reach the middle of the Tudor period.

If we would understand how exceptional a document *The Book of Margery Kempe* is, we must remember '1066 and all that'. English prose had made a brave beginning in the Dark Ages, thanks mainly to King Alfred; and during the century and a half which followed the death of that great king, England was leading Europe in the practice of writing in the vernacular. It was Englishmen who first began to write down in their vulgar tongue things which, till then, had been committed to writing only in Latin; so that in the development of English, instead of Latin, as an official language, 'England preceded the nations of Europe by some centuries'. Not only legal documents and sermons and translations, but stirring, if short, story came to be composed in the English tongue. But the Norman Conquest changed all that. In vain had England seemed to be escaping before its time from the Latinized Middle Ages into a new era in which the vernacular would become the literary language of educated people. This was not yet to be, and England was, as it were, dragged forcibly back into the Middle

Ages by the muscular arm of William the Conqueror. England, so far from preceding the other European nations in the use of vernacular prose, began to fall behind them; and, compared with countries like France or Iceland, was in a century or two very much behind indeed. Nevertheless, the decline was not instantaneous; it did not happen catastrophically within a year or two of the Battle of Hastings; the only biography which we know to have been written in the English tongue before that of Margery Kempe was a Life of Wulfstan of Worcester, the one English bishop who managed to retain his see throughout the Conqueror's reign, till his death in the reign of Rufus. Wulfstan's Life was written by his chaplain and chancellor Colman, a generation or more after the Norman Conquest. Yet Latin was rapidly ousting English, and it is significant that this Life has come down to us only in a Latin translation: and so it does not deprive *The Book of Margery Kempe* of its claim to be the first extant biography in the English tongue.

During the later twelfth century, the thirteenth century, and most of the fourteenth century, Latin or Norman-French prose entirely displaced English prose, except for purposes of preaching and devotion. During these centuries the rule holds that 'to save some one's soul, or to improve some one's morals, were seemingly the only motives which could suffice to persuade an Englishman to write his native language, except in verse'. In the Guildhall to-day may be seen the charter, *in English*, in which William the Conqueror promised to the citizens of London the retention of their ancestral privileges. But when we come to the reigns of Edward I, Edward II and Edward III, we find that, despite the flourishing national feeling which expresses itself in contemporary English poetry, the City Merchants and artisans wrote everything in either Latin or French. So England has nothing in original prose narrative to set against the great masterpieces of prose which were being written abroad — the Story of *Burnt Njal*, the *Life of St. Louis*, Froissart's *History*. There is magnificent narrative in Medieval English: Chaucer's *Troilus and Criseyde*, or the amazing story of *Sir Gawayne and the Green Knight*; but these are in verse. In prose we have, of course, the *Voyages and Travels* of Sir John Mandeville, which will often remind us of the more truthful and hardly less exciting voyages and travels undertaken by Margery Kempe to Jerusalem or Rome. But the English Mandeville is merely a translation of an original written in the Low Countries.

And so the great interest of *The Book of Margery Kempe* is, that whilst it no doubt follows precedent in being written from a wish to improve people's morals, it is our first extant prose narrative in English on a large scale: original, not translated, not a mere succession of Chronicle entries, but a continuous biography.

Margery was the daughter of John Burnham, one of the leading citizens of Lynn, at a time when Lynn was one of the leading towns of England. The modern visitor to Lynn will be struck with the large space enclosed within the circuit of its now almost entirely demolished walls, and the long distance he has to go from the centre of the city before he reaches the South Gate. Margery's narrative helps us to imagine this vacant space filled with vanished churches and shrines; the houses of the Black and the Grey, the White and the Austin Friars, of which to-day we can see nothing, save the tower of the Franciscans and the gateway of the Carmelites.

It is noteworthy, that though Margery was born into one of the prosperous families of this prosperous town, her education did not include any instruction in Latin, or, what is much more surprising, French. Of course, Margery had learnt a few words and phrases of Latin from the services of the Church. But during her pilgrimages abroad in later life we find that she had not enough Latin to make even the most rudimentary confession to a priest. She was compelled to confess to an evangelist, who appeared to her in a vision. She said *Benedicite*, and the evangelist replied *Dominus*; we gather that the rest of the conversation was in English. Margery found *bon* to be a useful word, as did the English private soldier between the years 1914 and 1918: *No bon*. But Margery's conversation was, of course, more sanctified than that of Mr. Thomas Atkins: *Bon Christian, pray pur me* would have astonished the keeper of an estaminet as much as did the subaltern who (according to *Punch*) purchased great quantities of food and drink *pour la messe*.

It is natural that our first biography in English should be that of a citizen of Lynn, for the Norfolk towns, to judge from the regulations of their guilds, had been the first in England to abandon the official use of Latin and French. Norfolk was notorious for ignorance of French: as is shown by a passage in *Piers Plowman* (B. text) written when Margery Kempe was a baby. Langland depicts 'Avarice' as being asked by his confessor whether he has ever made restitution, and as replying, Yes, he was once lodged with a company of merchants:

I rose when they were a-rest, and rifled their males.

4

Poor Avarice is reproved for thus betraying, simultaneously, his dishonesty and his ignorance; and he replies:

'I weened rifling were restitution, for I learned never read on book,
And I know no French, in faith, but of the farthest end of Norfolk.'

With Margery Kempe, Capgrave, and the English of its guilds, Lynn, at the farthest end of Norfolk, has an important part to play in the history of English prose.

Nevertheless, *The Book of Margery Kempe* may disappoint and even shock the reader, unless he is careful to ask from it only those things which it can give him.

One of the remarkable discoveries of the last few years has been that of a considerable English religious literature of the fourteenth and fifteenth centuries. Its masterpieces are Hilton's *Scale of Perfection*, *The Cloud of Unknowing*, the *Revelations* of Dame Julian of Norwich, and the translation of *The Mirror of the Life of Christ*, wrongly attributed to St. Bonaventura, and turned into English by Nicholas Love, prior to the same Carthusian house of Mountgrace to which *The Book of Margery Kempe* once belonged. These books of religion had indeed never been lost, and their popularity in medieval times is shown by the fact that they are for the most part extant in a considerable number of manuscripts. But after the Reformation they ceased to attract many English readers. Although some of them were still studied devoutly in the seventeenth century by the English Catholic refugees abroad, they passed out of the body of generally remembered English literature. By historians of English literature they have been almost entirely ignored. But during the past dozen years they have again begun to attract thousands of readers. And when it was announced that *The Book of Margery Kempe* had been discovered, we naturally expected a book of devotion, comparable to *The Scale of Perfection* or the *Revelations* of Dame Julian. Some noble fragments from Margery's book had come down to us. Brief extracts had been combined into a 'short treatise' and printed by Wynkyn de Worde in 1501. Of this little book only one copy had survived, in the University Library of Cambridge, but this, together with some short devotional tracts by other writers, had been edited by that beloved and saintly scholar whom we have recently lost, Edmund Gardner. These fragments from *The Book of Margery Kempe* were enough to arouse great expectations; and to those who had hoped to find a new *Scale of Perfection* Margery's book must be, from certain points of view, painful.

The reader should therefore be warned at the outset that poor Margery is to be classed with those hotels which Baedeker describes as 'variously judged'. You must come to her not expecting too much, and prepared for anything. She was variously judged in her own day; it would seem that her townsfolk were divided into two classes: those who regarded her as something of a saint, and those who were sure she was a good deal of a hypocrite. Most modern readers will probably hesitate to put her into either of these classes. Nevertheless, in fifteenth-century Lynn, it must have taxed the patience of even good-natured Christians to have a friend who, when she heard mirth or melody, was visited with full plenteous and abundant tears of high devotion, with great sobbings and sighings after the bliss of heaven, and cries of 'It is full merry in

Heaven'. The good burgesses of Lynn knew their neighbour Margery chiefly as an unsuccessful brewer and an unsuccessful miller, neither of which callings, with reverence be it spoken, has ever had any particular associations with sanctity. It is impossible not to sympathize with their retort, 'Why speak ye so of the mirth that is in Heaven? Ye know it not, and ye have not been there, no more than we.'

Things might have been easier for Margery, if she had been a recluse. At large, in the world, people found her a nuisance. In a cell, where people could come and speak to her when they wished, and depart when they liked, Margery would have fitted better into medieval life. But that she should wander about, rehearsing tales of scripture, was felt to be irregular.

Yet the novelty of Margery's book lies in the fact that we are not dealing with the revelations of a recluse, but the life of a religious enthusiast remaining in the world. So that the interest of her book is two-fold — that which concerns Margery herself, and that which concerns her relations to her contemporaries.

As to Margery herself: she had come under the influence not only of Hilton's *Scale* and the writings of Richard Rolle of Hampole, but also of the writings of St. Bridget, and this influence must have been increased by her presence in Rome when the celebrations took place over the confirmation of St. Bridget's canonization. What judgment we are to pass upon Margery's own spiritual experiences is a question upon which the present writer is entirely unqualified to speak. There are no doubt plenty of people who will be able and ready to do so, and poor Margery may again become as much a bone of contention as she was five hundred years ago. Students of mysticism, and of psycho-analysis, may dispute whether she really had not read too much of the revelations of St. Bridget.

But when we leave Margery's revelations for the story of her adventures, we can hardly deny that students of English literature and of English history have every reason to be grateful to her. A full discussion of the light she throws upon contemporary life would fill a book at least as long as her own. But the subject may be illustrated by considering what we are told about her interviews with Philip Repington, bishop of Lincoln, and with Thomas Arundel, archbishop of Canterbury.

Philip Repington had been one of the stoutest of Wiclif's supporters at Oxford, and had got into very serious trouble as a Lollard. But, in 1382, he publicly abjured his heresies. From that time on, he remained a pillar of orthodoxy. He was restored to his place in the schools of Oxford; he became abbot of his old monastery of St. Mary, Leicester, and for three years he was Chancellor of the University of Oxford. He was an intimate friend of Henry IV, and very frankly reproved that king for not carrying out the reforms which he had promised, upon his happy entrance into the kingdom of England. Far from resenting this reproof, Henry, after his victory at Shrewsbury, made proclamation through his army that, if there were any servant of the Abbot of Leicester present, he should report himself; immediately a servant came forward, and through him Henry sent the ring from his own finger, to announce to the Lord Philip, abbot of Leicester, that the King lived, and had obtained victory over his enemies, blessed be God.

8

Repington became the King's Confessor, Bishop of Lincoln, and Cardinal.

Repington, then, is a man upon whose character there can never be agreement. That he was an able man is clear; and if a critic chooses to think that he deserted Lollardy and became orthodox either from fear of punishment or hope of reward, I do not see how the critic can be refuted. But you have got to put yourself in the place of contemporaries. There were many people who sympathized with Wiclif's earlier pronouncements, but who were alienated when they saw the lengths to which Wiclif was prepared to go. Wiclif, it must be remembered, came to disapprove of all learning save that of the Scriptures, and would have disendowed, which I think means destroyed, the Universities. Now we have all of us enough toleration to be complacent about schemes of confiscation which failed more than five hundred years ago. But people like Repington had to face a Lollardy which, whatever its beginnings, was growing to be a danger to many things they loved. It is easy to call Repington a renegade, and to say that he was unwilling to sacrifice his career in Church and University. But perhaps there were other things which he was unwilling to sacrifice — what we broadly call civilization.

It was in the presence of this man that Margery Kempe and her husband had found themselves (after waiting three weeks, since at first the Bishop was not at home in his palace). What happened to her can be read in Chapter 15 (p. 60). It is interesting that Repington should have advised Margery to have her contemplations written down; a man so definitely opposed to Lollardy might have been expected to feel doubts about the writing down of a book of religious topics *in English* — a book, moreover, of a dangerously enthusiastic character. The hesitation of the bishop's council as to professing Margery with the mantle and the ring and the white clothes, without better advisement, is quite intelligible. Evidently the bishop's council (and perhaps the bishop himself when he had had time to think things over) were afraid that, if they gave official approval to this wild enthusiast, she might compromise them by her eccentricities. Bishop Repington's past was, after all, not so orthodox that he could afford to be made responsible for any doubtful people. Yet the bishop seems to have taken quite meekly Margery's reproach, 'that he dreadeth more the shames of the world than the perfect love of God'. But he pointed out to her that she was not of his diocese, and suggested that she should go to the Archbishop of Canterbury, Arundel, 'and pray him to grant leave to me, Bishop of Lincoln, for to give the mantle and the ring'. Margery thought that this was a mean subterfuge: 'This cause he feigned, through counsel of his clerks, for they loved not this creature.' Margery made a somewhat truculent answer — 'I will go to my lord of Canterbury with right good will, for other causes and matters which I have to show to his reverence. As for this cause I shall not go, for God will not that I ask *him* thereafter': in other words, her message had been to the Bishop of Lincoln, and she would receive an answer from no one else.

Then she took leave of the Bishop and he gave her twenty-six shillings and eight pence, to buy her clothing with, and for to pray for him.

Bishop Repington of Lincoln must have been a long-suffering and forgiving man. His Lollard enemies called him Rampington, but to Margery he seemed to have ramped as gently as any sucking dove.

So Margery and her husband came to Archbishop Arundel. How she visited him, and how she reproved him for the bad behaviour of his clergy and his household, and how their dalliance continued till the stars appeared in the firmament, will be found in Chapter 16 (p. 65). In justice to Margery and the Archbishop, it must be remembered that 'dalliance' has in Margery's book nothing of its modern meaning of amorous toying. It signifies pious and religious conversation.

Arundel was, of course, a very different man from Repington: a mighty statesman-prelate, of noble birth on his father's side, and of royal birth on his mother's. The gentle way in which he took Margery's reproof must count to his credit.

Indeed, these two interviews of Margery, which, more than five centuries after they took place, have been thus suddenly revealed to us, deserve our consideration. She was a difficult and morbid religious enthusiast. Perhaps harsher terms might justly be used. When this book is published, it will be interesting to see how many of Margery's reviewers will treat her with the forbearance which was shown by these two proud prelates — men of whose forbearance history has had very little good to say. And note how Margery got them both on their weak spot. She charged Philip Repington of Lincoln with want of moral courage: the very thing that his enemies were saying at the time, and historians have said ever since. She charged the high-born Arundel with not rising to the responsibilities of the supreme position to which he had been called. If Margery had tried to 'dally' in this way with two English prelates of the nineteenth or even of the twentieth century, I am not sure that the interview would have gone off so pleasantly. I am reminded of the inscription on a monument to an early nineteenth-century bishop in Exeter Cathedral — I don't remember the bishop's name; only that he was

> A successful exposer of pretence and enthusiasm; indulgent candour sweetened his government.

I think a modern prelate would have exposed the pretence and enthusiasm of Margery Kempe, with more of the candour of, say, the year 1936 than of the indulgence of the year 1414.

These are only two examples, out of scores which might be chosen, of the light which *The Book of Margery Kempe* throws upon the bustling life of the fifteenth century. Margery, like Chaucer's Wife of Bath,

> hadde passed many a straunge streem.

But besides the more usual pilgrimages, to Jerusalem, to Rome, and to St. James of Compostella, which both the Wife of Bath and Margery had made, Margery, as was not surprising in the wife of a citizen of Lynn, travelled also in the Baltic:

> And so they sailed forth to a place which is cleped Strawissownd. If the names of the places be not right written, let no man marvel, for she studied more about contemplation than the names of the places, and he that wrote them had never seen them, and therefore have him excused.

'Strawissownd' is, of course, Stralsund. The great brass of Robert Braunche, in St. Margaret's Church in Lynn, has, I think, its closest counterpart in the brass of Albrecht Hovener at Stralsund. That is only one tiny example of the intercourse between Lynn and the Baltic ports. I remember, some thirty-seven years ago, spending nine hours grovelling on the floor of St. Margaret's Church in Lynn, making a rubbing of the brass of Robert Braunche and his wives, wondering what kind of folk were these wealthy citizens of the great seaport. It is in its answer to a question like that, in the light which it throws upon the life of the fifteenth century, as it was lived in one of the more important English towns, and on the roads from shrine to shrine, and from town to town, that the value of *The Book of Margery Kempe* chiefly consists.

R. W. CHAMBERS

EDITOR'S NOTE

W HEN writing the foreword to someone else's autobiography it is usual to give some information regarding the author which, for modesty or other reasons, he may have omitted from his book. This presupposes a knowledge of, or some acquaintance with, the writer of it. In the case of Margery Kempe, however, a few lines in the *Dictionary of National Biography* are all that was hitherto available. She is therein credited with the authorship of two small books, one lost, the other extant in the form of a single copy, printed in London by Wynkyn de Worde in 1501, and now preserved in the University Library at Cambridge. It is a small book of eight pages and consists of extracts from her autobiography.

This autobiography, lost for several centuries, has now come to light. A manuscript book in my possession, some 250 pages in length, has recently been identified as the missing work. It was at first believed to be the actual original manuscript, begun in 1436, and written by her friend the priest 'from her own tongue', but expert examination has formed the opinion that it is an early copy. The grounds for this are, firstly, that the paper on which it is written was probably made in Holland about 1440, and, secondly, the writer says, at the end of the proem, that 'when he had written a quire, he added a leaf there-to, and then wrote he this proem'.

An inspection of the binding of my MS. shews that

the first quire is a complete one, with no leaf added. So, much as one may regret that the original is still lost, and likely to remain so, the possession of the only existing copy, and that, a fine manuscript one, written so soon after the original, is no small compensation.

The facsimile of a page of it is produced as a frontispiece, the one chosen being that on which Margery Kempe's name appears in full for the only time in the book, and thus provides the evidence of authorship.

An edition, published by the Early English Text Society, is a literal copy of the manuscript. That will meet the demands of experts and scholars, but the archaic spelling and meanings preclude its easy perusal by the ordinary reader.

But, apart from its mystical side, the narrative of her life in England, and her voyages to Palestine, Rome, Germany and elsewhere over five hundred years ago, is so interesting that I am impelled to produce this edition, sufficiently modernized to present no difficulty to anyone. Except to those particularly interested in it, the great amount of mystical matter would probably prove wearisome. Certain chapters, entirely devoted to that subject have therefore been removed from the body of the book and printed as an appendix. This arrangement does not affect the sequence.

This text almost exactly follows the manuscript. Marginal figures and letters show the beginning of each page of the manuscript, and are provided for readers who are inclined to compare the two editions. Except for the spelling, my modernization is slight, and I have not hesitated to keep original words, the meaning of which is obvious.

Words long obsolete, or whose meaning has entirely changed, have been replaced by modern equivalents. For instance, when a horse is described as 'craske and lykand', it has been changed to 'sturdy and gentle'.

Then, if a child were described as 'buxom to its father', a wrong meaning would be conveyed. 'Buxom' at that time meant 'obedient', 'willing' or 'kindly'. It had none of its present meaning of 'bonny' or 'handsome'.

But 'boisterous', a favourite word of Margery's, meant then very much what it means now, so it remains, though, in the case where she uses it to describe a nail at the Crucifixion, I have changed it to 'coarse'.

Her description of herself throughout as a 'creature' is, of course, in humble contradistinction to the Creator.

Place-names are modernized, except in the Second Book, where her own spelling of foreign names is retained in view of her apology for it.

I have kept 'Lynne' throughout, as it is her usual rendering of the name of her native place, though she spells it in several other ways. Its full title was Lynne Bishop, or Bishop's Lynne, until King Henry VIII, in a new charter, renamed it King's Lynn.

The word 'Duche' or 'Dewch' also remains, as it refers to a somewhat indeterminate area covering part of the present Germany, Holland and Belgium.

The names of her friends and acquaintances have not been modernized, because the old form would occur in wills or contemporary documents.

Words shewn in parenthesis are later marginal or interlinear notes in the MS., without provable authority.

A key to the extracts which make up Wynkyn de Worde's little book is given at the end.

EDITOR'S NOTE

I will conclude by expressing my thanks to Miss Hope Emily Allen, who, in the first instance, read the original manuscript and identified the authoress; to Professor Sanford B. Meech, who undertook the transcription and editing of the manuscript for publication by the Early English Text Society; to Dr. C. T. Onions, c.b.e., for the footnotes on pages 137 and 198; and to Mr. Francis Needham for much advice and assistance in the production of this modern version. To all these, I am most grateful. I am further indebted to Professor Meech for lending me his typewritten transcript. From that I drew this work, which he later checked with the original. It would, however, be unfair to him, if, for that reason, he were held accountable for its faults in any way, as, in modernizing, I have sometimes taken my own line, with the responsibilities inherent to that course.

W. Butler-Bowdon

THE BOOK OF MARGERY KEMPE

this boke is of montegracc[1]

[1] See Note A.

A short treatise of a creature set in great pomp and pride of the world, who later was drawn to Our Lord by great poverty, sickness, shames and great reproofs in many divers countries and places, of which tribulations some shall be shewn hereafter, not in the order in which they befell, but as the creature could have mind of them, when they were written. For it was twenty years and more from the time she had forsaken the world and busily cleft unto Our Lord, ere this book was written.

Notwithstanding, this creature had great counsel to have written her tribulations and her feelings, and a White Friar[1] proferred her to write freely, if she would. And she was warned in her spirit that she should not write so soon; and many years after, she was bidden in her spirit to write.

And then it was written first by a man who could neither well write English nor Duch, so it was unable to be read save only by special grace, for there was so much obloquy and slander of this creature that but few men would believe this creature.

So, at the last, a priest was sore moved to write this treatise, and he could not well read it for four years together. Later, at the request of this creature and compelled by his own conscience, he essayed again to read it, and it was much more easy than it was aforetime.

And so he began to write in the year of Our Lord 1436, on the day next after Mary Magdalene, after the information of this creature.

[1] *See* Note J.

CHAPTER 1

W HEN this creature was twenty years of age, or some deal more, she was married to a worshipful burgess (of Lynne) and was with child within a short time, as nature would. And after she had conceived, she was belaboured with great accesses till the child was born and then, what with the labour she had in childing, and the sickness going before, she despaired of her life, weening she might not live. And then she sent for her ghostly father, for she had a thing on her conscience which she had never shewn before that time in all her life. For she was ever hindered by her enemy, the devil, evermore saying to her that whilst she was in good health she needed no confession, but to do penance by herself alone and all should be forgiven, for God is merciful enough. And therefore this creature oftentimes did great penance in fasting on bread and water, and other deeds of alms with devout prayers, save she would not shew that in confession.

And when she was at any time sick or dis-eased, the devil said in her mind that she should be damned because she was not shriven of that default. Wherefore after her child was born, she, not trusting to live, sent for her ghostly father, as is said before, in full will to be shriven of all her lifetime, as near as she could. And when she came to the point for to say that thing which she had so long concealed, her confessor was a little too hasty and began sharply to reprove her, before she had fully said her intent, and so she would no more say for aught he might do. Anon, for the dread she had of damnation on the one side, and his sharp reproving of her on the other side, this creature went out of her mind and was wondrously vexed and laboured with spirits for half a year, eight weeks and odd days.

And in this time she saw, as she thought, devils opening their mouths all inflamed with burning waves of fire, as if they would have swallowed her in, sometimes ramping at her, sometimes threatening her, pulling her and hauling her, night and day during the aforesaid time. Also the devils cried upon her with great threatenings, and bade her that she should forsake Christendom, her faith, and deny her God, His Mother and all the Saints in Heaven, her good works and all good virtues, her father, her mother and all her friends. And so she did. She slandered her husband, her friends and her own self. She said many a wicked word, and many a cruel word; she knew no virtue nor goodness; she desired all wickedness; like as the spirits tempted her to say and do, so she said and did. She would have destroyed herself many a time at their stirrings and have been damned with them in Hell, and in witness thereof, she bit her own hand so violently, that the mark was seen all her life after.

And also she rived the skin on her body against her heart with her nails spitefully, for she had no other instruments, and worse she would have done, but that she was bound and kept with strength day and night so that she might not have her will. And when she had long been laboured in these and many other temptations, so that men weened she should never have escaped or

4b

lived, then on a time as she lay alone and her keepers were from her, Our Merciful Lord Jesus Christ, ever to be trusted, worshipped be His Name, never forsaking His servant in time of need, appeared to His creature who had forsaken Him, in the likeness of a man, most seemly, most beauteous and most amiable that ever might be seen with man's eye, clad in a mantle of purple silk, sitting upon her bedside, looking upon her with so blessed a face that she was strengthened in all her spirit, and said to her these words: —

'Daughter, why hast thou forsaken Me, and I forsook never thee?'

And anon, as He said these words, she saw verily how the air opened as bright as any lightning. And He rose up into the air, not right hastily and quickly, but fair and easily, so that she might well behold Him in the air till it was closed again.

And anon this creature became calmed in her wits and reason, as well as ever she was before, and prayed her husband as soon as he came to her, that she might have the keys of the buttery to take her meat and drink as she had done before. Her maidens and her keepers counselled him that he should deliver her no keys, as they said she would but give away such goods as there were, for she knew not what she said, as they weened.

Nevertheless, her husband ever having tenderness and compassion for her, commanded that they should deliver to her the keys; and she took her meat and drink as her bodily strength would serve her, and knew her friends and her household and all others that came to see how Our Lord Jesus Christ had wrought His grace in

5a

her, so, blessed may He be, Who ever is near in tribulation. When men think He is far from them, He is full near by His grace. Afterwards, this creature did all other occupations as fell to her to do, wisely and soberly enough, save she knew not verily the call of Our Lord.

CHAPTER 2

W<small>HEN</small> this creature had thus graciously come again to
her mind, she thought that she was bound to God and
that she would be His servant. Nevertheless, she would
not leave her pride or her pompous array, which she had
used beforetime, either for her husband, or for any other
man's counsel. Yet she knew full well that men said of
her full much villainy, for she wore gold pipes on her
head, and her hoods, with the tippets, were slashed. Her
cloaks also were slashed and laid with divers colours between the slashes, so that they should be the more staring
to men's sight, and herself the more worshipped.

And when her husband spoke to her to leave her pride,
she answered shrewdly and shortly, and said that she was
come of worthy kindred — he should never have wedded
her — for her father was sometime Mayor of the town of
N . . .[1] and afterwards he was alderman of the High Guild
of the Trinity in N . . . And therefore she would keep the
worship of her kindred whatever any man said.

She had full great envy of her neighbours, that they
should be as well arrayed as she. All her desire was to be
worshipped by the people. She would not take heed of
any chastisement, nor be content with the goods that God
had sent her, as her husband was, but ever desired more
and more.

5b

---

[1] Lynne, now King's Lynn, is evidently referred to. This anonymity is
dropped later on.

Then for pure covetousness, and to maintain her pride, she began to brew, and was one of the greatest brewers in the town of N . . . for three years or four, till she lost much money, for she had never been used thereto. For, though she had ever such good servants, cunning in brewing, yet it would never succeed with them. For when the ale was as fair standing under barm as any man might see, suddenly the barm would fall down, so that all the ale was lost, one brewing after another, so that her servants were ashamed and would not dwell with her.

Then this creature thought how God had punished her aforetime — and she could not take heed — and now again, by the loss of her goods. Then she left and brewed no more.

Then she asked her husband's mercy because she would not follow his counsel aforetime, and she said that her pride and sin were the cause of all her punishing, and that she would amend and that she had trespassed with good will.

Yet she left not the world altogether, for she now bethought herself of a new housewifery. She had a horse-mill. She got herself two good horses and a man to grind men's corn, and thus she trusted to get her living. This enterprise lasted not long, for in a short time after, on Corpus Christi Eve, befell this marvel. This man, being in good health of body, and his two horses sturdy and gentle, had pulled well in the mill beforetime, and now he took one of these horses and put him in the mill as he had done before, and this horse would draw no draught in the mill for anything the man might do. The man was sorry and essayed with all his wits how he should make this horse pull. Sometimes he led him by the head, sometimes

28

he beat him, sometimes he cherished him and all availed not, for he would rather go backward than forward. Then this man set a sharp pair of spurs on his heels and rode on the horse's back to make him pull, and it was never the better. When the man saw it would work in no way, he set up this horse again in the stable, and gave him corn, 6a and he ate well and freshly. And later he took the other horse and put him in the mill, and like his fellow did, so did he, for he would not draw for anything the man might do. Then the man forsook his service and would no longer remain with the aforesaid creature. Anon, it was noised about the town of N . . . that neither man nor beast would serve the said creature.

Then some said she was accursed; some said God took open vengeance on her; some said one thing and some said another. Some wise men, whose minds were more grounded in the love of Our Lord, said that it was the high mercy of Our Lord Jesus Christ that called her from the pride and vanity of the wretched world.

Then this creature, seeing all these adversities coming on every side, thought they were the scourges of Our Lord that would chastise her for her sin. Then she asked God's mercy, and forsook her pride, her covetousness, and the desire that she had for the worship of the world, and did great bodily penance, and began to enter the way of everlasting life as shall be told hereafter.

ON a night, as this creature lay in her bed with her husband, she heard a sound of melody so sweet and delectable, that she thought she had been in Paradise, and therewith she started out of her bed and said: —

'Alas, that ever I did sin! It is full merry in Heaven.'

This melody was so sweet that it surpassed all melody that ever might be heard in this world, without any comparison, and caused her, when she heard any mirth or melody afterwards, to have full plenteous and abundant tears of high devotion, with great sobbings and sighings after the bliss of Heaven, not dreading the shames and the spites of this wretched world. Ever after this inspiration, she had in her mind the mirth and the melody that was in Heaven, so much, that she could not well restrain herself from speaking thereof, for wherever she was in any company she would say oftentimes: — 'It is full merry in Heaven.'

And they that knew her behaviour beforetime, and now heard her speaking so much of the bliss of Heaven, said to her: —

'Why speak ye so of the mirth that is in Heaven? Ye know it not, and ye have not been there, any more than we.' And were wroth with her, for she would not hear nor speak of worldly things as they did, and as she did beforetime.

And after this time she had never desired to commune

30

fleshly with her husband, for the debt of matrimony was so abominable to her that she would rather, she thought, have eaten or drunk the ooze and the muck in the gutter than consent to any fleshly communing, save only for obedience.

So she said to her husband:—'I may not deny you my body, but the love of my heart and my affections are withdrawn from all earthly creatures, and set only in God.'

He would have his will and she obeyed, with great weeping and sorrowing that she might not live chaste. And oftentimes this creature counselled her husband to live chaste, and said that they often, she knew well, had displeased God by their inordinate love, and the great delectation they each had in using the other, and now it was good that they should, by the common will and consent of them both, punish and chastise themselves wilfully by abstaining from the lust of their bodies. Her husband said it was good to do so, but he might not yet. He would when God willed. And so he used her as he had done before. He would not spare her. And ever she prayed to God that she might live chaste; and three or four years after, when it pleased Our Lord, he made a vow of chastity, as shall be written afterwards, by leave of Jesus.

And also, after this creature heard this heavenly melody, she did great bodily penance. She was shriven sometimes twice or thrice on a day, and specially of that sin she so long had (hid), concealed and covered, as is written in the beginning of the book.

She gave herself up to great fasting and great watching; 7a she rose at two or three of the clock, and went to church, and was there at her prayers unto the time of noon and

also all the afternoon. Then she was slandered and reproved by many people, because she kept so strict a life.
She got a hair-cloth from a kiln, such as men dry malt on,
and laid it in her kirtle as secretly and privily as she might,
so that her husband should not espy it. Nor did he, and
she lay by him every night in his bed and wore the hair-
cloth every day, and bore children in the time.

Then she had three years of great labour with temptations which she bore as meekly as she could, thanking
Our Lord for all His gifts, and was as merry when she
was reproved, scorned and japed for Our Lord's love, and
much more merry than she was beforetime in the worship
of the world. For she knew right well she had sinned
greatly against God and was worthy of more shame and
sorrow than any man could cause her, and despite of the
world was the right way Heavenwards, since Christ Himself had chosen that way. All His apostles, martyrs, confessors and virgins, and all that ever came to Heaven,
passed by the way of tribulation, and she, desiring nothing
so much as Heaven, then was glad in her conscience when
she believed that she was entering the way that would lead
her to the place she most desired.

And this creature had contrition and great compunction
with plenteous tears and many boisterous sobbings for her
sins and for her unkindness against her Maker. She repented from her childhood for unkindness, as Our Lord
would put it in her mind, full many a time. Then, beholding her own wickedness, she could but sorrow and
weep and ever pray for mercy and forgiveness. Her weeping was so plenteous and continuing, that many people
thought she could weep and leave off, as she liked. And
7b   therefore many men said she was a false hypocrite, and

wept before the world for succour and worldly goods. Then full many forsook her that loved her before while she was in the world, and would not know her. And ever, she thanked God for all, desiring nothing but mercy and forgiveness of sin.

CHAPTER 4

The first two years when this creature was thus drawn to Our Lord, she had great quiet in spirit from any temptations. She could well endure to fast, and it did not trouble her. She hated the joys of the world. She felt no rebellion in her flesh. She was so strong, as she thought, that she dreaded no devil in Hell, as she did such great bodily penance. She thought that she loved God more than He did her. She was smitten with the deadly wound of vainglory, and felt it not, for she many times desired that the crucifix should loosen His hands from the Cross, and embrace her in token of love. Our Merciful Lord Jesus Christ, seeing this creature's presumption, sent her, as is written before, three years of great temptations, one of the hardest of which I purpose to write as an example to those who come after, so that they should not trust in themselves, or have joy in themselves, as she had. For, no dread, our ghostly enemy sleepeth not, but he full busily searcheth our complexions and dispositions and where he findeth us most frail, there, by Our Lord's sufferance, he layeth his snare, which no man may escape by his own power.

So he laid before this woman the snare of lechery, when she believed that all fleshly lust had wholly been quenched in her. And so for a long time she was tempted with the sin of lechery, for aught that she could do. Yet she was often shriven, she wore her hair-cloth, and did great bodily penance and wept many a bitter tear, and prayed full often to Our Lord that He should preserve her and keep her, so that she should not fall into temptation, for she thought she would rather be dead than consent thereto. All this time she had no lust to commune with her husband; but it was very painful and horrible unto her. 8a

In the second year of her temptation, it so fell that a man whom she loved well, said unto her on St. Margaret's Eve before evensong that, for anything, he would lie by her and have his lust of his body, and she should not withstand him, for if he did not have his will that time, he said he would anyhow have it another time; she should not choose. And he did it to see what she would do, but she thought that he had meant it in full earnest at that time, and said but little thereto. So they parted then and both went to hear evensong, for her church was that of Saint Margaret.[1] This woman was so laboured with the man's words that she could not hear her evensong, nor say her Paternoster, or think any other good thought, but was more troubled than ever she was before.

The devil put into her mind that God had forsaken her, or else she would not be so tempted. She believed the devil's persuasion, and began to consent because she could think no good thought. Therefore thought she that God had forsaken her, and when evensong was done, she went to the man aforesaid, so that he could have his lust, as she thought he had desired, but he made such simulation that she could not know his intent, and so they parted asunder for that night. This creature was so laboured and vexed all that night, that she never knew what she might do. She lay by her husband, and to commune with him

[1] *See* Note E.

was so abominable to her that she could not endure it, and yet it was lawful unto her, in lawful time, if she would. But ever she was laboured with the other man, to sin with him inasmuch as he had spoken to her. At last, through the importunity of temptation, and lack of discretion, she was overcome and consented in her mind, and went to the man to know if he would then consent to her, and he said he never would, for all the gold in this world; he would rather be hewn as small as flesh for the pot.

8b

She went away all shamed and confused in herself at seeing his stability and her own instability. Then thought she of the grace that God had given her before; how she had had two years of great quiet in her soul, repenting of her sin with many bitter tears of compunction, and a perfect will never again to turn to her sin, but rather to die. Now she saw how she had consented in her will to do sin, and then fell she half into despair. She thought she must have been in Hell for the sorrow she felt. She thought she was worthy of no mercy, for her consent was so wilfully done, nor ever worthy to do Him service, because she was so false to Him. Nevertheless she was shriven many times and often, and did whatever penance her confessor would enjoin her to do, and was governed by the rules of the Church. That grace, God gave his creature, blessed may He be, but He withdrew not her temptation, but rather increased it, as she thought.

Therefore she thought He had forsaken her, and dared not trust to His mercy, but was afflicted with horrible temptations to lechery and despair all the next year following. But Our Lord, of His mercy, as she said herself, gave her each day for the most part two hours of sorrow for her sins, with many bitter tears. Afterwards, she was laboured with temptation to despair as she was before, and was as far from feelings of grace, as they that never felt any, and that she could not bear, and so she gave way to despair. But for the time that she felt grace, her labours were so wonderful that she could evil fare with them, but ever mourned and sorrowed as though God had forsaken her.

[Here follows Chapter 5]

CHAPTER 6

Another day, she gave herself up to meditation as she had been bidden and lay still, not knowing what she might best think of. Then she said to Our Lord Jesus Christ: 'Jesus, of what shall I think?'

Our Lord answered to her mind:—'Daughter, think of My Mother, for she is the cause of all the grace that thou hast.'

Then, anon, she saw Saint Anne, great with child, and she prayed Saint Anne that she might be her maiden, and her servant. And anon, Our Lady was born, and then she arranged to take the child to herself and keep it till it was twelve years of age, with good meat and drink, with fair white clothing and white kerchiefs.

Then she said to the blessed child:—'Lady, you shall be the Mother of God.'

The blessed child answered and said:—'I would I were worthy to be the handmaiden of her that should conceive the Son of God.'

The creature said:—'I pray you, Lady, if that grace befall, you renounce not my service.'

The blessful child passed away for a certain time, the creature being quiet in contemplation, and afterwards came again and said:—

'Daughter, now am I become the Mother of God.'

And then the creature fell down on her knees with great reverence and great weeping and said:—

'I am not worthy, Lady, to do you service.'

'Yes, daughter,' said she, 'follow thou me, thy service 10a
liketh me well.'

Then went she forth with Our Lady and with Joseph,
bearing with her a pottle of wine and honey, and spices
thereto. Then went they forth to Elizabeth, Saint John
the Baptist's mother, and when they met together, each
worshipped the other, and so they dwelt together, with
great grace and gladness twelve weeks. And Saint John
was born, and Our Lady took him up from the earth with
all manner of reverence, and gave him to his mother,
saying of him that he should be a holy man, and blessed
him. Afterwards they took leave of each other with compassionate tears. Then the creature fell down on her
knees to Saint Elizabeth, and begged her to pray for her
to Our Lady that she might do her service and pleasure.

'Daughter,' said Elizabeth, 'me-seemeth thou dost right
well thy duty.'

Then went the creature forth with Our Lady to Bethlehem and purchased her shelter every night with great
reverence, and Our Lady was received with glad cheer.
Also she begged for Our Lady fair white cloths and kerchiefs to swathe her Son in, when He was born; and when
Jesus was born, she provided bedding for Our Lady to lie
in with her Blessed Son. Later she begged meat for Our
Lady and her Blessed Child, and she swathed Him with
bitter tears of compassion, having mind of the sharp death
He would suffer for love of sinful men, saying unto Him:—

'Lord, I shall fare fair with You. I will not bind You
tight. I pray You be not displeased with me.'

CHAPTER 7

A<small>ND</small> afterwards on the twelfth day, when three Kings came with their gifts, and worshipped Our Lord in His Mother's lap, this creature, Our Lady's handmaiden, beholding all the process in contemplation, wept wondrous sore.

And when she saw that they would take their leave to go home again into their country, she could not bear that they should go from the Presence of Our Lord, and for wonder that they should go, she cried wondrous sore. Soon after came an angel, and bade Our Lady and Joseph to go from the country of Bethlehem into Egypt. Then went this creature forth with Our Lady, day by day finding her harbourage with great reverence and many sweet thoughts and high meditations, and also high contemplation, sometimes continuing in weeping two hours and often longer in mind of Our Lord's Passion without ceasing, sometimes for her own sin, sometimes for the sin of the people, sometimes for the souls in Purgatory, sometimes for them that were in poverty and dis-ease, for she desired to comfort them all.

Sometimes she wept full plenteously and full boisterously for desire of the bliss of Heaven, and because she was so long deferred therefrom. She greatly coveted to be delivered out of this wretched world. Our Lord Jesus Christ said to her mind that she should abide and languish in love, 'for I have ordained thee to kneel before the

10b

Trinity, to pray for all the world, for many hundred thousand souls shall be saved by thy prayers. So ask, daughter, what thou wilt, and I will grant thee thine asking.'

The creature said:—'Lord, I ask mercy and preservation from everlasting damnation for me and all the world. Chastise us here how Thou wilt and in Purgatory also, and of Thy great mercy, keep us from damnation.'

CHAPTER 8

Another time, as this creature lay in her prayer, the Mother of Mercy, appearing to her, said:—

'Daughter, blessed may thou be, thy seat is made in Heaven, before my Son's knee, and Whom thou wilt have with thee.'

Then asked her Blessed Son:—'Daughter, whom wilt thou have fellow with thee?'

'My dearworthy Lord, I ask for my ghostly father, Master N...'

'Why asketh thou more for him than thine own father or thine husband?'

'Because I may never requite him for his goodness to me, and the gracious labour he has taken over me in hearing my confession.'

'I grant thee thy desire for him; yet shall thy father be saved, and thy husband also, and all thy children.'

Then this creature said:—'Lord, after Thou has forgiven me my sin, I make Thee mine executor of all the good works that Thou workest in me. In praying, in thinking, in weeping, in going on pilgrimage, in fasting, or in speaking any good word, it is fully my will, that Thou give Master N... half of it to the increase of his merit, as if he did them himself. And the other half, Lord, spread on Thy friends and Thine enemies, and on my friends and mine enemies, for I will have but Thyself for my share.'

'Daughter, I shall be a true executor to thee and fulfil all thy will; and for the great charity that thou hast to comfort thy fellow Christians, thou shalt have double reward in Heaven.'

Another time, as she prayed to God that she might live chaste by leave of her husband, Christ said to her: —

'Thou must fast on Friday, both from meat and drink, and thou shalt have thy desire ere Whitsunday, for I shall suddenly slay (the fleshly lust in) thy husband.'

Then on the Wednesday in Easter week, after her husband would have had knowledge of her, as he was wont before, and when he came nigh to her, she said: —'Jesus Christ, help me,' and he had no power to touch her at that time in that way, nor ever after with any fleshly knowledge.

It befell on a Friday before Whitsun Eve, as this creature was in a church of Saint Margaret at N . . . hearing her Mass, she heard a great noise, and a dreadful. She was sore amazed through fear of the voice of the people, who said God should take vengeance on her. She knelt on her knees, holding down her head, with her book in her hand, praying Our Lord Jesus Christ for grace and mercy.

Suddenly there fell down from the highest part of the church roof, from under the foot of the spar, on her head and back, a stone which weighed three pounds, and a short end of a beam weighing six pounds, so that she thought her back was broken asunder, and she feared she would be dead in a little while.

Soon afterwards, she cried 'Jesus, mercy!' and anon, her pain was gone.

A good man, called John of Wyreham, seeing this wonder and supposing she had been greatly injured, came 11b and pulled her by the sleeve and said:—

'Dame, how fare ye?'

The creature, whole and sound, then thanked him for his cheer and his charity, much marvelling and greatly a-wonder that she felt no pain, having had so much a little before. For twelve weeks afterwards, she felt no pain. Then the spirit of God said to her soul: —

'Hold this for a great miracle, and if the people will not believe this, I will work many more.'

A worshipful doctor of divinity, named Master Aleyn, a White Friar, hearing of this wonderful work, inquired of this creature all the details of the process. He, desiring the work of God to be magnified, got the same stone that fell on her back and weighed it, and then got the beam-end that fell on her head, which one of the keepers of the church had laid on the fire to burn. This worshipful doctor said it was a great miracle, and Our Lord was highly to be magnified for preserving this creature against the malice of her enemy, and told it to many people and many people magnified God much in this creature. Many also would not believe it, and thought it more a token of wrath and vengeance, rather than believe it was any token of mercy and kindness.

CHAPTER 10

Soon after, this creature was urged in her soul to go and visit certain places for ghostly health, inasmuch as she was cured, but might not without the consent of her husband. She asked her husband to grant her leave, and he, full trusting it was the will of God, soon consenting, they went to such places as she was inclined.

Then Our Lord Jesus Christ said to her: — 'My servants desire greatly to see thee.'

Then she was welcomed and made much of in divers places, wherefore she had great dread of vainglory, and was much afraid. Our Merciful Lord Jesus Christ, worshipped be His Name, said to her: —

'Dread not, daughter, I will take vainglory from thee, for they that worship thee, worship Me; they that despise thee, despise Me and I will chastise them therefor. I am in thee and thou in Me, and they that hear thee, hear the voice of God. Daughter, there is no so sinful man living on earth, that, if he will forsake his sin and live after thy counsel, such grace as thou promiseth him, I will confirm for thy love.'

Then her husband and she went forth to York and divers other places.

12a

46

IT befell on a Friday on Midsummer Eve in right hot weather, as this creature was coming from York-ward carrying a bottle with beer in her hand, and her husband a cake in his bosom, that he asked his wife this question: —

'Margery, if there came a man with a sword, who would strike off my head, unless I should commune naturally with you as I have done before, tell me on your conscience — for ye say ye will not lie — whether ye would suffer my head to be smitten off, or whether ye would suffer me to meddle with you again, as I did at one time?'

'Alas, sir,' said she, 'why raise this matter, when we have been chaste these eight weeks?'

'For I will know the truth of your heart.'

And then she said with great sorrow: — 'Forsooth, I would rather see you being slain, than that we should turn again to our uncleanness.'

And he replied: — 'Ye are no good wife.'

She then asked her husband what was the cause that he had not meddled with her for eight weeks, since she lay with him every night in his bed. He said he was made so afraid when he would have touched her, that he dare do no more.

'Now, good sir, amend your ways, and ask God's mercy, for I told you nearly three years ago that ye[1] should be slain suddenly, and now is this the third year,

[1] i.e. 'your lust'. *See* p. 44 line 5.

and so I hope I shall have my desire. Good sir, I pray you grant me what I ask, and I will pray for you that ye shall be saved through the mercy of Our Lord Jesus Christ, and ye shall have more reward in Heaven than if ye wore a hair-cloth or a habergeon.[1] I pray you, suffer me to make a vow of chastity at what bishop's hand God wills.'

'Nay,' he said, 'that I will not grant you, for now may I use you without deadly sin, and then might I not do so.'

12b Then she said to him: — 'If it be the will of the Holy Ghost to fulfil what I have said, I pray God that ye may consent thereto; and if it be not the will of the Holy Ghost, I pray God ye never consent to it'.

Then they went forth towards Bridlington in right hot weather, the creature having great sorrow and dread for her chastity. As they came by a cross, her husband sat down under the cross, calling his wife to him and saying these words unto her: — 'Margery, grant me my desire, and I shall grant you your desire. My first desire is that we shall still lie together in bed as we have done before; the second, that ye shall pay my debts, ere ye go to Jerusalem; and the third, that ye shall eat and drink with me on the Friday as ye were wont to do.'

'Nay, sir,' said she, 'to break the Friday, I will never grant you whilst I live.'

'Well,' said he, 'then I shall meddle with you again.'

She prayed him that he would give her leave to say her prayers, and he granted it kindly. Then she knelt down beside a cross in the field and prayed in this manner, with a great abundance of tears: —

[1] A habergeon, or coat of mail, was worn as a penance, in addition to its primary purpose of bodily protection.

'Lord God, thou knowest all things. Thou knowest
what sorrow I have had to be chaste in my body to Thee
all these three years, and now might I have my will, and
dare not for love of Thee. For if I should break that
manner of fasting which Thou commandest me to keep on
the Friday, without meat or drink, I should now have my
desire. But, Blessed Lord, Thou knowest that I will not
contravene Thy will, and much now is my sorrow unless
I find comfort in Thee. Now, Blessed Jesus, make Thy
will known to me unworthy, that I may follow it thereafter
and fulfil it with all my might.'

Then Our Lord Jesus Christ with great sweetness,
spoke to her, commanding her to go again to her husband,
and pray him to grant her what she desired, 'And he shall
have what he desireth. For, my dearworthy daughter,
this was the cause that I bade thee fast, so that thou
shouldst the sooner obtain and get thy desire, and now it
is granted to thee. I will no longer that thou fast. Therefore I bid thee in the Name of Jesus, eat and drink as
thy husband doth.'

Then this creature thanked Our Lord Jesus Christ for
His grace and goodness, and rose up and went to her
husband, saying to him: —

13a

'Sir, if it please you, ye shall grant me my desire, and
ye shall have your desire. Grant me that ye will not come
into my bed, and I grant you to requite your debts ere I
go to Jerusalem. Make my body free to God so that ye
never make challenge to me, by asking any debt of
matrimony. After this day, whilst ye live, I will eat and
drink on the Friday at your bidding.'

Then said her husband: — 'As free may your body be
to God, as it hath been to me.'

This creature thanked God, greatly rejoicing that she had her desire, praying her husband that they should say three Paternosters in worship of the Trinity for the great grace that He had granted them. And so they did, kneeling under a cross, and afterwards they ate and drank together in great gladness of spirit. This was on a Friday on Midsummer's Eve. Then went they forth Bridlington-ward and also to many other countries and spoke with God's servants, both anchorites and recluses, and many others of Our Lord's lovers, with many worthy clerks, doctors of divinity and bachelors also, in divers places. And this creature, to many of them, shewed her feelings and her contemplations, as she was commanded to do, to find out if any deceit were in her feelings.

CHAPTER 12

THIS creature was sent by Our Lord to divers places of religion, and among them she came to a place of monks, where she was right welcome for Our Lord's love, save that there was a monk, who bore great office in that place, who despised her and set her at naught. Nevertheless she was set at meat with the Abbot, and many times, of the meat, she said many good words, as God would put them into her mind, the same monk who had so despised her being present and many others to hear what she would say. And through her conversation, his affection began greatly to incline towards her, and he began to have great savour in her words. And so, afterwards, this monk came to her and said, she being in church and he also, at the time: —

'Damsel, I hear it said that God speaketh unto thee. I pray thee tell me whether I shall be saved or not, and in what sins I have most displeased God, for I will not believe but that thou can tell me my sin.'

The creature said to the monk: — 'Go to your Mass, and if I may weep for you, I hope to have grace for you.' 13b

He followed her counsel and went to his Mass. She wept wondrously for his sins. When Mass was ended, the creature said to Our Lord Christ Jesus: —

'Blessed Lord, what answer shall I give to this man?'

'My dearworthy daughter, say in the name of Jesus

E 51

that he hath sinned in lechery, in despair, and in worldly goods keeping.'

'Ah! Gracious Lord, this is hard for me to say. He will do me much shame, if I tell him a lie.'

'Dread thee not, but speak boldly in My name, for they are not lies.'

Then she said again to Our Lord Jesus Christ: — 'Good Lord, shall he be saved?'

'Yea,' said Our Lord, 'if he will forsake his sin, and live after thy counsel. Charge him that he forsake his sin and be shriven thereof, and also the office that he holdeth outside.'

Then came the monk again. 'Margery, tell me my sins.'

She said: — 'I pray you, sir, ask not thereafter, for I undertake, for your soul, ye shall be saved, if ye will do after my counsel.'

'Forsooth, I will not believe you, unless ye tell me my sin.'

'Sir, I understand that ye have sinned in lechery, in despair, and in keeping worldly goods.'

Then the monk stood still, somewhat abashed, and afterwards said: —

'Say whether I have sinned with wives or single women?'

'Sir, with wives.'

Then he said: — 'Shall I be saved?'

'Yea, sir, if ye will do after my counsel. Sorrow for your sin, and I will help you to sorrow. Be shriven thereof, and forsake it wilfully. Leave the office ye hold outside, and God shall give you grace, for my love.'

The monk took her by the hand, and led her into a

fair house of office, made her a great dinner, and afterwards gave her gold to pray for him, and so she took her leave at that time.

Another time, when the creature came again to that place, the aforesaid monk had forsaken his office at her counsel, and was turned from his sin, and was made Sub-prior of the place, a well behaved man and well disposed, thanked be God, and made her great cheer and highly blessed God that ever he saw her.

CHAPTER 13

14a   O<small>N</small> a time, as this creature was at Canterbury in the church amongst the monks, she was greatly despised and reproved because she wept so fast, both by the monks and priests, and by secular men, nearly all day both forenoon and afternoon also, so much indeed that her husband went away from her as if he had not known her, and left her alone amongst them, choose how she might. Further comfort had she none of him that day.

So an old monk, who had been Treasurer with the Queen whilst he was in secular clothing, a rich man, and greatly dreaded by many people, took her by the hand, saying unto her: —

'What canst thou say of God?'

'Sir,' she said, 'I will both speak of Him, and hear of Him,' repeating to the monk a story of Scripture.

The monk said: — 'I would thou wert enclosed in a house of stone, so that, there, no man should speak with thee.'

'Ah! Sir,' she said, 'ye should maintain God's servants. Ye are the first that hold against them. Our Lord amend you.'

Then a young monk said to her: — 'Either thou hast the Holy Ghost, or else thou hast the devil within thee, for what thou speakest to us here is Holy Writ, and that hast thou not of thyself.'

Then said this creature: — 'I pray you, sir, give me leave to tell you a tale.'

Then the people said to the monk: — 'Let her say what she will.'

Then she said: — 'There was once a man who had sinned greatly against God, and when he was shriven, his confessor enjoined him as part of his penance, that he should for one year hire men to chide him and reprove him for his sins, and he should give them silver for their labour. And one day he came amongst many great men, such as are now here, God save you all, and stood among them as I do now amongst you, despising him as ye do me, the man laughing and smiling and having good game at their words. The greatest master of them said to the man: —

' "Why laughest thou, wretch? Thou art greatly despised!"

' "Ah! Sir, I have great cause to laugh, for I have many days put silver out of my purse and hired men to chide me for remission of my sin, and this day I may keep my silver in my purse. I thank you all."

'Right so I say to you, worshipful sirs. Whilst I was at home in my own country, day by day with great weeping and mourning, I sorrowed because I had no shame, scorn or contempt, as I was worthy. I thank you all, sirs, highly for what, forenoon and afternoon, I have had in good measure this day, blessed be God for it.'

Then she went out of the monastery, they following and crying upon her: —

'Thou shalt be burnt, false Lollard. Here is a cartful of thorns ready for thee, and a tun[1] to burn thee with.'

14b

---

[1] There is at least one recorded case of a Lollard being burnt under a tun.

55

And the creature stood outside the gates of Canterbury, for it was in the evening, many people wondering at her.

Then said the people: — 'Take and burn her!'

She stood still, trembling and quaking full sore in her flesh, without any earthly comfort, and knew not where her husband had gone.

Then prayed she in her heart to Our Lord in this manner: —

'Here came I, Lord, for Thy love. Blessed Lord, help me and have mercy on me.'

And anon, after she had made her prayer in her heart to Our Lord, there came two fair young men, who said to her: —

'Damsel, art thou neither heretic nor Lollard?'

And she said: — 'No, sirs, I am neither heretic nor Lollard.'

They asked her, where was her inn. She said she knew not what street; nevertheless it would be at a Dewchman's house. Then these two young men brought her home to her hostel, and made her great cheer, asking her to pray for them, and there she found her husband.

And many people in N . . . had said evil of her whilst she was out, and slandered her over many things she was said to have done whilst she was in the country.

Then, after this, she was in great rest of soul a long while, and had high contemplation day by day, and much holy speech and dalliance with Our Lord Jesus Christ, both forenoon and afternoon with many sweet tears of high devotion, so plenteously and continually, that it was a marvel that her eyes endured, or that her heart should last, without being consumed with the ardour of

love, which was kindled with the holy dalliance of Our 15a
Lord, when He said to her many times: —

'Dear daughter, love thou Me with all thy heart, for I
love thee with all My heart and the might of My Godhead,
for thou wert a chosen soul without beginning in My
sight and a pillar of Holy Church. My merciful eyes are
ever upon thee. It would be impossible for thee to suffer
the scorn and contempt that thou shalt have, were not
My grace supporting thee.'

[Here follows Chapter 14]

Tʜɪs creature, when Our Lord had forgiven her her sin, as has been written before, had a desire to see those places where He was born, and where He suffered His Passion, and where He died, with other holy places where He was in His life, and also after His resurrection.

As she was in these desires, Our Lord bade her, in her mind, two years ere she went, that she should go to Rome, to Jerusalem and to Saint James,[1] and she would fain have gone but she had no money.

And then she said to Our Lord: — 'Where shall I get money to go with to these Holy Places?'

Our Lord answered to her: — 'I shall send thee friends enough in divers countries of England to help thee. And, daughter, I shall go with thee in every country and provide for thee. I shall lead thee thither, and bring thee back again in safety. And no Englishman shall die in the ship that thou art in. I shall keep thee from all wicked men's power. And daughter, I say to thee that I will that thou wearest clothes of white and no other colour, for thou shalt be arrayed after My will.'

'Ah! Dear Lord, if I go arrayed in other manner than other chaste women do, I dread the people will slander me. They will say I am a hypocrite and wonder at me.'

'Yea, daughter, the more ridicule that thou hast for My love, the more thou pleasest Me.'

[1] Santiago de Compostella, in north-western Spain.

Then this creature durst not otherwise do than she was commanded in her soul.

And so she went forth with her husband into the country, for he was ever a good man and an easy man to her, though he sometimes, for vain dread, let her alone for a time. Yet he resorted evermore again to her, and had compassion on her, and spoke for her as he durst for dread of the people; but all others that went with her, forsook her, and full falsely they accused her, through temptation of the devil, of things that she was never guilty of.   16b

And so did one man whom she greatly trusted on, and who proffered himself to go with her into the country, whereat she was right glad, trusting he would well support her and help her when she had need, for he had been dwelling a long time with an anchorite, commencer in divinity, and that anchorite was this woman's confessor.

And so his servant took leave, of his own stirring, to go with this creature into the country, and her own maiden went with her also as long as they fared well and no man said anything against them.

But as soon as the people, through the enticing of our ghostly enemy, and by the sufferance of Our Lord, spake against this creature because she wept so sore, and said she was a false hypocrite, and falsely deceived the people, and threatened her to be burnt, then the aforesaid man who was held to be so holy, and whom she trusted so much upon, utterly reproved her and foully despised her, and would go no further with her. Her maiden seeing discomfort on every side, waxed boisterous against her mistress. She would not obey, or follow her counsel. She let her go alone into many good towns and would not go with her.

And ever her husband was ready when all others failed, and went with her where Our Lord would send her, always trusting that all was for the best and would come to a good end, when God willed.

And at this time, he led her to speak with the Bishop of Lincoln, who was called Philip,[1] and they abode three weeks ere they might speak with him, for he was not at home at his palace.

When the Bishop had come home, and heard it said how such a woman had awaited him so long to speak with him, anon he sent for her in great haste to learn her will. And she came to his presence and saluted him, and he warmly welcomed her and said he had long desired to speak with her, and he was right glad of her coming. So she prayed him that she might speak with him in counsel and show him the secrets of her soul, and he settled her a time convenient thereto.

17a When the time came, she shewed him her meditations, and high contemplations, and other secret things both of the quick and the dead, as Our Lord shewed to her soul. He was right glad to hear them, and suffered her benignly to say what she listed, and commended greatly her feelings and her contemplations, saying they were high matters and full devout matters, and inspired by the Holy Ghost, counselling her seriously that her feelings should be written.

And she said that it was not God's will that they should be written so soon; nor were they written for twenty years and more.

Then she said furthermore: — 'My lord, if it pleases you, I am commanded in my soul that ye shall give me

[1] Philip Repingdon.

the mantle and the ring, and clothe me all in white clothes. And if ye clothe me on earth, Our Lord Jesus Christ will clothe you in Heaven, as I understand by revelation.'

Then the Bishop said to her: — 'I will fulfil your desire, if your husband will consent thereto.'

Then she said to the Bishop: — 'I pray you, let my husband come into your presence, and ye shall hear what he will say.'

And so her husband came before the Bishop, and the Bishop asked him: —

'John, is it your will that your wife take the mantle and the ring and live chaste, and both of you?'

'Yes, my lord,' said he, 'and in token that we both vow to live chaste, I offer my hands into yours,' and he put his hands between the Bishop's hands.

And the Bishop did no more to us that day, save that he made us right good cheer and said we were right welcome.

Another day this creature came to meat at the request of the Bishop, and she saw him giving with his hands, ere he sat down to meat, to thirteen poor men, thirteen pence and thirteen loaves with other meat. And so he did every day.

This creature was stirred to high devotion at this sight, and gave God praise and worship because He gave the Bishop grace to do these good deeds, with plenteous weeping, in so much that all the Bishop's household was greatly marvelling what ailed her.

And afterwards she was set to meat with many worthy clerks and priests and squires of the Bishop's, and the Bishop himself sent her full kindly from his own table.

The clerks asked this creature many hard questions, 17b

61

which she, by the grace of Jesus, solved, so that her answers pleased the Bishop right well, and the clerks had full great marvel at her that she answered so readily and pregnantly.

When the Bishop had eaten, he sent for her to his chamber, saying to her: —

'Margery, ye and your husband spake to me to give you the mantle and the ring, for which cause I have taken counsel, and my counsel will not allow me to profess you in such singular clothing, without better advice. And ye say, by the grace of God, that ye will go to Jerusalem. Therefore pray to God that it may wait over till ye come back from Jerusalem, so that ye are better proved and known.'

On the next day, this creature went to church and prayed to God with all her spirit that she might have knowledge how she might be governed in this matter, and what answer she might give to the Bishop.

Our Lord Jesus Christ answered to her mind in this manner: —

'Daughter, say to the Bishop that he dreadeth more the shames of the world than the perfect love of God. Say to him that I would as well have excused him if he had fulfilled my will, as I did the children of Israel when I bade them borrow the goods of the people of Egypt and go away therewith. Therefore, daughter, tell him, though he will not do it now, it shall be done another time when God willeth.'

And so she gave her message to the Bishop of Lincoln as she had been commanded. Then he prayed her to go to the Archbishop of Canterbury, — Arundel, — 'and pray him to grant leave to me, the Bishop of Lincoln,' to give her the mantle and the ring, inasmuch as she was not of his diocese. This cause he feigned through counsel of his clerks, for they loved not this creature.

She said: — 'Sir, I will go to my lord of Canterbury with right good will, for other causes and matters which I have to show to his reverence. As for this cause, I shall not go, for God willeth not that I ask him thereafter.' 18a

Then she took her leave of the Bishop of Lincoln and he gave her twenty-six shillings and eight pence to buy her clothes with, and to pray for him.

CHAPTER 16

T HEN went this creature forth to London with her husband unto Lambeth, where the Archbishop lay at that time; and as they came into the hall in the afternoon, there were many of the Archbishop's clerks and other reckless men, both squires and yeomen, who swore many great oaths and spoke many reckless words, and this creature boldly reprehended them, and said they would be damned unless they left off their swearing and other sins that they used.

And with that, there came forth another woman of the same town in a furred cloak, who forswore this creature, banned her, and spoke full cursedly to her in this manner: —

'I would thou wert in Smithfield, and I would bring a faggot to burn thee with. It is a pity thou art alive.'

This creature stood still and answered not, and her husband suffered it with great pain, and was full sorry to hear his wife so rebuked.

Then the Archbishop sent for this creature into his garden. When she came into his presence, she saluted him as best she could, praying him of his gracious lordship to grant her authority to choose her confessor and to be houselled[1] every Sunday, if God would dispose her thereto, under his letter and his seal through all his province. And he granted her full benignly all her desire

[1] To go to Holy Communion.

without any silver or gold, nor would he let his clerks take anything for the writing or the sealing of the letter.

When this creature found this grace in his sight, she was well comforted and strengthened in her soul, and so she showed this worshipful lord her manner of life, and such grace as God wrought in her mind and in her soul, to find out what he would say thereto, and whether he found any default either in her contemplation or in her weeping.

And she told him also the cause of her weeping, and the manner of dalliance that Our Lord spoke to her soul; and he found no default in her, but praised her manner of living, and was right glad that Our Merciful Lord Christ Jesus showed such grace in our days, blessed may He be.

Then this creature boldly spoke to him for the correction of his household, saying with reverence: —

'My lord, Our Lord of all, Almighty God has not given you your benefice and great worldly wealth to keep His traitors and them that slay Him every day by great oaths swearing. Ye shall answer for them, unless ye correct them, or else put them out of your service.'

Full benignly and meekly he suffered her to speak her intent, and gave her a fair answer, she supposing it would then be better. And so their dalliance continued till stars appeared in the firmament. Then she took her leave, and her husband also.

Afterwards they came again to London, and many worthy men desired to hear her dalliances and communication, for her communication was so much in the love of God that her hearers were often stirred thereby to weep right sadly.

And so she had there right great cheer, and her husband because of her, as long as they remained in the city.

Afterwards they came again to Lynne, and then went this creature to the anchorite at the Preaching Friars[1] in Lynne and told him what cheer she had had, and how she had sped whilst she was in the country. And he was right glad of her coming home, and held it was a great miracle, her coming and going to and fro.

And he said to her: — 'I have heard much evil language of you since ye went out, and I have been sore counselled to leave you and no more to associate with you, and there are promised me great friendships, on condition that I leave you. And I answered for you thus: —

19a

"If ye were in the same plight as ye were when we parted asunder, I durst well say that ye were a good woman, a lover of God, and highly inspired by the Holy Ghost. And I will not forsake her for any lady in this realm, if speaking with the lady means leaving her. Rather would I leave the lady and speak with her, if I might not do both, than do the contrary".'

[1] *See* Note L.

On a day, long before this time, while this creature was bearing children and she was newly delivered of a child, Our Lord Jesus Christ said to her that she should bear no more children, and therefore He bade her to go to Norwich.

And she said: — 'Ah! dear Lord, how shall I go? I am both faint and feeble.'

'Dread thee not. I shall make thee strong enough. I bid thee go to the Vicar of Saint Stephen's[1] and say that I greet him well, and that he is a highly chosen soul of Mine, and tell him he pleaseth Me much with his preaching and shew him thy secrets, and My counsels such as I shew thee.'

Then she took her way Norwich-ward, and came into his church on a Thursday a little before noon. And the Vicar went up and down with another priest, who was his ghostly father, who lived when this book was made. And this creature was clad in black clothing at that time.

She saluted the Vicar, praying him that she might speak with him an hour or else two hours at afternoon, when he had eaten, in the love of God.

He, lifting up his hands and blessing her, said: — 'Benedicite. How could a woman occupy an hour or two hours in the love of Our Lord? I shall never eat meat till I learn what ye can say of Our Lord God in the time of an hour.'

[1] *See* Note Q.

F

67

19b Then he sat himself down in the church. She, sitting a little aside, showed him all the words that God had revealed to her in her soul. Afterwards she shewed him all her manner of life from her childhood, as nigh as it would come to her mind; how unkind she had been against Our Lord Jesus Christ, how proud and vain she had been in her behaviour, how obstinate against the laws of God, and how envious against her fellow Christians. Later, when it pleased Our Lord Christ Jesus, how she was chastised with many tribulations and horrible temptations and afterwards how she was fed and comforted with holy meditations and specially in the memory of Our Lord's Passion.

And, while she conversed on the Passion of Our Lord Jesus Christ, she heard so hideous a melody that she could not bear it. Then this creature fell down, as if she had lost her bodily strength, and lay still a great while, desiring to put it away, and she might not. Then she knew well, by her faith, that there was great joy in Heaven where the least point of bliss, without any comparison, passeth all the joy that ever might be thought or felt in this life.

She was greatly strengthened in her faith and more bold to tell the Vicar her feelings, which she had by revelation both of the quick and the dead, and of his own self.

She told him how sometimes the Father of Heaven spoke to her soul as plainly and as verily as one friend speaks to another by bodily speech. Sometimes the Second Person in Trinity, sometimes all Three Persons in Trinity, and one substance in Godhead spoke to her soul, and informed her in her faith and in His love, how she should love Him, worship Him and dread Him, so excellently that she never heard of any book, either Hylton's book or Bride's[1] book, or Stimulus Amoris, or Incendium Amoris, or any other that she ever heard read, that spoke so highly of the love of God. But she felt that, as highly working in her soul, as if she could have shewn what she felt.

Sometimes Our Lady spoke to her mind; sometimes St. Peter, sometimes St. Paul, sometimes St. Katherine, 2ca or whatever Saint in Heaven she had devotion to, appeared in her soul and taught her how she should love Our Lord, and how she should please Him. Her dalliance was so sweet, so holy and so devout, that this creature might not oftentimes bear it, but fell down and wrested with her body, and made wondrous faces and gestures with boisterous sobbings, and great plenty of tears, sometimes saying 'Jesus, Mercy', sometimes, 'I die'.

And therefore many people slandered her, not believing that it was the work of God, but that some evil spirit vexed her in her body or else that she had some bodily sickness.

Notwithstanding the rumours and the grutching of the people against her, this holy man, the Vicar of Saint Stephen's Church of Norwich, whom God hath exalted, and through marvellous works shewn and proved for holy, ever held with her and supported her against her enemies, unto his power, after the time that she, by the bidding of God, had shewn him her manner of governance and living, for he trustfully believed that she was well learned in the law of God, and endued with the grace of the Holy Ghost, to Whom it belongeth to inspire where He will. And though His voice be heard, it is not known

[1] Saint Bridget of Sweden.

in the world from whence it cometh or whither it goeth.

This holy Vicar, after this time, was confessor to this creature always when she came to Norwich, and houselled her with his own hands.

And when she was at one time admonished to appear before certain officers of the Bishop, to answer to certain articles which would be put against her by the stirring of envious people, the good Vicar, preferring the love of God before any shame of the world, went with her to hear her examination, and delivered her from the malice of her enemies. And then it was revealed to this creature that the good Vicar would live seven years after, and then should pass hence with great grace, and he did as she foretold.

CHAPTER 18

THIS creature was charged and commanded in her soul 20b
that she should go to a White Friar, in the same city of
Norwich, called William Sowthfeld, a good man and a
holy liver, to shew him the grace that God wrought in
her, as she had done to the good Vicar before. She did as
she was commanded and came to the friar on a forenoon,
and was with him in a chapel a long time, and shewed him
her meditations, and what God had wrought in her soul,
to find out if she were deceived by any illusion or not.

This good man, the White Friar, ever whilst she told
him her feelings, holding up his hands, said: — 'Jesu
Mercy and gramercy.'

'Sister,' he said, 'dread not for your manner of living,
for it is the Holy Ghost working plenteously His grace
in your soul. Thank Him highly for His goodness, for
we all be bound to thank Him for you, Who now in our
days will inspire His grace in you, to the help and comfort
of us all, who are supported by your prayers and by such
others as ye be. And we are preserved from many
mischiefs and diseases which we should suffer, and
worthily, for our trespass. Never were such good creatures
amongst us. Blessed be Almighty God for His goodness.
And therefore, sister, I counsel you that ye dispose yourself to receive the gifts of God as lowly and meekly as ye
can, and put no obstacle or objection against the goodness
of the Holy Ghost, for He may give His gifts where He

71

will, and of unworthy He maketh worthy, of sinful He maketh rightful. His mercy is ever ready unto us, unless the fault be in ourselves, for He dwelleth not in a body subject to sin. He flieth all false feigning and falsehood: He asketh of us a lowly, a meek and a contrite heart, with a good will. Our Lord sayeth Himself: — "My Spirit shall rest upon a meek man, a contrite man, and one dreading My words."

'Sister, I trust to Our Lord that ye have these conditions either in your will or your affection, or else in both, and I believe not that Our Lord suffereth them to be deceived endlessly, that set all their trust in Him, and seek and desire nothing but Him only, as I hope ye do. And therefore believe fully that Our Lord loveth you and worketh His grace in you. I pray God to increase it and continue it to His everlasting worship, for His mercy.'

The aforesaid creature was much comforted both in body and in soul by this good man's words, and greatly strengthened in her faith.

Then she was bidden by Our Lord to go to an anchoress in the same city, named Dame Jelyan,[1] and so she did, and showed her the grace that God put into her soul, of compunction, contrition, sweetness and devotion, compassion with holy meditation and high contemplation, and full many holy speeches and dalliance that Our Lord spake to her soul; and many wonderful revelations, which she shewed to the anchoress to find out if there were any deceit in them, for the anchoress was expert in such things, and good counsel could give.

The anchoress, hearing the marvellous goodness of Our Lord, highly thanked God with all her heart for His

---

[1] Now more usually known as Dame (or Mother) Juliana.

72

visitation, counselling this creature to be obedient to the
will of Our Lord God and to fulfil with all her might
whatever He put into her soul, if it were not against the
worship of God, and profit of her fellow Christians, for
if it were, then it were not the moving of a good spirit,
but rather of an evil spirit. 'The Holy Ghost moveth
ne'er a thing against charity, for if He did, He would be
contrary to His own self for He is all charity. Also He
moveth a soul to all chasteness, for chaste livers are called
the Temple of the Holy Ghost, and the Holy Ghost
maketh a soul stable and steadfast in the right faith, and
the right belief.

'And a double man in soul is ever unstable and unstead-
fast in all his ways. He that is ever doubting is like the
flood of the sea which is moved and born about with the
wind, and that man is not likely to receive the gifts of
God.

'Any creature that hath these tokens may steadfastly   21b
believe that the Holy Ghost dwelleth in his soul. And
much more when God visiteth a creature with tears of contrition, devotion, and compassion, he may and ought to
believe that the Holy Ghost is in his soul. Saint Paul
saith that the Holy Ghost asketh for us with mourning
and weeping unspeakable, that is to say, he maketh us to
ask and pray with mourning and weeping so plenteously
that the tears may not be numbered. No evil spirit may
give these tokens, for Saint Jerome saith that tears torment
more the devil than do the pains of Hell. God and the
devil are ever at odds and they shall never dwell together
in one place, and the devil hath no power in a man's soul.

'Holy Writ saith that the soul of a rightful man is the
seat of God, and so I trust, sister, that ye be. I pray God

grant you perseverance. Set all your trust in God and fear not the language of the world, for the more despite, shame and reproof that ye have in the world, the more is your merit in the sight of God. Patience is necessary to you, for in that shall ye keep your soul.'

Much was the holy dalliance that the anchoress and this creature had by communing in the love of Our Lord Jesus Christ the many days that they were together.

This creature shewed her manner of living to many a worthy clerk, to worshipful doctors of divinity, both religious men and others of secular habit, and they said that God wrought great grace with her, and bade her she should not be afraid — there was no deceit in her manner of living. They counselled her to be persevering, for their greatest dread was that she should turn and not keep her perfection. She had so many enemies and so much slander, that they thought she might not bear it without great grace and a mighty faith.

Others who had no knowledge of her manner of governance, save only by outward sight or else by jangling of other persons perverting the judgment of truth, spoke full evil of her and caused her much enmity and much distress, more than she would otherwise have had, had their evil language never been spoken. Nevertheless the anchorite of the Preaching Friars in Lynne, who was the principal ghostly father of this creature, as is written before, took it on charge of his soul that her feelings were good and sure, and that there was no deceit in them, and he by the spirit of prophecy, told her that, when she should go Jerusalem-ward, she would have much tribulation with her maiden, and how Our Lord would try her sharply and prove her full straitly.

22a

Then said she to him: — 'Ah! Good sir, what shall I do when I am far from home, and in strange countries, and my maiden is against me? Then is my bodily comfort gone, and ghostly comfort from any confessor such as ye be, I wot not where to get.'

'Daughter, dread ye nothing, for Our Lord Himself shall comfort you His own self, Whose comfort surpasseth all other, and when all your friends have forsaken you, Our Lord will make a broken-backed man lead you forth whither ye will go.'

And so it befell as the anchorite had prophesied in every point, and as, I trust, shall be written more fully afterwards.

Then this creature, in a manner complaining, said to the anchorite:—

'Good sir, what shall I do? He that is my confessor in your absence is right sharp with me; he will not believe my feelings; he setteth naught by them; he holdeth them but trifles and japes, and that is great pain to me, for I love him well and would fain follow his counsel.'

The anchorite answering her, said:—'It is no wonder, daughter, if he cannot believe in your feelings so soon. He knoweth well that ye have been a sinful woman, and therefore he weeneth that God would not be homely with you in so short a time. After your conversion, I would not for all this world be so sharp to you as he is. God, for your merit, hath ordained him to be your scourge, and he fareth with you as a smith with a file maketh the iron bright and clean to the sight, which before appeared rusty, dirty, and evil-coloured. The more sharp he is to you the more clearly shineth your soul in the sight of God, and God hath ordained me to be your nurse and your 22b

75

comfort. Be ye lowly and meek and thank God for both one and the other.'

On a time, before this creature went to her prayers to find out what answer she should give to the widow, she was commanded in her spirit to bid the widow leave her confessor, that was, at that time if she would please God, and go to the anchorite at the Preaching Friars in Lynne and show him her life.

When this creature gave this message, the widow would not believe her words, nor her ghostly father either, unless God should give her the same grace that He gave this creature, and she charged this creature that she should no more come to her place.

And because this creature told her that she had to feel love and affection for her ghostly father, therefore the widow said it had been good for this creature that her love and her affection were set as hers was.

Then Our Lord bade this creature write a letter and send it her. A master of divinity wrote a letter at her request and sent it to the widow with these clauses that follow:

One clause was that the widow should never have the grace that this creature had. Another was that, though this creature never came into her house, it would please God right well.

Our Lord soon after said to this creature: 'It were better for her than all this world, if her love were set as thine is, and I bid thee go to her ghostly father and tell him that, as he will not believe thy words, they shall be parted asunder sooner than he thinketh, and they that be not of her counsel shall know it ere he does, whether he will or not. Lo! Daughter, here mayest thou see how hard it is to part a man from his own will.'

And all this procedure was fulfilled in truth, as the creature had said, before twelve years after. Then this creature suffered much tribulation and great grief, because she said these words, as Our Lord bade her. And ever she increased in the love of God and was more bold than she was before.

23a BEFORE this creature went to Jerusalem, Our Lord sent
her to a worshipful lady, so that she should speak with
her in counsel and do His errand unto her. The lady
would not speak with her unless her ghostly father were
present, and she said she was well pleased. And then,
when the lady's ghostly father had come, they went into
a chapel, all three together, and then this creature said
with great reverence and many tears:—

'Madam, Our Lord Jesus Christ bade me tell you that
your husband is in Purgatory, and that ye shall be saved,
but that it shall be long ere ye come to Heaven.'

And then the lady was displeased, and said her husband
was a good man — she believed not that he was in Purgatory. Her ghostly father held with this creature, and
said it might right well be as she said, and confirmed her
words with many holy tales.

And then this lady sent her daughter, with many others
of her household with her, to the anchorite who was
principal confessor to this creature, so that he should forsake her or else he would lose her friendship. The
anchorite said to the messengers that he would not forsake this creature for any man on earth, because to such
creatures as would inquire of him her manner of governance and what he thought of her, he said she was God's
own servant, and also he said that she was the tabernacle
of God.

And the anchorite said unto her own person to strengthen her in her faith:—

'Though God take from you all tears and dalliance, believe nevertheless that God loveth you and that ye shall be right sure of Heaven for what ye have had beforetime, for tears with love are the greatest gift which God may give on earth, and all men that love God ought to thank Him for you.'

Also, there was a widow who prayed this creature to pray for her husband, and find out if he had any need of help. And as this creature prayed for him, she was answered that his soul would be thirty years in Purgatory, unless he had better friends on earth. Thus she told the widow and said:—

'If ye will give alms, three pounds or four, in Masses and alms-giving to poor folk, ye shall highly please God and give the soul great ease.'

The widow took little heed of her words and let it pass.

Then this creature went to the anchorite and told him how she had felt, and he said the feeling was of God, and the deed in itself was good, even though the soul had no need there-of, and counselled that it should be fulfilled. Then this creature told this matter to her ghostly father, so that he should speak to the widow, and so for a long time this creature heard no more of this matter.

Afterwards Our Lord Jesus Christ said to this creature:— 'That thing I bade should be done for the soul, it is not done. Ask now thy ghostly father.'

And so she did, and he said it was not done.

She said again:—'My Lord Jesus Christ told me so right now.'

23b

79

CHAPTER 20

ON a day as this creature was hearing her Mass, a young man and a good priest was holding up the Sacrament in his hands, over his head, and the Sacrament shook and flickered to and fro, as a dove flickereth with her wings. And when he held up the Chalice with the Precious Sacrament, the Chalice moved to and fro, as if it would have fallen out of his hands. When the Consecration was done, this creature had great marvel of the stirring and moving of the Blessed Sacrament, desiring to see more Consecrations, and watching if it would do so again.

Then said Our Lord Jesus Christ to the creature: — 'Thou shalt no more see It in this manner; therefore thank God that thou hast seen. My daughter, Bride, saw Me never in this wise.'

Then said this creature, in her thought: —

'Lord, what betokeneth this?'

'It betokeneth vengeance.'

'Ah! Good Lord, what vengeance?'

Then said Our Lord again to her: — 'There shall be an earthquake; tell it to whom thou wilt, in the name of Jesus. For I tell thee forsooth, right as I spoke to Saint Bride, right so I speak to thee, daughter, and I tell thee truly that it is true, every word that is written in Bride's book, and by thee it shall be known for very truth. And thou shalt fare well, daughter, in spite of all thine enemies; the more envy they have of thee for My grace, the better shall I love thee. I were not rightful God unless [I loved][1] thee, for I know thee better than thou dost thyself, [whatsoever men][1] say of thee. Thou sayest I have great patience in the sin of the people, and thou sayest truth, but if thou saw the sin of the people as I do, then wouldst thou have much more marvel in My patience and much more sorrow in the sin of the people than thou hast.'

24a

Then the creature said: — 'Alas! dearworthy Lord, what shall I do for the people?'

Our Lord answered: — 'It is enough to thee to do as thou dost.'

Then she prayed: — 'Merciful Lord Christ Jesus, in Thee is all mercy and grace and goodness. Have mercy, pity and compassion on them. Show Thy mercy and Thy goodness to them, help them, send them true contrition, and never let them die in their sin.'

Our Merciful Lord said: — 'I may no more, daughter, of My rightfulness do for them than I do. I send them preaching and teaching, pestilence and battles, hunger and famine, loss of their goods with great sickness and many other tribulations, and they will not believe My words, nor will they know My visitation. And therefore I shall say to them thus: —

' "I made My servants pray for you and ye despised their works and their living." '

---

[1] Words missing owing to damage to the MS.

Aᴛ the time that this creature had revelations, Our Lord said to her: — 'Daughter, thou art with child.'

She said to Him: — 'Ah! Lord, what shall I do for the keeping of my child?'

Our Lord said: — 'Dread thee not. I shall arrange for a keeper.'

'Lord, I am not worthy to hear Thee speak, and thus to commune with my husband. Nevertheless, it is to me great pain and great dis-ease.'

'Therefore it is no sin to thee, daughter, for it is rather to thee reward and merit, and thou shalt have never the less grace, for I will that thou bring Me forth more fruit.'

Then said the creature: — 'Lord Jesus, thus manner of living belongeth to Thy holy maidens.'

'Yea, daughter, trow thou right well that I love wives also, and specially those wives who would live chaste if they might have their will, and do their business to please Me as thou dost; for, though the state of maidenhood be more perfect and more holy than the state of widowhood, and the state of widowhood more perfect than the state 24b of wedlock, yet, daughter, I love thee as well as any maiden in the world. No man may hinder Me in loving whom I will, and as much as I will, for love, daughter, quencheth all sin. And therefore ask of Me the gifts of love. There is no gift so holy as is the gift of love, nor

82

anything to be desired so much as love, for love may purchase what it can desire. And therefore, daughter, thou mayest no better please God than continually to think on His love.'

Then this creature asked Our Lord how she should best love Him, and Our Lord said: —

'Have mind of thy wickedness and think of My goodness.'

She said again: — 'I am the most unworthy creature that ever Thou shewedest grace unto on earth.'

'Ah! daughter,' said Our Lord, 'fear thee nothing. I take no heed what a man hath been, but I take heed what he will be. Daughter, thou hast despised thyself; therefore thou shalt never be despised of God. Have mind, daughter, what Mary Magdalene was, Mary of Egypt, Saint Paul, and many other saints that are now in Heaven, for of unworthy, I make worthy, and of sinful, I make rightful. And so have I made thee worthy. To Me, once loved, and ever more loved by Me. There is no saint in Heaven that thou wilt speak with, but he shall come to thee. Whom God loveth, they love. When thou pleasest God, thou pleasest His Mother, and all the saints in Heaven. Daughter, I take witness of My Mother, of all the angels in Heaven, and of all the saints in Heaven, that I love thee with all My heart, and I may not forget thy love.'

Our Lord said then to His Blissful Mother: — 'Blessed Mother, tell ye My daughter of the greatness of the love I have unto her.'

Then this creature lay still, all in weeping and sobbing as if her heart would have burst for the sweetness of speech that Our Lord spoke unto her soul.

Immediately afterwards, the Queen of Mercy, God's Mother, dallied to the soul of this creature, saying: —

'My dearworthy daughter, I bring thee sure tidings, as witness my sweet Son Jesus, with all the angels and all the saints in Heaven who love thee full highly. Daughter, I am thy Mother, thy Lady and thy Mistress, to teach thee in all wise how thou shalt please God best.'

25a

She taught this creature and informed her so wonderfully, that she was abashed to say it or tell it to any — the matters were so high and so holy — save only to the anchorite who was her principal confessor, for he had most knowledge of such things. And he charged this creature, by virtue of obedience, to tell him whatever she felt, and so she did.

[Here follows Chapter 22]

CHAPTER 23

THERE came once a vicar to this creature, praying her to pray for him, and to find out whether he would more please God by leaving his cure and his benefice, or by keeping it still, for he thought he profited not among his parishioners. The creature being at her prayers, having mind of this matter, Christ said unto her spirit:—

'Bid the vicar keep still his cure and his benefice, and be diligent in preaching and teaching them in person, and sometimes to procure others to teach them My laws and My commandments, so that there be no default on his part, and if they do never the better, his merit shall be never the less.'

So she gave her message as she was commanded, and the vicar still kept his cure.

As this creature was in a church of Saint Margaret in the choir, where a corpse was present, and he that was husband of the same corpse, whilst she lived, was there in good health to offer her Mass-penny, as was the custom of the place, Our Lord said to the aforesaid creature:— 26b

'Lo! Daughter, the soul of this corpse is in Purgatory, and he that was her husband is now in good health, and yet he shall be dead in a short time.'

And so it befell, as she felt by revelation.

Also, as this creature lay in the choir at her prayers, a priest came to her and prayed her to pray for a woman who lay at point of death. As this creature began to pray for her, Our Lord said to her: —

'Daughter, there is great need to pray for her, for she hath been a wicked woman, and she shall die.'

And she answered: — 'Lord, as thou lovest me, save her soul from damnation.'

Then she wept with plenteous tears for that soul, and Our Lord granted her mercy for the soul, commanding her to pray for her.

This creature's ghostly father came to her, moving her to pray for a woman who lay at point of death, to man's sight, and anon Our Lord said she should live and fare well, and so she did.

A good man, who was a great friend of this creature and helpful to the poor people, was very sick for many weeks together. And much mourning was made for him, for men thought he would never have lived, his pain was so amazing in all his joints and all his body. Our Lord Jesus said to her spirit: —

'Daughter, be not afraid for this man, he shall live and fare right well.'

And so he lived many years after, in good health and prosperity.

Another good man, who was a reader, lay sick also, and when this creature prayed for him, it was answered to her mind that he should linger a while, and later would be dead of the same sickness, and so he was a short time after.

Also a worshipful woman, and as men believed, a holy woman, who was a special friend of this creature, was right sick, and many people thought she should have been dead. Then, this creature praying for her, Our Lord said: —

'She shall not die these ten years, for ye shall, after this, make full merry together, and have full good communication as ye have had before.'

And so it was, in truth. This holy woman lived many years after.

Many more such revelations this creature had in feel- 27a ing; to write them all would be hindrance, peradventure, of more profit.

These are written to show the homeliness and goodliness of Our Lord Jesus Christ, and for no commendation of this creature.

These feelings and many more than are written, both of living and of dying, of some to be saved, of some to be damned, were to this creature great pain and punishment. She would rather have suffered any bodily penance than these feelings, if she might have put them away, for the dread she had of illusions and deceits of her ghostly enemies. She had sometimes such great trouble with such feelings when they fell not true to her understanding, that her confessor feared that she would have fallen into despair therewith. And then, after her trouble and her great fears, it would be shewn unto her soul how the feelings should be understood.

THE priest who wrote this book, to prove this creature's feelings many and divers times asked her questions, and information of things that were to come, unknown and uncertain at that time to any creature as to what would be the outcome, praying her, though she was loath and unwilling to do such things, to pray to God therefore, and ascertain, when Our Lord would visit her with devotion, what would be the outcome, and truly, without any feigning, tell him how she felt, or else he would not gladly write the book.

And so this creature, compelled somewhat for fear that he would not otherwise have followed her intent to write this book, did as he prayed her, and told him her feelings as to what would befall in such matters as he asked her, if her feelings were truth. And thus he proved them for very truth. And yet he would not always give credence to her words, and that hindered him in the manner that followeth.

It befell on a time, that there came a young man to this priest, which young man the priest had never seen before, complaining to the priest of poverty and distress into which he had fallen by misfortune, explaining the cause of the misfortune, saying also that he had taken holy orders to be a priest. For a little hastiness, defending himself, as he had no choice unless he was to be dead through the pursuit of his enemies, he smote a man, or perhaps

27b

88

two, where-through, as he said, they were dead or like to die.

And so he had fallen into irregularities and might not execute his orders without dispensation of the Court of Rome, and for this reason he fled from his friends, and dared not go into his country for dread of being taken for their death.

The aforesaid priest, giving credence to the young man's words inasmuch as he was an amiable person, fair featured, well favoured in cheer and countenance, sober in his language and dalliance, priestly in his gesture and vesture, having compassion on his distress, purposing to get him friends unto his relief and comfort, went to a worshipful burgess in Lynne, a mayor's equal, and a merciful man, who lay in great sickness, and long had done so, complaining to him and his wife, a full good woman, of the misfortune of this young man, trusting to have fair alms as he oftentimes had for others that he asked for.

It happened that the creature, of whom this book is written, was present there and heard how the priest pleaded for the young man, and how the priest praised him. And she was sore moved in her spirit against that young man, and said they had many poor neighbours whom, they knew well enough, had great need of being helped and relieved, and it should rather be alms to help them that they knew well for well disposed folk, and their own neighbours, than strangers that they knew not, for many speak and seem full fair outwardly to the sight of the people. God knoweth what they are in their souls!

The good man and his wife thought she spoke right well, and therefore they would grant him no alms.

At that time the priest was evil-pleased with this

creature, and when he met her alone, he repeated how she had hindered him so that he could get no alms for the young man, who was a well-disposed man, as he thought, and much commended his behaviour.

28a

The creature said:—'Sir, God knoweth what his behaviour is, for, as far as I know, I have never seen him and yet I have understanding what his behaviour should be; and therefore, Sir, if ye will act by my counsel, and after what I feel, let him choose and help himself as well as he can, and meddle ye not with him, for he will deceive you at the last.'

The young man resorted always to the priest, flattering him and saying that he had good friends in other places, who would help him if they knew where he was, and that in a short time; and also they would thank those persons who had supported him in his distress. The priest, trusting it would be as this young man told him, lent him silver, with good will, to help him. The young man prayed the priest to hold him excused if he saw him not for two days or three, for he would go a little way, and come again in a short time and bring him back his silver right well and truly. The priest, having confidence in his promise, was well content, granting him good love and leave unto the day on which he had promised to come again.

When he was gone, the aforesaid creature, understanding by feeling in her soul that Our Lord would show that he was an untrue man, and would come back no more, she, to prove whether her feeling was true or false, asked the priest where the young man was, that he had praised so much.

The priest said he had walked a little way and he trusted that he would come again. She said she supposed he would no more see him, and no more he did ever after. And then he repented that he had not done after her counsel.

A short time after this was past, there came another false rascal, an old man, to the same priest and proffered him a breviary, a good little book, for sale. The priest went to the aforesaid creature, praying her to pray for him, and find out whether God willed that he should buy the book or not, and while she prayed, he cheered the man as well as he could, and then came again to this creature and asked how she felt.

'Sir,' she said, 'buy no book from him, for he is not to be trusted, and that ye will well know if ye meddle with him.'

Then the priest prayed the man that he might see his book. The man said he had not got it on him. The priest asked how he came by it. He said he was executor to a priest who was of his kindred, and he charged him to sell it, and dispose of it for him.

'Father,' said the priest — because of reverence — 'why do ye offer me this book rather than other men or other priests, when there are so many more thriftier and richer priests in this church than I am, and I wot well ye had no knowledge of me before this time?'

'Forsooth, Sir,' he said, 'no more I had. Nevertheless I have good will toward your person, and also it was his will, who owned it before, that, if I knew any young priest that me-thought quiet and well disposed, he should have this book before any other man, and for less price than any other man, that he might pray for him, and these causes make me come to you rather than to another.'

The priest asked him where he dwelt.

28b

'Sir,' he said, 'but five miles from this place in Penteney[1] Abbey.'

'There have I been,' said the priest, 'but I have not seen you.'

'No, Sir,' said he again, 'I have been there but a little while, and now have I there an allowance of food, thanks be to God.'

The priest prayed him that he might have a sight of the book and see if they might agree.

He said: — 'Sir, I hope to be here again next week and to bring it with me, and, Sir, I promise you, ye shall have it before any other man, if ye like it.' The priest thanked him for his good will and so they parted asunder, but the man never came to the priest afterwards, and the priest knew well that the aforesaid creature's feeling was true.

[1] *See* Note B.

Furthermore, here followeth a right notable matter of the creature's feeling, and it is written here for convenience inasmuch as it is, in feeling, like the matters that be written before, notwithstanding that it befell long after the matters which follow.

It happened in a worshipful town where there was one parish church and two chapels annexed, the chapels having and administering all the Sacraments, except only christening and purifications, through sufferance of the parson, who was a monk of Saint Benedict's Order, sent from the house of Norwich, keeping residence with three of his 29a brethren in the worshipful town before written.

Through some of the parishioners desiring to make the chapels like the parish church by pursuance of a bull from the Court of Rome, there befell great dispute and great trouble between the prior, who was their parson and curate, and the aforesaid parishioners, who desired to have fonts and purifications in the chapels, as there were in the parish church. And especially in the one chapel[1] which was the greater and fairer, they would have a font.

There was pursued a bull, under which a font was granted to the chapel, provided that it was no derogation to the parish church. The bull was put in plea and divers days were spent in form of law to prove whether the font, if it were put in, would be derogatory to the parish church

---

[1] St. Nicholas' Chapel, King's Lynn. *See* Notes F and G.

or not. The parishioners who pursued were right strong, and had great help of lordship, and also, most of all, they were rich men, worshipful merchants, and had gold enough, that can speed in every need; and it is ruth that need should speed ere truth.

Nevertheless, the prior who was their parson, though he was poor, manfully withstood them with the help of some of his parishioners who were his friends, and loved the worship of their parish church. So long was this matter in plea that it began to irk them on both sides, and it was never the nearer an end.

Then was the matter put to my lord of Norwich — Alnewyk — to see if he might by treaty bring it to an end. He laboured this matter diligently; and to set it at rest and peace, he proffered the aforesaid parishioners much of their desire with certain conditions, insomuch that they that held with the parson and with their parish church, were full sorry, dreading greatly that they that sued to have a font would obtain and get their intent and so make the chapel equal to the parish church.

Then the priest who afterwards wrote this book, went to the creature of whom this treatise maketh mention, as he had done before in time of plea, and asked her how she felt in her soul on this matter, whether they should have a font in the chapel or not.

29b 'Sir,' said the creature, 'dread ye not, for I understand in my soul, though they should give [even][1] a bushel of nobles[2] they could not have it.'

'Ah! Mother,' said the priest, 'my lord of Norwich hath offered it to them on certain conditions, and they

[1] Word missing in MS.
[2] The value of a noble was six shillings and eightpence.

94

have a time for consideration to say nay or yea, whichever they will, and therefore I am afraid they will not refuse it, but be right glad to have it.'

This creature prayed to God that His will might be fulfilled, and, forasmuch as she had the revelation that they would not have it, she was the more bold to pray Our Lord to withstand their intent and slacken their boasting.

And so, as Our Lord willed, they obeyed not nor liked the conditions which were offered them, for they trusted fully to get their intent by lordship and process of law; and, as God willed, they were deceived of their intent, and because they would have all, they lost all.

And so, blessed may God be, the parish church stood fast in their worship and her degree, as she had done for two hundred years before and more, and the inspiration of Our Lord was by experience proved very true and sure in the aforesaid creature.

CHAPTER 26

W HEN the time came that this creature should visit
those holy places where Our Lord was quick and dead,
as she had by revelation years before, she prayed the
parish priest of the town where she was dwelling, to say
for her in the pulpit, that, if any man or woman claimed
any debt from her husband or herself, they should come
and speak with her ere she went, and she, with the help of
God would make a settlement with each of them, so that
they should hold themselves content. And so she did.

Afterwards, she took her leave of her husband and of
the holy anchorite, who had told her, before, the process
of her going and the great dis-ease that she would suffer
by the way, and when all her fellowship forsook her, how
a broken-backed man would lead her forth in safety,
through the help of Our Lord.

And so it befell indeed, as shall be written afterward.

3ca   Then she took her leave of Master Robert, and prayed
him for his blessing, and so, forth of other friends. Then
she went forth to Norwich, and offered at the Trinity, and
afterwards she went to Yarmouth and offered at an image
of Our Lady, and there she took her ship.

And next day they came to a great town called
Zierikzee, where Our Lord of His high goodness visited
this creature with abundant tears of contrition for her
own sins, and sometime for other men's sins also. And
especially she had tears of compassion in mind of Our

96

Lord's Passion. And she was houselled each Sunday where there was time and place convenient thereto, with great weeping and boisterous sobbing, so that many men marvelled and wondered at the great grace that God had wrought in His creature.

This creature had eaten no flesh and drunk no wine for four years ere she went out of England, and so now her ghostly father charged her, by virtue of obedience, that she should both eat flesh and drink wine. And so she did a little while; afterwards she prayed her confessor that he would hold her excused if she ate no flesh, and suffer her to do as she would for such time as pleased him.

And soon after, through the moving of some of her company, her confessor was displeased because she ate no flesh, and so were many of the company. And they were most displeased because she wept so much and spoke always of the love and goodness of Our Lord, as much at the table as in other places. And therefore shamefully they reproved her, and severely chid her, and said they would not put up with her as her husband did when she was at home and in England.

And she answered meekly to them: — 'Our Lord, Almighty God, is as great a Lord here as in England, and as good cause have I to love Him here as there, blessed may He be.'

At these words, her fellowship was angrier than before, and their wrath and unkindness to this creature was a matter of great grief, for they were held right good men and she desired greatly their love, if she might have it to the pleasure of God.

And then she said to one of them specially: — 'Ye cause 30b me much shame and great grievance.'

He answered her anon: — 'I pray God that the devil's death may overcome thee soon and quickly,' and many more cruel words he said to her than she could repeat.

And soon after some of the company in whom she trusted best, and her own maiden also, said she could no longer go in their fellowship. And they said that they would take away her maiden from her, so that she should no strumpet be, in her company. And then one of them, who had her gold in keeping, left her a noble with great anger and vexation to go where she would and help herself as she might, for with them, they said, she should no longer abide; and they forsook her that night.

Then, on the next morning, there came to her one of their company, a man who loved her well, praying her that she would go to his fellows and meeken herself to them, and pray them that she might go still in their company till she came to Constance.

And so she did, and went forth with them till she came to Constance with great discomfort and great trouble, for they did her much shame and much reproof as they went, in divers places. They cut her gown so short that it came but little beneath her knee, and made her put on a white canvas, in the manner of a sacken apron, so that she should be held a fool and the people should not make much of her or hold her in repute. They made her sit at the table's end, below all the others, so that she ill durst speak a word.

And, notwithstanding all their malice, she was held in more worship than they were, wherever they went.

And the good man of the house where they were hostelled, though she sat lowest at the table's end, would always help her before them all as well as he could, and sent her from his own table such service as he had, and that annoyed her fellowship full evil.

As they went by the way Constance-ward, it was told them that they would be robbed and have great discomfort unless they had great grace.

Then this creature came to a church and went in to make her prayer, and she prayed with all her heart, with great weeping and many tears, for help and succour against their enemies. 31a

Then Our Lord said to her mind:— 'Dread thee naught, daughter, thy fellowship shall come to no harm whilst thou art in their company.'

And so, blessed may Our Lord be in all His works, they went forth in safety to Constance.

CHAPTER 27

W<small>HEN</small> this creature and her fellowship had come to Constance, she heard tell of an English friar, a master of divinity, and the Pope's legate, who was in that city. Then she went to that worshipful man and shewed him her life from the beginning till that hour, as nigh as she might in confession, because he was the Pope's legate and a worshipful clerk.

And afterwards she told him what discomfort she had with her fellowship. She told him also what grace God gave her of contrition and compunction, of sweetness and devotion and of many divers revelations that God had revealed to her, and the fear that she had of illusions and deceits of her ghostly enemies, of which she lived in great dread, desiring to put them away, and to feel none, if she might withstand them.

And when she had spoken, the worshipful clerk gave her words of great comfort, and said it was the work of the Holy Ghost, commanding and charging her to obey them and receive them when God should give them and to have no doubts, for the devil hath no power to work such grace in a soul. And also he said that he would support her against the evil will of her fellowship.

Afterwards, when it pleased her fellowship, they prayed this worthy doctor to dinner, and the doctor told the aforesaid creature, warning her to sit at the meat in his presence as she did in his absence, and to keep the same manner of behaviour as she kept when he was not there.

When the time had come for them to sit at meat, every man took his place as he liked; the worshipful legate and doctor sat first, and then the others, and, at the last, the said creature at the board's end, sitting and speaking no word, as she was wont to do, when the legate was not there.

31b

Then the legate said to her: —

'Why are ye no merrier?'

And she sat still and answered not, as he himself had commanded her to do.

When they had eaten, the company made great complaint against this creature to the legate, and said that, utterly, she could no longer be in their company, unless he commanded her to eat flesh as they did and stop her weeping, and that she should not talk so much of holiness.

Then the worshipful doctor said:—'Nay, sirs, I will not make her eat flesh whilst she can abstain and be the better disposed to Our Lord. If one of you made a vow to go to Rome barefoot, I would not dispense him of his vow whilst he could fulfil it, nor will I bid her to eat flesh whilst our Lord giveth her strength to abstain. As for her weeping, it is not in my power to restrain it, for it is the gift of the Holy Ghost. As for her speaking, I will pray her to cease till she cometh where men will hear her with better will than ye do.'

The company was wroth, and in great anger. They gave her over to the legate and said utterly that they would no more associate with her. He full benignly and kindly received her as though she had been his mother, and received her gold, about twenty pounds, and yet one of them withheld wrongfully about sixteen pounds.

And they withheld also her maiden, and would not let

her go with her mistress, notwithstanding that she had promised her mistress and assured her that she would not forsake her for any need.

And the legate made arrangements for this creature and made her his charge as if she had been his mother.

Then this creature went into a church and prayed Our Lord that He would provide her with a leader.

And anon Our Lord spoke to her and said: —

'Thou shalt have right good help and a good leader.'

Immediately afterwards there came to her an old man with a white beard. He was from Devonshire, and said: —

'Damsel, will ye pray me for God's love, and for Our Lady's, to go with you and be your guide, for your countrymen have forsaken you?'

32a   She asked, what was his name?

He said: — 'My name is William Wever.'

She prayed him, by the reverence of God and of Our Lady, that he would help her at her need, and she would well reward him for his labour, and so they agreed.

Then went she to the legate and told him how well Our Lord had ordained for her, and took her leave of him and of her company who so unkindly had rejected her, and also of her maiden who was bounden to have gone with her. She took her leave with full heavy face and rueful, having great grief in as much as she was in a strange country, and knew not the language, or the man who would lead her, either.

And so the man and she went forth in great dread and gloom. As they went together, the man said to her: —

'I am afraid thou wilt be taken from me, and I shall be beaten for thee, and lose my jacket.'

She said: — 'William, dread you not. God will keep us right well.'

And this creature had every day mind of the Gospel which telleth of the woman that was taken in adultery, and brought before Our Lord.

And she prayed: — 'Lord, as thou drove away her enemies, so drive away mine enemies, and keep well my chastity that I vowed to Thee, and let me never be defiled, for if I am, Lord, I make my vow, that I will never come back to England whilst I live.'

Then they went forth day by day and met with many jolly men. And they said no evil word to this creature, but gave her and her man meat and drink, and the good wives where they were housed, laid her in their own beds for God's love, in many places where they came.

And Our Lord visited her with great grace of ghostly comfort as she went by the way. And so God brought her forth till she came to Bologna.[1] And after she had come there, there came thither also her other fellowship, which had forsaken her before. And when they heard say that she had come to Bologna ere they had, then had they great wonder, and one of their fellowship came to her praying her to go to his fellowship and try if they would receive her again into their fellowship. And so she did.

'If ye will go in our fellowship, ye must make a new covenant, and that is this — ye shall not speak of the Gospel where we are, but shall sit still and make merry, as we do, both at meat and at supper.'   32b

She consented and was received again into their fellowship. Then went they forth to Venice and dwelt there thirteen weeks; and this creature was houselled

[1] In MS. 'Boleyn de Grace'. Bologna was called 'the Fat'.

every Sunday in a great house of nuns, and had great cheer among them, where Our Lord Jesus Christ visited this creature with great devotion and plenteous tears, so that the good ladies of the place were much marvelled thereof.

Afterwards, it happened, as this creature sat at meat with her fellowship, that she repeated a text of the Gospel that she had learnt beforetime with other good words, and then her fellowship said she had broken covenant. And she said:—

'Yea, sirs, forsooth I may no longer keep your covenant, for I must needs speak of My Lord Jesus Christ, though all this world had forbidden it me.'

Then she took to her chamber and ate alone for six weeks, unto the time that Our Lord made her so sick that she weened to have been dead, and then suddenly He made her whole again. And all the time her maiden let her alone and made the company's meat and washed their clothes, and, to her mistress, under whom she had taken service, she would no deal attend.

CHAPTER 28

ALSO this company, which had put the aforesaid creature from their table, so that she should no longer eat
amongst them, engaged a ship for themselves to sail in.
They bought vessels for their wine, and obtained bedding
for themselves, but nothing for her. Then she, seeing
their unkindness, went to the same man where they had
been, and bought herself bedding as they had done, and
came where they were and shewed them what she had
done, purposing to sail with them in that ship which they
had chartered.

Afterwards, as this creature was in contemplation, Our
Lord warned her in her mind that she should not sail in
that ship, and He assigned her to another ship, a galley,
that she should sail in. Then she told this to some of the
company, and they told it forth to their fellowship, and
then they durst not sail in the ship they had chartered. So 33a
they sold away their vessels which they had got for their
wines, and were right fain to come to the galley where she
was, and so, though it was against her will, she went forth
with them in their company, for they durst not otherwise
do.

When it was time to make their beds, they locked up
her clothes, and a priest, who was in their company, took
away a sheet from the aforesaid creature, and said it was
his. She took God to witness that it was her sheet. Then
the priest swore a great oath, by the book in his hand,

that she was as false as she might be, and despised her and strongly rebuked her.

And so she had ever much tribulation till she came to Jerusalem. And ere she came there, she said to them that she supposed they were grieved with her.

'I pray you, Sirs, be in charity with me, for I am in charity with you, and forgive me that I have grieved you by the way. And if any of you have in anything trespassed against me, God forgive it you, and I do.'

So they went forth into the Holy Land till they could see Jerusalem. And when this creature saw Jerusalem, riding on an ass, she thanked God with all her heart, praying Him for His mercy that, as He had brought her to see His earthly city of Jerusalem, He would grant her grace to see the blissful city of Jerusalem above, the city of Heaven. Our Lord Jesus Christ, answering her thought, granted her to have her desire.

Then for the joy she had, and the sweetness she felt in the dalliance with Our Lord, she was on the point of falling off her ass, for she could not bear the sweetness and grace that God wrought in her soul. Then two pilgrims, Duchemen, went to her, and kept her from falling; one of whom was a priest, and he put spices in her mouth to comfort her, thinking she had been sick. And so they helped her on to Jerusalem, and when she came there, she said:—

'Sirs, I pray you be not displeased though I weep sore in this holy place where Our Lord Jesus Christ was quick and dead.'

Then went they to the temple in Jerusalem and they were let in on the same day at evensong time, and abode there till the next day at evensong time. Then the friars lifted up a cross and led the pilgrims about from one

place to another where Our Lord suffered His[1] ... and   33b
His Passion, every man and woman bearing a wax candle
in one hand. And the friars always, as they went about,
told them what Our Lord suffered in every place. The
aforesaid creature wept and sobbed as plenteously as
though she had seen Our Lord with her bodily eye,
suffering His Passion at that time. Before her in her soul
she saw Him verily by contemplation, and that caused
her to have compassion. And when they came up on to
the Mount of Calvary, she fell down because she could
not stand or kneel, and rolled and wrested with her body,
spreading her arms abroad, and cried with a loud voice
as though her heart burst asunder; for, in the city of her
soul, she saw verily and clearly how Our Lord was crucified. Before her face, she heard and saw, in her ghostly
sight, the mourning of Our Lady, of Saint John, and
Mary Magdalene and of many others that loved Our
Lord.

And she had such great compassion and such great
pain, at seeing Our Lord's pain that she could not keep
herself from crying and roaring though she should have
died for it. And this was the first cry[2] that ever she cried
in any contemplation. And this manner of crying endured
many years after this time, for aught any man might do,
and therefore, suffered she much despite and much reproof. The crying was so loud and so wonderful that it
made the people astounded unless they had heard it
before, or unless they knew the cause of the crying. And
she had them so often that they made her right weak in
her bodily might, and especially if she heard of Our Lord's
Passion.

[1] Word missing in MS.   [2] Outcry; scream.

107

And sometimes, when she saw the crucifix, or if she saw a man with a wound, or a beast, whichever it were, or if a man beat a child before her, or smote a horse or other beast with a whip, if she saw it or heard it, she thought she saw Our Lord being beaten or wounded, just as she saw it in the man or the beast either in the field or the town, and by herself alone as well as amongst the people.

34a First when she had her cryings in Jerusalem, she had them often, and in Rome also. And when she came home to England, first at her coming home, it came but seldom, as it were once a month, then once a week, afterwards daily, and once she had fourteen in one day, and another day she had seven, and so on, as God would visit her, sometimes in church, sometimes in the street, sometimes in her chamber, sometimes in the fields, whenever God would send them, for she never knew the time nor the hour when they would come. And they never came without passing great sweetness of devotion and high contemplation. And as soon as she perceived that she would cry, she would keep it in as much as she might that the people should not hear it, to their annoyance. For some said that a wicked spirit vexed her; some said it was a sickness; some said she had drunk too much wine; some banned her; some wished she was in the harbour; some wished she was on the sea in a bottomless boat; and thus each man as he thought. Other ghostly men loved her and favoured her the more. Some great clerks said Our Lady cried never so, nor any saint in Heaven, but they knew full little what she felt, nor would they believe that she could not stop crying if she wished.

And therefore when she knew that she would cry, she kept it in as long as she might, and did all she could to withstand it or put it away, till she waxed as livid as any lead, and ever it would labour in her mind more and more till the time it broke out. And when the body might no longer endure the ghostly labour, but was overcome with the unspeakable love that wrought so fervently in her soul, then she fell down and cried wondrous loud, and the more she laboured to keep it in or put it away, so much the more would she cry, and the louder. Thus she did on the Mount of Calvary, as is written before.

Thus she had as very contemplation in the sight of her soul, as if Christ had hung before her bodily eye in His 34b Manhood. And when through the dispensation of the high mercy of Our Sovereign Saviour Christ Jesus, it was granted to this creature to behold so verily His precious tender body, all rent and torn with scourges, fuller of wounds than ever was a dove-house of holes, hanging on the Cross with the crown of thorns upon His head, His beautiful hands, His tender feet nailed to the hard tree, the rivers of blood flowing out plenteously from every member, the grisly and grievous wound in His precious side shedding blood and water for her love and her salvation, then she fell down and cried with a loud voice, wonderfully turning and wresting her body on every side, spreading her arms abroad as if she would have died, and could not keep herself from crying, and from these bodily movements for the fire of love that burnt so fervently in her soul with pure pity and compassion.

It is not to be marvelled at, if this creature cried and made wondrous faces and expressions, when we may see each day with the eye both men and women, some for the loss of worldly goods, some for affection of their kindred, or worldly friendships, through over much study and earthly affection, and most of all for inordinate love and fleshly affection, if their friends are parted from them, they will cry and roar and wring their hands as if they had no wits or senses, and yet know they well that they are displeasing God.

And, if a man counsel them to leave or cease their weeping and crying, they will say that they cannot; they loved their friend so much, and he was so gentle and so kind to them, that they may in no way forget him. How much more might they weep, cry, and roar, if their most beloved friends were with violence taken in their sight and with all manner of reproof, brought before the judge, wrongfully condemned to death, and especially so spiteful a death as Our Merciful Lord suffered for our sake. How would they suffer it? No doubt they would both cry 35a and roar and avenge themselves if they might, or else men would say they were no friends.

Alas! Alas! for sorrow that the death of a creature, who hath often sinned and trespassed against their Maker, shall be so immeasurably mourned and sorrowed. And it is an offence to God, and a hindrance to the souls beside them.

And the compassionate death of Our Saviour by which we are all restored to life, is not kept in mind by us unworthy and unkind wretches, nor do we support Our Lord's own secretaries whom He hath endued with love, but rather detract and hinder them as much as we may.

Wᴴᴇɴ this creature with her fellowship came to the grave where Our Lord was buried, anon, as she entered that holy place, she fell down with her candle in her hand, as if she would have died for sorrow. And later she rose up again with great weeping and sobbing, as though she had seen Our Lord buried even before her.

Then she thought she saw Our Lady in her soul, how she mourned and how she wept for her Son's death, and then was Our Lady's sorrow her sorrow.

And so, wherever the friars led them in that holy place, she always wept and sobbed wonderfully, and especially when she came where Our Lord was nailed on the Cross. There cried she, and wept without measure, so that she could not restrain herself.

Also they came to a stone of marble that Our Lord was laid on when He was taken down from the Cross, and there she wept with great compassion, having mind of Our Lord's Passion.

Afterwards she was houselled on the Mount of Calvary, and then she wept, she sobbed, she cried so loud that it was a wonder to hear it. She was so full of holy thoughts and meditations and holy contemplations on the Passion of Our Lord Jesus Christ, and holy dalliance that Our Lord Jesus Christ spoke to her soul, that she could never express them after, so high and so holy were they. Much was the grace that Our Lord shewed to this creature whilst she was three weeks in Jerusalem.

Another day, early in the morning, they went again 5b amongst great hills, and their guides told her where Our Lord bore the Cross on His back, and where His Mother met with Him, and how she swooned and fell down and He fell down also. And so they went forth all the forenoon till they came to Mount Sion. And ever this creature wept abundantly, all the way that she went, for compassion of Our Lord's Passion. On Mount Sion is a place where Our Lord washed His disciples' feet and, a little therefrom, He made His Maundy with His disciples.

And therefore this creature had great desire to be houselled in that holy place where Our Merciful Lord Christ Jesus first consecrated His precious Body in the form of bread, and gave it to His disciples. And so she was, with great devotion and plenteous tears and boisterous sobbings, for in this place is plenary remission, and so there is in four other places in the Temple. One is on the Mount of Calvary; another at the grave where Our Lord was buried; the third is at the marble stone that His precious Body was laid on, when It was taken from the Cross; the fourth is where the Holy Cross was buried; and in many other places in Jerusalem.

And when this creature came to the place where the apostles received the Holy Ghost, Our Lord gave her great devotion. Afterwards she went to the place where Our Lady was buried, and as she knelt on her knees the time of two masses, Our Lord Jesus Christ said to her: —

'Thou comest not hither, daughter, for any need except merit and reward, for thy sins were forgiven thee ere thou came here and therefore thou comest here for the increasing of thy reward and thy merit. And I am well pleased with thee, daughter, for thou standest under obedience to Holy Church, and because thou wilt obey thy confessor and follow his counsel who, through authority of Holy Church, hath absolved thee of thy sins and dispensed thee so that thou shouldst not go to Rome and Saint James unless thou wilt thine own self. Notwithstanding all this, I command thee in the Name of Jesus, daughter, that thou go visit these holy places and do as I bid thee, for I am above Holy Church, and I shall go with thee and keep thee right well.'

Then Our Lady spoke to her soul in this manner, saying: — 36a

'Daughter, well art thou blessed, for my Son Jesus shall flow so much grace into thee that all the world shall wonder at thee. Be not ashamed, my dearworthy daughter, to receive the gifts that my Son shall give thee, for I tell thee in truth, they shall be great gifts that He shall give thee. And therefore, my dearworthy daughter, be not ashamed of Him that is thy God, thy Lord and thy love, any more than I was, when I saw Him hanging on the Cross — my sweet Son, Jesus — to cry and to weep for the pain of my sweet Son Jesus Christ. Mary Magdalene was not ashamed to cry and weep for my Son's love. Therefore, daughter, if thou will be partaker in our love, thou must be partaker in our sorrow.'

This sweet speech and dalliance had this creature at Our Lady's grave, and much more than she could ever repeat.

Afterwards she rode on an ass to Bethlehem, and when she came to the temple and the crib where Our Lord was born, she had great devotion, much speech and dalliance in her soul, and high ghostly comfort with much weeping and sobbing, so that her fellows would not let her eat in their company, and therefore she ate her meat by herself alone.

And then the Grey Friars,[1] who had led her from place to place, received her to them and set her with them at the meat so that she should not eat alone. And one of the friars asked one of her fellowship if she were the woman of England whom, they had heard said, spoke with God. And when this came to her knowledge, she knew well that it was the truth that Our Lord said to her, ere she went out of England: —

'Daughter, I will make all the world to wonder at thee, and many a man and many a woman shall speak of Me for love of thee, and worship Me in thee.'

[1] *See* Note I.

CHAPTER 30

ANOTHER time, this creature's fellowship would go to the Flood of Jordan and would not let her go with them. Then this creature prayed Our Lord that she might go with them, and He bade that she should go with them whether they would or not. Then she went forth by the grace of God, and asked no leave of them.

36b

When she came to the Flood of Jordan, the weather was so hot that she thought her feet would have burnt for the heat that she felt.

Afterwards she went with her fellowship to Mount Quarentyne.[1] There Our Lord fasted forty days, and there she prayed her fellowship to help her up on to the Mount. And they said, 'Nay', for they could not well help themselves. Then had she great sorrow, because she might not come on to the hill. And anon, happed a Saracen, a well-favoured man, to come by her, and she put a groat into his hand, making him a sign to bring her on to the Mount. And quickly the Saracen took her under his arm and led her up on to the high Mount, where Our Lord fasted forty days.

Then was she sore a-thirst, and had no comfort in her fellowship. Then God, of His great goodness, moved the Grey Friars with compassion, and they comforted her, when her countrymen would not know her.

[1] A 'quarentine' is a period of forty days. The Mount is now generally known as the 'Hill of Temptation'.

And so she was ever more strengthened in the love of Our Lord and the more bold to suffer shame and reproof for His sake in every place where she came, for the grace that God wrought in her of weeping, sobbing, and crying, which grace she might not withstand when God would send it. And ever she proved her feelings true, and those promises that God had made her while she was in England and other places also. They befell her in effect just as she had felt before, and therefore she durst the better receive such speeches and dalliance, and the more boldly work thereafter.

Afterwards, when this creature came down from the Mount, as God willed, she went forth to the place where Saint John the Baptist was born. And later she went to Bethania, where Mary and Martha dwelt, and to the grave where Lazarus was buried and raised from death into life. And she prayed in the chapel where Our Blessed Lord appeared to His blissful Mother on Easter Day at morn, first of all others. And she stood in the same place where Mary Magdalene stood when Christ said to her: —

'Mary, why weepest thou?'

And so she was in many more places than be written, for she was three weeks in Jerusalem and the country thereabout, and she had ever great devotion as long as she was in that country.

The friars of the Temple made her great cheer and gave her many great relics, desiring that she should have dwelt still amongst them if she would, for the faith they had in her. Also the Saracens made much of her, and conveyed her, and led her about the country wherever she would go; and she found all people good to her and gentle, save only her own countrymen.

37a

And as she came from Jerusalem unto Rafnys,[1] then would she have turned again to Jerusalem for the great grace and ghostly comfort that she felt when she was there, and to purchase herself more pardon.

Then Our Lord commanded her to go to Rome and, so, forth home into England, and said to her: —

'Daughter, as oftentimes as thou sayest or thinkest "Worshipped be those Holy Places in Jerusalem that Christ suffered bitter pain and Passion in", thou shalt have the same pardon as if thou wert there with thy bodily presence, both to thyself and to all that thou wilt give it to.'

And as she went forth to Venice, many of her fellowship were right sick, and Our Lord said to her: —

'Dread thee not, daughter, no man shall die in the ship that thou art in.'

And she found her feelings right true. When Our Lord had brought them again to Venice in safety, her countrymen forsook her and went away from her, leaving her alone. And some of them said that they would not go with her for a hundred pound.

When they had gone away from her, then Our Lord Jesus Christ, Who ever helpeth at need, and never forsaketh His servants who truly trust in His mercy, said to this creature: —

'Dread thee not, daughter, for I will provide for thee right well, and bring thee in safety to Rome and home again into England without any villainy to thy body, if thou wilt be clad in white clothes, and wear them as I said to thee whilst thou wert in England.' 37b

Then this creature, being in great grief and distress, answered Him in her mind: —

[1] *See* Note R.

117

'If Thou be the spirit of God that speaketh in my soul, and I may prove Thee for a true spirit with the counsel of the Church, I shall obey Thy will; and if Thou bringest me to Rome in safety, I shall wear white clothes, though all the world should wonder at me, for Thy love.'

'Go forth, daughter, in the Name of Jesus, for I am the spirit of God, which shall help thee in all thy need, go with thee, and support thee in every place, and therefore mistrust Me not. Thou foundest Me never deceivable, and I bid thee nothing do, but that which is worship to God, and profit to thy soul. If thou will do thereafter, then I shall flow on thee great plenty of grace.'

Then anon, as she looked on one side, she saw a poor man sitting, who had a great hump on his back. His clothes were all clouted and he seemed a man of fifty winter's age. Then she went to him and said: —

'Good man, what aileth your back?'

He said: — 'Damsel, it was broken in a sickness.'

She asked, what was his name, and what countryman he was. He said his name was Richard, and he was of Ireland. Then thought she of her confessor's words, who was a holy anchorite, as is written before, who spoke to her whilst she was in England in this manner: —

'Daughter, when your fellowship hath forsaken you, God will provide a broken-backed man to lead you forth, wherever you will go.'

Then she, with a glad spirit, said to him: —

'Good Richard, lead me to Rome, and you shall be rewarded for your labour.'

'Nay, damsel,' said he, 'I wot well thy countrymen have forsaken thee, and therefore it were hard on me to lead thee. Thy countrymen have both bows and arrows with which they might defend both thee and themselves, and I have no weapon save a cloak full of clouts, and yet I dread me that mine enemies will rob me, and perad- 38a venture take thee away from me and defile thy body, and therefore I dare not lead thee, for I would not, for a hundred pounds, that thou hadst a villainy in my company.'

And she said again: — 'Richard, dread you not; God shall keep us both right well and I shall give you two nobles for your labour.'

Then he consented and went forth with her. Soon after, there came two Grey Friars and a woman that came with them from Jerusalem, and she had with her an ass, which bore a chest and an image therein, made after Our Lord.

Then said Richard to the aforesaid creature: — 'Thou shalt go forth with these two men and the woman and I will meet thee morning and evening, for I must get on with my job and beg my living.'

So she did after his counsel and went forth with the two friars and the woman. And none of them could understand her language, and yet they provided for her every day, meat, drink, and harbourage as well as they did for themselves and rather better, so that she was ever bounden to pray for them.

Every evening and morning, Richard with the broken back came and comforted her as he had promised.

The woman who had the image in the chest, when they came into good cities, took the image out of her chest, and set it in worshipful wives' laps; and they would put shirts thereon, and kiss it as if it had been God Himself.

When the creature saw the worship and reverence that they gave to the image, she was taken with sweet devotion and sweet meditations, so that she wept with great sobbing and loud crying; and she was moved so much the more, because while she was in England, she had high meditations on the birth and the childhood of Christ, and she thanked God forasmuch as she saw these creatures having as great faith in what she saw with her bodily eye, as she had had before with her ghostly eye.

38b When these good women saw this creature weeping, sobbing and crying so wonderfully and mightily that she was nearly overcome therewith, then they arranged a good soft bed and laid her thereon, and comforted her as much as they could for Our Lord's sake, blessed may He be.

The aforesaid creature had a ring, which Our Lord had commanded her to have made whilst she was at home in England, and she had engraved thereon, 'Jesus Cryst est amor meus'. She had much thought how she should keep this ring from thieves and stealing, as she went about the countries, for she thought she would not have lost the ring for a thousand pounds and much more, because she had it made by the bidding of God; and also, she wore it by His bidding, for she purposed beforetime, ere she had it by revelation, never to have worn a ring.

So it happed her to be harboured in a good man's house, and many neighbours came in to cheer her for her perfection and her holiness, and she gave them the measure of Christ's grace which they received full kindly, having great joy thereof, and thanked her highly therefor.

Afterwards this creature went to her chamber and let her ring hang by her purse-string, which she bore at her breast. In the morning on the next day, when she would have taken her ring, it was gone. She could not find it. Then had she great grief, and complained to the good wife of the house, saying in this wise: —

'Madam, my good wedding ring to Jesus Christ, as one might say, it is away.'

The good wife, understanding what she meant, prayed her to pray for her, and she changed her face and countenance strangely, as though she had been guilty.

Then this creature took a candle in her hand and sought all about her bed where she had lain all night, and the good wife of the house took another candle in her hand and busied herself seeking also about the bed; and at last she found the ring under the bed on the boards. And with great joy she told the good wife that she had found her ring. Then the good wife, submitting herself, prayed this creature for forgiveness, as well as she could. 'Good Christian, pray for me.'

39ª

Afterwards this creature came to Assisi, and there she met with a Friar Minor,[1] an Englishman; and a devout clerk, he was held to be. She told him of her manner of living, of her feelings, of her revelations, and of the grace that God wrought in her soul by holy inspirations and high contemplations, and how Our Lord dallied to her soul in a manner of speaking. Then the worshipful clerk said she was much beholden to God, for he said he had never heard of anyone living in this world, who was so homely with God by love and homely dalliance, as she was, thanked be God for His gifts, for it is His goodness, and no man's merit.

Upon a time, as this creature was in church at Assisi, there was shewn Our Lady's kerchief which she wore here on earth, with many lights and great reverence. Then this creature had great devotion. She wept, she sobbed, she cried with great plenty of tears and many holy thoughts. She was also there on Lammas Day, when there is great pardon with plenary remission, to purchase grace, mercy and forgiveness for herself, for all her friends, for all her enemies, and for all the souls in Purgatory.

And there was a lady who had come from Rome to

[1] *See* Note I.

purchase her pardon. Her name was Margaret Florentyne, and she had with her many Knights of Rhodes, many gentlewomen, and much good baggage.

Then Richard, the broken-backed man, went to her, praying her that this creature might go with her to Rome, and himself also, so as to be kept from the peril of thieves. And then that worshipful lady received them into her company and let them go with her to Rome, as God willed. When the aforesaid creature had come into Rome, they that were her fellows aforetime, who had put her out of their company, were in Rome also, and having heard that such a woman had come thither, they had great wonder how she came there in safety.

39b

Then she went and got her white clothes and was clad all in white, as she was commanded to do, years before, in her soul by revelation, and now it was fulfilled in effect.

Then was this creature received into the Hospital of Saint Thomas of Canterbury[1] in Rome, and she was houselled every Sunday with great weeping, boisterous sobbing, and loud crying, and was highly beloved by the Master of the Hospital and all his brethren. And then, through the stirring of her ghostly enemy, there came a priest, that was held a holy man in the Hospital and also in other places of Rome, who was one of her fellows, and one of her own countrymen. And notwithstanding his holiness, he spoke so evil of this creature and slandered so her name in the Hospital that, through his evil language, she was put out of the Hospital, so that she might no longer be shriven or houselled therein.

[1] This hospice was built in 1362 by John Shepherd, an Englishman, for the accommodation of pilgrims. It fell into disrepair, and in 1572 it was transformed into the English College for English students for the priesthood, which it still is.

Wₕₑₙ this creature saw she was forsaken and put from amongst the good men, she was full grieved, most because she had no confessor, and could not be shriven then as she wished. Then prayed she Our Lord, of His mercy, that He would dispose for her as was most pleasing to Him, with great plenty of tears.

And later, she called to herself the aforesaid Richard with the broken back, praying him to go over to a church against the Hospital, and inform the parson of the church of her manner of governance, and what sorrow she had, and how she wept because she could not be shriven nor houselled, and what compunction and contrition she had for her sins.

Then Richard went to the parson and informed him of this creature, and how Our Lord gave her contrition and compunction with great plenty of tears, and how she desired to be houselled every Sunday if she might, and that she had no priest to be shriven to. And the parson, hearing of her contrition and compunction, was right glad and bade that she should come to him in the name of Jesus, and say her 'Confiteor', and he would housel her his own self, for he could not understand any English.

Then Our Lord sent Saint John the Evangelist to hear her confession, and she said, 'Benedicite'. And he said 'Dominus' verily into her soul, so that she saw him and heard him in her ghostly understanding as she would have done another priest by her bodily wits. Then she told him

40a

all her sins, and all her troubles with many grievous tears, and he heard her full meekly and benignly and afterwards, he enjoined her the penance that she should do for her trespass, and absolved her of her sins with sweet words and meek ones, highly strengthening her to trust in the mercy of Our Lord Jesus Christ, and bade her that she should receive the Sacrament of the Altar, in the Name of Jesus.

And then he passed away from her.

When he was gone, she prayed with all her heart all the time, as she heard her Mass: —

'Lord, as surely as Thou art not wroth with me, grant me a well of tears, whereby I may receive Thy Precious Body with all manner of tears of devotion to Thy worship and to the increase of my merit; for Thou art my joy, Lord, my bliss, my comfort and all the treasure I have in this world; for other worldly joys covet I not, but only Thee. And therefore my dearworthy Lord and my God, forsake me not.'

Then Our Blissful Lord Christ Jesus answered to her soul and said: —

'My dearworthy daughter, I swear by My Majesty that I shall never forsake thee. And, daughter, the more shame, despite, and reproof that thou sufferest for My love, the better I love thee, for I am like a man that loveth well his wife. The more envy that men have of her, the better he will array her in despite of her enemies. And right so shall I fare with thee. In anything thou dost, daughter, thou mayest no better please God than by believing that He loveth thee; for if it were possible that I might weep with thee, I would weep with thee, daughter, for the compassion that I have of thee. Time shall come when thou shalt hold thyself right well pleased, for it shall be verified in thee, the common proverb, that men 40b say: — "He is well blessed that may sit on his well-stool and tell of his woe-stool."

'And so shalt thou do, daughter, and all thy weeping and thy sorrow shall turn into joy and bliss, which thou shalt never miss.'

CHAPTER 33

Another time as this creature was at Saint John Lateran's Church in Rome, before the altar, hearing Mass, she thought that the priest who said Mass seemed a good man and devout. She was sore moved in spirit to speak with him. Then she prayed her man with the broken back to go to the priest and pray him to speak with her. The priest understood no English and knew not what she said, and she knew no other language but English. Therefore they spoke by an interpreter, a man who told each what the other said.

Then she prayed the priest, in the Name of Jesus, that he should make his prayers to the Blissful Trinity, to Our Lady, and to all the saints in Heaven, also stirring others that loved Our Lord to pray for him, that he might have grace to understand her language and her speech in such things as she, by the grace of God, would say and shew unto him.

The priest was a good man, and by his birth he was a Ducheman, a good clerk and a well learned man, highly beloved, well cherished and much trusted in Rome, and he had one of the greatest offices of any priest in Rome.

Desiring to please God, he followed the counsel of this creature and made his prayers to God, as devoutly as he could, every day, that he might have grace to understand what the aforesaid creature would say to him, and also he made other lovers of Our Lord to pray for him.

Thus they prayed thirteen days. And after thirteen days the priest came again to her to prove the effect of their prayers, and then he understood what she said in English to him, and she understood what he said. And yet he understood not English that other men spoke; though they spoke the same words that she spoke, yet he understood them not, unless she spoke herself.

Then was she confessed to this priest of all her sins, as near as her memory would serve her, from her childhood unto that hour, and received her penance full joyfully.

41a Afterwards, she shewed him the secret things, of revelations and of high contemplations, and how she had such mind of His Passion, and such great compassion when God would give it, that she fell down therewith and could not bear it. Then she wept bitterly; she sobbed boisterously, and cried full loud and horribly, so that the people were oftentimes afraid and greatly astonished, deeming she had been vexed with some evil spirit or a sudden sickness, not believing it was the work of God, but rather some evil spirit, or a sudden sickness, or else simulation and hypocrisy, falsely feigned by her own self.

The priest had great trust that it was the work of God, and when he mistrusted, Our Lord sent him such tokens by the aforesaid creature of his own misbehaviour and of his living, which no man knew but God and he, that Our Lord shewed to her by revelation, and bade her tell him, so that he knew well thereby that her feelings were true.

And this priest received her full meekly and reverently, as for his mother and his sister, and said he would support her against her enemies. And so he did, as long as she was in Rome, and suffered many evil words and much tribulation.

And also he forsook his office, because he would support her in her sobbing and in her crying when all her countrymen had forsaken her; for they were ever her greatest enemies, and caused her much grief in every place where they came, for they would that she never sobbed or cried. And she had no choice; but that, they would not believe. And there they were, ever against her and against the good man who supported her.

Then this good man, seeing this woman so wonderfully sobbing and crying, and especially on Sunday when she would be houselled amongst all the people, determined to prove whether it were the gift of God, as she said, or else her own feigning by hypocrisy, as the people said, and took her alone another Sunday into another church when Mass was done, and all the people were home, no man knowing thereof save himself and the clerk only. And when he would housel her, she wept so plenteously and sobbed and cried so loud that he was astonished himself, for it seemed to his hearing that she never cried so loud before that time. And he believed 41b fully that it was the working of the Holy Ghost and neither feigning nor hypocrisy of her own self.

Then afterwards, he was not abashed to hold with her and to speak against them that would defame her and speak evil of her, till he was detracted by the enemies of virtue nearly as much as she, and it pleased him well to suffer tribulation for God's cause.

Many people in Rome, that were disposed to virtue, loved him much the more, and her also, and often prayed her to meat and made her right great cheer, praying her to pray for them. And ever her own countrymen were obstinate, and especially a priest that was amongst them.

He stirred many people against her and said much evil of her, because she wore white clothing more than did others, who were holier and better than ever was she, as he thought.

The cause of his malice was that she would not obey him, and she knew full well that it was against the health of her soul to obey him as he would that she should have done.

CHAPTER 34

Then the good man, the Duche priest, that she was shriven unto, through the stirring of the English priest who was her enemy, asked her if she would be obedient to him or not.

And she said: — 'Yea, sir.'

'Will ye do, then, as I bid you do?'

'With right good will, sir.'

'I charge you that ye leave off your white clothes and wear again your black clothes.'

And she did his commandment, and then had she feeling that she pleased God by her obedience.

Then suffered she many scorns from the wives of Rome. They asked her if highwaymen had robbed her, and she said: —

'Nay, madame.'

Afterwards when she went on pilgrimage, it happed her to meet with the priest who was her enemy, and he rejoiced greatly that she was put from her will, and said unto her: —

'I am glad that ye go in black clothing as ye were wont to do.'

And she answered to him: — 'Sir, Our Lord was not displeased, though I wore white clothes, for He wills that I do so.'   42a

Then the priest said to her again: — 'Now wot I well

thou hast a devil within thee, for I hear him speaking in thee to me.'

'Ah! Good sir, I pray you, drive him away from me, for God knoweth I would right fain do well, and please Him if I could.'

Then he was right wroth and said full many cruel words; and she said to him: —

'Sir, I hope I have no devil within me, for, if I had a devil within me, know well I should be wroth with you. And sir, methinketh I am nothing wroth with you for anything that ye can do to me.' And then the priest parted from her with heavy face.

Then Our Lord spoke to this creature, in her soul, and said: —

'Daughter, dread thee not whatever he saith to thee, for though he run every year to Jerusalem, I have no liking for him, for as long as he speaketh against thee, he speaketh against Me, for I am in thee, and thou art in Me. And hereby mayest thou know that I suffer many cruel words, for I have oftentimes said to thee that I should be crucified anew in thee by cruel words, for thou shalt not otherwise be slain than by cruel words suffering. As for this priest that is thine enemy, he is but a hypocrite.'

Then the good priest, her confessor, bade her by virtue of obedience, and also as part of her penance, that she should serve an old woman who was a poor creature in Rome. And she did so, six weeks. She served her as she would have done Our Lady; and she had no bed to lie in, nor any clothes to be covered with, save her own mantle. Then was she full of vermin and suffered great pain therewith. Also she fetched home water, and sticks on her neck for the poor woman, and begged meat and wine, both, for her; and when the poor woman's wine was sour, this creature herself drank that sour wine, and gave the poor woman good wine that she had bought for her own self.

[Here follow Chapters 35 and 36]

'DAUGHTER, thou art obedient to My will, and cleavest as sore to Me as the skin of a stockfish cleaveth to a man's hands when it is seethed, and wilt not forsake Me for any shame that any man may do to thee.

And thou sayest also that, though I stood before thee in Mine own Person and said to thee that thou shouldst never have My love, never come to Heaven, never see My face, yet sayest thou, daughter, that thou wouldst never forsake Me on earth, nor ever love Me the less, nor ever do the less business to please Me, though thou shouldst lie in Hell without end, because thou mayest not do without My love on earth, nor canst thou have any other comfort but Me only, Who am I, thy God, and am all joy and bliss to thee.

'Therefore I say to thee, dearworthy daughter, it is impossible that any such soul should be damned or parted from Me, who hath such great meekness and charity towards me. And therefore, daughter, dread thee never, for all the great promises that I have made to thee and thine, and to all thy ghostly fathers, shall ever be true and truly fulfilled when the time cometh. Have no doubt thereof.'

Another time, when she was in Rome, a little before Christmas, Our Lord Jesus Christ commanded her to go to her ghostly father, Wenslawe by name, and bid him give her leave to wear again her white clothes, for he had

45a

put her therefrom by virtue of obedience, as is written before. And when she told him the will of Our Lord, he durst not once say 'nay'. So wore she white clothes ever after.

Then Our Lord bade her that she should, at Christmas, go home again to her host's house, where she was at hostel before. And then she went to a poor woman, that she served at that time by the bidding of her confessor, as is written before, and told the poor woman how she must go from her. Then the poor woman was right sorry and made great trouble over her departure. This creature told her how it was the will of God that it should be so, and then she took it the more easily.

Afterwards, when this creature was in Rome, Our Lord bade her give away all her money, and make herself bare for His love. And anon she, with a fervent desire to please God, gave away such money as she had, and such as she had borrowed also from the broken-backed man who went with her. When he found that she had given away his money, he was greatly moved and evil pleased because she had done so, and spake right sharply to her. Then she said to him: —

'Richard, by the grace of God, we shall come home into England right well, and ye shall come to me in Bristol in the Whitsun week, and there shall I pay you right well and truly, by the grace of God. For I trust right well that He Who bade me give it away for His love, will help me to pay it again.'

And so He did.

Aᴜᴛᴇʀ this creature had thus given away her money,
and had neither penny nor halfpenny to help herself
with, as she lay in Saint Marcellus' Church in Rome
thinking and studying where she should get her living, inasmuch as she had no silver to provide herself withal, Our
Lord answered to her mind and said: —

45b   'Daughter, thou art not yet so poor as I was, when I
hung naked on the cross for thy love, for thou hast clothes
on thy body and I had none. And thou hast counselled
other men to be poor for My sake, and therefore thou
must follow thine own counsel.

'But dread thee not, daughter, for gold is to thee-ward,
and I have promised thee beforetime that I would never
fail thee. And I shall pray Mine Own Mother to beg for
thee, for thou hast many times begged for Me and for My
Mother also. And therefore, dread thee not. I have
friends in every country, and will make My friends
to comfort thee.'

When Our Lord had thus sweetly dallied to her soul,
she thanked Him for this great comfort, having good
trust it would be as He said.

Afterwards, she, rising up, went into the street and met
casually with a good man. And so they fell into good
communication as they went together by the way, and to
him she told many good tales and many good exhortations
till God visited him with tears of devotion and compunc-

tion, to his high comfort and consolation. And then he gave her money, by which she was well relieved and comforted a good while.

Then, one night, she saw in a vision, how Our Lady, she thought, sat at the meat with many worshipful persons and asked meat for her. And then thought this creature that Our Lord's words were fulfilled ghostly in that vision, for He promised this creature a little before that He would pray His Mother to beg for her.

A short time after this vision, she met with a worshipful lady, Dame Margaret Florentyne, the same lady that brought her from Assisi into Rome; and neither of them could well understand the other, but by signs and tokens and a few common words. And then the lady said to her : —

'Margerya in poverté?'

She, understanding what the lady meant, said to her : — 'Yea, grand poverté, Madam.'

Then the lady commanded her to eat with her every Sunday and set her at her own table above herself, and laid her meat with her own hands. Then this creature sat and wept full sore, thanking Our Lord that she was so cheered and cherished, for His love, by them that could not understand her language.

When they had eaten, the good lady used to take her a hamper with other stuff, that she might make her potage 46a therewith, as much as would serve her for two days' meat, and filled her bottle with good wine, and sometimes she gave her eight bolendines[1] thereto.

---

[1] In MS. 'an viii bolendinys'. Bolendines were coins current in Rome in the fifteenth century. Forty-eight went to the ducat. The use of 'a(n)' with a numeral is idiomatic, as in Chaucer's 'wommen a gret route . . . well a ten or twelve', 'of a twenty yeer and three'. For its use with a coin, compare 'a six-pence'.

Then another man in Rome, who was called Marcelle, bade her to meat two days in the week. His wife was great with child, and highly desired to have this creature for godmother to her child when it had been born, but she abode not so long in Rome.

And also there was a holy maiden who gave this creature her meat on the Wednesday. Other days, when she was not purveyed, she begged her meat from door to door.

CHAPTER 39

ANOTHER time, right as she came to a poor woman's house, the poor woman called her into her house, and made her sit by her little fire, giving her wine to drink in a cup of stone. And she had a little man-child, which sucked a while on the mother's breast; another while, it ran to this creature, the mother sitting full of sorrow and sadness. Then this creature burst all into weeping, as if she had seen Our Lady and her Son at the time of His Passion, and had so many holy thoughts that she could never tell the half, but ever sat and wept plenteously a long time, so that the poor woman, having compassion on her weeping, prayed her to cease, not knowing why she wept.

Then Our Lord Jesus Christ said to this creature : —

'This place is holy.'

Then she rose up and went forth into Rome and saw much poverty amongst the people, and she thanked God highly for the poverty that she was in, trusting there-through to be partner with them in merit.

Then was there a great gentlewoman in Rome, praying this creature to be godmother to her child, and naming it after Saint Bridget, for they had knowledge of her in her lifetime. And so she did.

Afterwards, God gave her grace to have great love in Rome, both of men and women and great favour among the people.

When the Master and Brother of the Hospital of Saint Thomas, where she was refused beforetime, as is written already, heard it said what love and what favour she had in the city, they prayed her that she would come again to them, and she should be more welcome than ever she was before, for they were right sorry that they had put her away from them. And she thanked them for their charity and did their commandment. When she had come back to them, they made her right good cheer, and were right glad of her coming.

Then she found there, her that was her maiden beforetime, and, with right, should have been so still, dwelling in the hospital in much wealth and prosperity, for she was keeper of their wine.

And this creature went sometimes to her for cause of meekness and prayed her for meat and drink, and the maiden gave her with good will, and sometimes a groat thereto. Then she complained to her maiden, and said she thought with great grief of their parting, and what slander and evil words men said of her because they were asunder; but she would never the rather be with her again.

Afterwards this creature spake with Saint Bride's[1] maiden in Rome, but she could not understand what she said. Then had she a man who could understand her language, and that man told Saint Bridget's maiden what this creature said, and how she asked after Saint Bridget, her lady. Then the maiden said that her lady, Saint Bridget, was kind and meek to every creature and that she had a laughing face.

Also the good man where this creature was at host,

[1] St. Bridget of Sweden died in 1373 in Rome at the age of 71, was canonized in 1391, and her canonization was confirmed in 1415.

told her that he knew her himself, but he little thought
that she had been as holy a woman as she was, for she was
ever homely and kind to all creatures that would speak
with her.

She was in the chamber that Saint Bridget died in, and
heard a Duche priest preaching of her therein, and of her
revelations and her manner of life. She knelt also on the
stone on which Our Lord appeared to Saint Bridget and
told her what day she should die on. And this was one of
Saint Bridget's Days that this creature was in her chapel,
which beforetime was her chamber that she died in.

Our Lord sent such tempests of wind and rain, and
divers impressions of airs, that they that were in the fields
and at their labours out-of-doors were compelled to enter
houses in succouring their bodies, to avoid divers perils.

Through such tokens this creature supposed that Our
Lord wished His holy saint's day to be hallowed, and the
saint held in more worship than she was at that time.

And sometimes, when this creature would have done
the Stations,[1] Our Lord warned her in the night in her
bed, that she should not go out far from her hostel, for
He would send great tempests of lightning and thunder
that day. And so it was indeed. There were such great
tempests that year of thunder and lightning, of rains and
divers weather, that right old men, at that time dwelling

47a

---

[1] This does not refer to the 'Stations of the Cross' depicted on the walls of
every Catholic church, representing fourteen episodes in the Passion of Christ
from the trial to the burial, but to the ancient custom of paying visits, with
appropriate prayers, to certain churches in Rome. The ones to be so visited vary
according to the feast days. The visits may be made either with the clergy in
public procession or privately by individuals, this latter being what Margery
refers to here. Nowadays the churches visited are usually the four great basilicas
of St. Peter, St. John Lateran, St. Maria Maggiore, and St. Paul outside the
walls.

in Rome, said they had never seen such before; the lightning was so plenteous and so bright-shining in their houses, that they thought verily it would have burnt their houses, with the contents.

Then cried they upon the aforesaid creature to pray for them, fully trusting that she was the servant of Almighty God, and through her prayers they should be helped and succoured. This creature at their request praying Our Lord for mercy, He answered in her soul, saying:—

'Daughter, be not afraid, for no weather nor tempest shall harm thee, and therefore, distrust Me not, for I shall never deceive thee.'

And Our Merciful Lord Christ Jesus, as it pleased Him, withdrew the tempests, preserving the people from all mischief.

CHAPTER 40

T<small>HEN</small>, through the provision of Our Lord Christ Jesus, there came a priest, a good man, out of England into Rome, with another fellowship, speering and inquiring diligently after the said creature, whom he had never seen before, nor she him.

But while he was in England, he heard tell that such a woman was in Rome, with whom he longed highly to speak, if God would grant him grace. Wherefore, whilst he was in his own land, he, purposing to see this creature when he, through sufferance of Our Lord, might come where she was, purveyed gold to bring her in her relief, if she had need. Then, by inquiring, he came to the place where she was, and fully humbly and meekly, he called her 'Mother', praying her for charity to receive him as her son. She said that he was welcome to God and to her, as to his own mother.

So by holy dalliance and communication, she felt well that he was a good man. Then she, uncovering the secrets of her heart, revealed what grace God wrought in her soul through His holy inspiration, and somewhat of her manner of life. Then he would no longer suffer her to beg her meat from door to door, but prayed her to eat with him and his fellowship, unless good men and women, in the way of charity and for ghostly comfort, would pray her to meat. Then he would that she should take it in the name of Our Lord; and otherwise she ate with him and

47b

his fellowship every day and he gave her gold sufficient to come home to England.

Then was fulfilled what Our Lord said to her a little before:— 'Gold is to thee-ward.'

And so it was indeed, thanked be Almighty God.

Then some of her fellows whom she had been with in Jerusalem, came to this good priest, newly come to Rome, complaining of her, and saying that she was shriven to a priest who could not understand her language or her confession. Then this good priest, trusting to her as to his mother, desiring the health of her soul, asked her if her confessor understood her when she spoke to him or not.

'Good son, I beseech you pray him to dine with you and with your fellows, and let me be present, and then shall ye know the truth.'

Her confessor was prayed to meat, and, when the time came, set and served with this good priest and his fellowship, the said creature being present, the good priest of England chatting and communing in their own language, English.

The Duche priest, a worthy clerk, as is written before, confessor to the said creature, sat all still in a manner of gloom, because he understood not what they said in English, but only when they spoke Latin. And they did it on purpose, he unwitting, to prove if he understood English or not.

At the last, the said creature, seeing and well understanding that her confessor understood not their language, and that it was tedious to him, partly to comfort him and partly, or much more, to prove the work of God, told in her own language, in English, a story of Holy Writ,

48a

which she had learned of clerks whilst she was at home in England, for she would speak of no vanity nor of fantasies.

They asked her confessor if he understood what she had said, and he, anon, in Latin told them the same words that she had said before in English, for he could neither speak English nor understand it, save only from her tongue. And then had they great marvel, for they knew well that he understood what she said, and she understood what he said, and he could understand no other Englishman. So blessed may God be, Who made an alien to understand her, when her own countrymen had forsaken her, and would not hear her confession unless she would leave off her weeping and her speaking of holiness.

Yet she might not weep but when God gave it her, and oftentimes He gave it so plenteously, that she could not withstand it, but the more she tried to withstand it or put it away, the more strongly it wrought in her soul with such holy thoughts that she could not cease. She would sob and cry full loud, all against her will, so that many a man, and woman also, wondered at her therefor.

CHAPTER 41

Sᴏᴍᴇᴛɪᴍᴇs when the aforesaid creature was at sermons, where Duchemen and other men preached, teaching the laws of God, sudden sorrow and grief occupying her heart caused her to complain with mourning face for lack of understanding, desiring to be refreshed with some crumb of ghostly understanding unto her most trusted, and most entirely beloved Sovereign Lord, Christ Jesus, Whose melodious voice, sweetest of all delights, softly sounding in her soul, said:—

'I shall preach to thee, and teach thee Myself, for thy will and thy desire is acceptable unto Me.'

Then was her soul so delectably fed with the sweet dalliance of Our Lord, and so fulfilled of His love, that, as a drunken man, she turned herself first on one side, and then on the other with great weeping and sobbing, unable to keep herself stable for the unquenchable fire of love which burnt full sore in her soul.

48b   Then many people wondered at her, asking her what she ailed; to whom she, like a creature all wounded with love, and as if reason had failed, cried with a loud voice:—

'The Passion of Christ slayeth me.'

The good women, having compassion on her sorrow, and greatly marvelling at her weeping and her crying, much the more loved her. And therefore they, desiring to make her solace and comfort after her ghostly labour,

146

by signs and tokens — for she understood not their speech — prayed her, and in a manner compelled her, to come home to them, anxious that she should not go from them.

Then Our Lord sent her grace to have great love and great favour of many persons in Rome, both religious men and others. Some religious came to such persons of her countrymen as loved her and said: —

'This woman hath sown much good seed in Rome since she came hither; that is to say, shewn good example to the people, through which they love God more than they did before.'

On a time, this creature was in a church at Rome where the body of Saint Jerome lies buried, [1] which was miraculously translated from Bethlehem into that place, and, there, is now held in great worship beside the place where Saint Lawrence lies buried. To this creature's ghostly sight appeared Saint Jerome, saying to her soul: —

'Blessed art thou, daughter, in the weeping that thou weepest for the people's sins, for many shall be saved thereby. And daughter, dread thee nothing, for it is a singular and special gift that God hath given thee — a well of tears which man shall never take from thee.'

With such manner of dalliance, he highly comforted her spirit, and also he made great praising and thanking to God for the grace He wrought in her soul, for unless she had had such ghostly comforts, it would have been impossible for her to have borne the shames and wonderings which she suffered patiently and meekly for the grace that God shewed in her.

---

[1] At the Basilica of St. Maria Maggiore.

W HEN the time of Easter — or otherwise Pasch — was come and gone, this creature with her fellowship purposing to go again into their own native land, it was told them that there were many thieves by the way, who would despoil them of their goods, and peradventure slay them.

49a

Then the said creature, with many a bitter tear in her eye, prayed to Our Lord Jesus Christ saying: —

'Christ Jesus, in Whom is all my trust, as Thou hast promised me many times before that there should be no man molested in my company, and I was never deceived nor defrauded in Thy promise as long as I fully and truly trusted unto Thee, so hear the prayers of Thine unworthy servant all wholly trusting in Thy mercy, and grant that I and my fellowship, without hindrance of body or chattel — for over our souls, Lord, have they no power — may go home again into our land, as we came hither, for Thy love, and let never our enemies have power over us, Lord, if it pleaseth Thee. As Thou wilt, so may it be.'

Then Our Lord Jesus Christ said to her mind: —

'Dread thee not, daughter, for thou and all that be in thy company shall go as safe as if they were in Saint Peter's Church.'

Then thanked she God with all her spirit, and was bold enough to go where God willed, and took her leave of her friends in Rome, and most specially of her ghostly father,

who for Our Lord's love, had supported her and succoured her full tenderly against the wicked winds of her
envious enemies, and whose parting was full lamentable,
as witnessed well the pure water drops running down their
cheeks.

She, falling on her knees, received the benefit of his
blessing, and so they parted asunder, whom charity joined
in one, through which they trusted to meet again, when
Our Lord willed, in their common country when they had
passed this wretched worldly exile.

Thus she and her fellowship passed forth England-
ward. And when they were a little way out of Rome, the
good priest whom, as is before written, this creature had
received as her own son, had much dread of enemies.
Wherefore he said unto her: —

'Mother, I dread me to be dead and slain with enemies.'

She said: — 'Nay, son, ye shall fare right well, and
go safe, by the grace of God.'

And he was well comforted by her words, for he trusted
much in her feelings, and made her as good cheer by the
way as if he had been her own son, born of her body.

So they came forth to Middelburg, and then her
fellowship would take their journey into England on the
Sunday.

Then the good priest came to her, saying: —

'Mother, will ye go with your fellowship or not, on this 49b
good day?'

And she said: — 'Nay, son, it is not My Lord's will
that I should go so soon hence.'

And so she abode still with the good priest and some
others of her fellowship till the Saturday after, and many
of her fellowship went to ship on the Sunday. On the

Friday after, as this creature went to sport herself in the fields, and men of her own nation with her, whom she instructed in the laws of God as well as she could, and sharply she spake to them for swearing great oaths, and breaking the commandment of Our Lord God.

And as she was thus dallying with them, Our Lord Jesus Christ bade her go home in haste to her hostel, for there should come great weatherings and parlous. Then she hied her homewards with her fellowship, and as soon as they came to their hostel, the weather fell, as she had felt by revelation. And many times, as she went by the way, and in the fields, there fell great lightnings with hideous thunder, grisly and grievous, so that she feared it would have smitten her to death, and many great rains which caused her great dread and grief.

Then Our Lord Jesus Christ said to her: — 'Why art thou afraid while I am with thee? I am as mighty to keep thee here in the field as in the strongest church in all the world.'

And after that time she was not so greatly afraid as she was before, for ever she had great trust in His mercy, blessed may He be, That comforted her in every sorrow.

Afterwards there happed an Englishman to come to this creature, and swore a great oath. She, hearing that oath, wept, mourned and sorrowed without measure, without power to restrain herself from weeping and sorrowing, forasmuch as she saw her brother offending Our Lord God Almighty, and little heed would he take of his own default.

CHAPTER 43

O n the next day, betimes, came to this creature the good priest, who was as her son, and said: —

'Mother, good tidings! We have good wind, thanks be to God.'

And anon she gave praise to Our Lord, and prayed Him of His mercy to grant them perseverance of good wind and weather, so that they might come home in safety. And it was answered and commanded in her soul that they should go their way in the Name of Jesus.

When the priest knew that she would in any case go forward, he said: —

'Mother, there is no ship. There is but a little smack.'

She answered again: — 'Son, God is as mighty in a little ship as in a great ship, so I will go therein by leave of God.'

When they were in the little ship, it began to wax into great tempests and dark weather. Then they cried to God for grace and mercy, and anon the tempests ceased and they had fair weather, and sailed all night on end, and the next day till evensong time, and then they came to land. And when they were on the land, the aforesaid creature fell down on her knees, kissing the ground, highly thanking God who had brought them home in safety.

Then had this creature neither penny nor halfpenny in her purse. And so they happened to meet with other pilgrims, who gave her three halfpennies, inasmuch as she, in communing, told them good tales. Then she was right glad and merry, for she had some money which she might offer in the worship of the Trinity when she came to Norwich, as she did when she went outward from England.

And so, when she came there, she offered with right good will, and afterwards went with her fellowship to the Vicar of Saint Stephen's, Master Richard Castyr, who lived at that time, and he led them with him to the place where he went to board and made them right good cheer.

And he said to the aforesaid creature: — 'Margery, I marvel how ye can be so merry, and have had such great labour, and been so far hence.'

'Sir, for I have great cause to be merry, and to rejoice in Our Lord, Who hath helped me and succoured me and brought me back in safety, blessed and worshipped may He be.'

And so they dallied in Our Lord a good while and had full goodly cheer.

And then they took their leave, and she went to an anchorite, who was a monk of a far country, and dwelt in the chapel in the fields. He bore a name for great perfection, and aforetime had loved this creature right much. Afterwards, through evil language that he heard of her, he turned all against her, and therefore she went to him on purpose to meeken herself, and draw him to charity, if she might.

When she was come to him, he welcomed her home shortly, and asked her what she had done with her child which was begotten and born whilst she was out, as he had heard said.

And she said: — 'Sir, the same child that God hath sent me, I have brought home, for God knoweth that I did

50b

152

nothing since I went out, wherethrough I should have a child.'

And he would not believe her for aught she could say.

Yet nevertheless, she lowly and meekly shewed him, for the trust that she had in him, how it was Our Lord's will that she should be clad in white clothing, and he said: — 'God forbid it,' for she would then make all the world wonder at her.

And she answered: — 'Sir, it matters not, as long as God is pleased there-with.'

Then he bade her come again to him, and be governed by him, and by a good priest called Sir Edward,[1] and she said she should ask first whether it were the will of God or not, and therewith she took her leave at that time. And as she went from him by the way, Our Lord said to her soul: —

'I will not that thou be governed by him.'

And she sent him word what answer she had of God.

---

[1] It was then the custom to address priests as 'Sir' or 'Master'.

CHAPTER 44

T<small>HEN</small> prayed she to God, saying:—'As surely, Lord, as it is Thy will that I should be clad in white, as surely grant me a token of lightning, thunder and rain — so that it neither hinders nor harms anything — that I, unworthy, may the sooner fulfil Thy will.'

Then Our Lord answered and said unto His unworthy servant: —

'Daughter, doubt it not, thou shalt have thy token on the third day.' And so it was.

On the Friday next following, early in the morning, as she lay in her bed, she saw great lightning, she heard great thunder and great rain following, and as quickly it passed away, and was fair weather again.

Then she purposed herself fully to wear white clothes, but she had neither gold nor silver to buy her clothing.

Then Our Lord said to her soul: — 'I will provide for thee.'

So she went forth to a worshipful man in Norwich, to whom she was right welcome, and had great cheer; and as they sat together, telling good tales, ever Our Lord said in her soul: —

'Speak to this man, speak to this man!'

Then she said to that worshipful man: —

51a 'Would God, sir, that I might find a good man who would lend me two nobles till I might pay him again, to buy myself clothes with.'

And then he said: — 'That I will do, damsel, gladly. What clothes will ye wear?'

'Sir,' she said, 'white clothes, by the leave of God.'

So this good man bought white cloth, and had made for her a gown thereof, and a hood, a kirtle, and a cloak, and on the Saturday, which was the next day, at evening, he brought her this clothing and gave it her for God's love, and much more kindness did to her, for Our Lord's love, Christ Jesus be his reward and have mercy on his soul, and on all Christians.

On the Trinity Sunday next following, she was houselled all in white, and since then hath she suffered much abuse and much shame in many divers countries, cities, and towns, thanked be God of all.

Soon afterwards, her husband came from Lynne to Norwich to see how she fared and how she had sped, and so went they home together to Lynne.

And she, a short time afterwards, fell into great sickness, insomuch that she was anointed, for doubt of death. She desired, if it were the will of God, that she might seek Saint James ere she died, and suffer more shame for His love, as He had promised her before that she should do.

Then Our Lord Jesus Christ said to her in her soul that she should not die yet, and she thought herself that she should not have lived, for her pain was so great. And quickly afterwards she was hale and whole.

And it drew into winter-ward and she had so much cold that she knew not what she might do, for she was poor and had no money, and also she was in great debt. Then suffered she shame and reproof for wearing her white clothes, and because she cried so loud when God gave her mind of His Passion. And for the compassion that she had of Our Lord's Passion, she cried so wondrous loud, and they had never heard her cry before (at Lynne), so it was the more marvel unto them, for she had her first cry at Jerusalem, as is written before.

And many said there was never saint in Heaven who cried as she did, wherefore they would conclude that she had a devil within her, which caused that crying; and so they said, plainly, and much more evil.

51b And she took all patiently for Our Lord's love, for she knew well that the Jews said much worse of His own Person than men did of her, and therefore she took it the more meekly.

Some said she had the falling evil, for she, with the crying, wrested her body, turning from the one side to the other, and waxed all blue and livid, like the colour of lead. Then folk spat at her for horror of the sickness, and some scorned her and said that she howled as if she were a dog, and banned her and cursed her, and said she did much harm among the people. Then they that beforetime had given her both meat and drink for God's love, now they put her away, and bade her that she should not come in their places, because of the cruel tales that they heard of her.

Afterwards, when the time came that she should go to Saint James, she went to the best friends that she had in Lynne and told them her intent, how she purposed to go to Saint James if she could have money to go with, but she was poor and owed much debt. And her friends said to her: —

'Why have ye given away your money and other men's also? Where shall ye now get as much money as ye owe?'

And she answered: — 'Our Lord shall help right well, for He failed me never in any country, and therefore I trust Him right well.'

And suddenly came a good man, and gave her forty pence, and with some thereof, she bought herself a furred cloak.

And ever Our Lord said to her: — 'Daughter, study not for any money, for I shall provide for thee, but ever study how to love Me and to keep thy mind on Me, for I shall go with thee where thou go-est, as I have promised thee before.'

And afterwards there came a woman, a good friend to this creature, and gave her seven marks, that she should pray for her when she came to Saint James; and so she took her leave of her friends in Lynne purposing herself forward with all the haste she might.

And it was said in Lynne that there were many thieves by the way. Then had she great dread that they would rob her and take her gold away from her. Our Merciful Lord, comforting her, said unto her: —

'Go forth, daughter, in the Name of Jesus. There shall no thief have power over thee.'

So then she went forth and came to Bristol on the Wednesday in Whitsun week, and there found she ready the broken-backed man who had been with her in Rome, whom she left in Rome when she came hence two years before this time.

And while they were in Rome, she borrowed certain gold of him, and, by the bidding of God, she gave away to poor people all the money that she had, and what she had borrowed of him also, as is written before.

Then while she was in Rome, she promised him to pay him again in Bristol at this time, and so he had come thither for his payment.

52a

Our Lord Jesus Christ had so provided for her, as she went Bristol-ward, that there was given to her so much money, that she might well pay the aforesaid man all she owed him. And so she did, blessed be Our Lord therefor. And then she lay still in Bristol, by the bidding of God, to await shipping, six weeks, inasmuch as there were no English ships that would sail thither, for they were arrested and taken up for the King.

Other pilgrims that were at Bristol, desiring to speed their journey, went about from port to port, and sped never the more. And so they came back to Bristol, while she lay still and sped better than they, for all their labour.

And while she was thus still in Bristol, after the bidding of God, Our Merciful Lord Jesus Christ visited his creature with many holy meditations and many high contemplations and many sweet comforts.

And there she was houselled every Sunday, with plenteous tears, and boisterous sobbings, with loud cryings and shrill shriekings; and therefore many men and many women wondered at her, scorned her, and despised her, banned her and cursed her, said much evil of her, slandered her and bore false witness against her for having said a thing which she never said.

Then she wept full sore for her sins, praying God for mercy and forgiveness for them, saying to Our Lord:—

'Lord, as Thou saidest, hanging on the Cross, for Thy crucifiers: "Father, forgive them. They know not what they do," so, I beseech Thee, forgive the people all scorn and slanders, and all that they have trespassed if it be Thy will, for I have deserved much more, and of much more am I worthy.'

CHAPTER 45

O N Corpus Christi Day afterwards, as the priests bore 52b
the Sacrament about the town in solemn procession,
with many lights and great solemnity, as was worthy to be
done, the aforesaid creature followed, full of tears and
devotion, with holy thoughts, and meditation for weeping
and boisterous sobbing. Then came a good woman to this
creature and said: —

'Damsel, God give us grace to follow the steps of Our
Lord Jesus Christ.'

Then those words wrought so sorely in her heart and
in her mind that she could not bear it, so that she was fain
to take to a house. There she cried, 'I die, I die', and
roared so wonderfully, that people wondered upon her,
having great marvel of what she ailed. Yet Our Lord
made some to love and cherish her right much, and have
her home both to meat and drink, and they had full great
gladness in hearing her dallying in Our Lord. So there
was a man of Newcastle — his name was Thomas Marchale — who oftentimes had this creature to meat to hear
her dalliance, and he was so drawn by the good words that
God put into her to say of contrition and compunction, of
sweetness and devotion, that he was all moved as if he had
been a new man, with tears of contrition and compunction,
both days and nights as Our Lord would visit his heart
with grace, so that sometimes when he went into the fields,
he wept so sore for his sins and his trespass, that he fell

down and could not bear it, and told the aforesaid creature that he had been a full reckless man and misgoverned and therefore rued him, thanked be God. Then he blessed the time that he knew this creature and purposed himself fully to be a good man.

Also he said to the said creature: —

'Mother, I have here ten marks.[1] I pray you that it be yours, as your own, for I will help you to Saint James with God's grace; and what ye bid me give to any poor man or woman, I will do at your bidding — always one penny for you and another for myself.'

Then, as it pleased Our Lord, He sent a ship out of Britain into Bristol, which ship was made ready and arrayed for sailing to Saint James. Then the said Thomas Marchale went and paid the master for himself and for the said creature.

Then was there a rich man of Bristol who would not let the said creature sail in that ship, for he held her no good woman. And then she said to that rich man: —

'Sir, if ye put me out of the ship, My Lord Jesus shall put you out of Heaven; for I tell you, sir, Our Lord Jesus hath no liking for a rich man unless he is a good man and a meek man.'

And so she said many sharp words unto him without any glossing or flattering.

Then Our Lord said to her in her soul: — 'Thou shalt have thy will and go to Saint James at thy desire.'

And anon after, she was put up before the Bishop of Worcester, who lay three miles beyond Bristol, and admonished to appear before him where he lay. She rose up early on the next day, and went to the place where he lay —

53a

---

[1] The value of a mark was thirteen shillings and fourpence.

he being yet in bed — and happened to meet one of his wor-shipfullest men in the town, and so they dallied of God.

And when he had heard her dallying a good while, he prayed her to meat, and afterwards he brought her into the Bishop's hall.

When she came into the hall, she saw many of the Bishop's men, all slashed and pointed in their clothes. She, lifting up her hand, blessed herself.

And then they said: — 'What devil aileth thee?'

She said to them: — 'Whose men be ye?'

They answered back: — 'The Bishop's men.'

And then she said: — 'Nay, forsooth; ye are more like the devil's men.'

Then they were wroth, and chid her, and spoke angrily to her, and she suffered them well and meekly.

And afterwards she spoke so seriously against sin and their misbehaviour that they were in silence, and held themselves well pleased with her words, thanked be God, ere she left.

Then she went into the church and abode the coming of the Bishop; and when he came, she knelt down and asked what was his will, and why she was summoned to come before him; it was to her great hurt and hindrance inasmuch as she was a pilgrim, proposing by the grace of God to go Saint James-ward.

Then the Bishop said: — 'Margery, I have not sum-moned thee, for I know well enough that thou art John of Brunam's daughter, of Lynne. I pray thee be not wroth, but fare fair with me, and I shall fare fair with thee, for thou shalt eat with me this day.'

'Sir,' she said, 'I pray you hold me excused, for I have promised a good man in town to eat with him to-day.'

53b   And then he said:— 'Thou shalt eat with me, and he, also.'

So she abode with him till God sent wind so that she might sail, and had great cheer of him, and of his household also.

Afterwards she was shriven to the Bishop, and he prayed her to pray for him that he might die in charity, for it was warned him, by a holy man who had the revelation, that this Bishop should be dead within the turn of two years. And it fell so indeed.

And therefore he complained to this creature, and prayed her to pray for him that he might die in charity.

At last, she took her leave of him, and he gave her gold and his blessing, and commanded his household to lead her forth on her way. And he also prayed her, when she came back from Saint James, that she would come unto him.

So she went forth to her ship. Before she entered the ship, she made her prayers that God would keep them and preserve them from vengeance, tempests and perils on the sea, so that they might go and come in safety, for it was told to her that, if they had any tempest, they would cast her into the sea, for they said it would be because of her. And they said the ship was the worse because she was there-in.

Therefore she in her prayers said in this manner:— 'Almighty God, Christ Jesus, I beseech Thee for Thy mercy, if Thou wilt chastise me, spare me till I come again into England. And when I come again, chastise me right as Thou wilt.' And Our Lord granted her her boon.

So she took her ship in the Name of Jesus and sailed forth with her fellowship, whom God sent fair wind and weather, so that they came to Saint James on the seventh day.

Then they that were against her when they were at Bristol, now made her good cheer; and so they abode fourteen days in that land, and there had she great cheer, both bodily and ghostly, high devotion, and many great cries in mind of Our Lord's Passion, with plenteous tears of compassion.

And afterwards they came home again to Bristol in five days.

She abode not long there, but went forth to the Blood of Hayles,[1] and there she was shriven and had loud cries and boisterous weepings.

Then the religious men had her in amongst them, and made her good cheer, save they swore many great oaths and horrible. And she rebuked them therefor, after the Gospel, and thereof had they great wonder.

Nevertheless some were right well pleased, thanked be God for His goodness.   54a

---

[1] *See* Note D.

Afterwards, set she forth to Leicester, and a good man also — Thomas Marchale — of whom is written before; and there she came into a fair church where she beheld a crucifix that was piteously portrayed and lamentable to behold, through beholding which, the Passion of Our Lord entered her mind, so that she began all to melt and to relent by tears of pity and compassion. Then the fire of love kindled so eagerly in her heart that she could not keep it secret, for, whether she would or not, it caused her to break out with a loud voice and cry marvellously, and weep and sob so hideously that many a man and woman wondered on her therefor.

When it was overcome and she was going out of the church door, a man took her by the sleeve and said: —

'Damsel, why weepest thou so sore?'

'Sir,' she said, 'it is not you to tell.'

So she and the good man, Thomas Marchale went forth, and took her hostel and there ate their meat. When they had eaten, she prayed Thomas Marchale to write a letter and send it to her husband, that he might fetch her home. And while the letter was in writing, the hosteler came up to her chamber in great haste, and took away her scrip and bade her come quickly and speak with the Mayor. And so she did.

Then the Mayor asked her of what country she was, and whose daughter she was.

'Sir,' she said, 'I am of Lynne in Norfolk, a good man's daughter of the same Lynne, who hath been mayor five times of that worshipful borough, and alderman also many years; and I have a good man, also a burgess of the said town of Lynne, for my husband.'

'Ah!' said the Mayor, 'Saint Katherine told what kindred she came of, and yet ye are not like her, for thou art a false strumpet, a false Lollard, and a false deceiver of the people, and I shall have thee in prison.'

And she answered: — 'I am as ready, sir, to go to prison for God's love, as ye are ready to go to church.'

When the Mayor had long chidden her and said many evil and horrible words to her, and she, by the grace of Jesus, had reasonably answered to all that he could say, he commanded the jailer's man to lead her to prison. 54b

The jailer's man, having compassion on her with weeping tears, said to the Mayor: —

'Sir, I have no house to put her in, unless I put her amongst men.'

Then she was moved with compassion for the man who had compassion on her. Praying for grace and mercy to that man, as for her own soul, she said to the Mayor: —

'I pray you, sir, put me not among men, that I may keep my chastity, and my bond of wedlock to my husband, as I am bound to do.'

Then said the jailer his own self to the Mayor: —

'Sir, I will be under bond to keep this woman in safe ward till ye will have her back.'

Then was there a man of Boston, who said to the good wife, where she was at hostel: —

'Forsooth,' he said, 'in Boston this woman is held to be a holy woman and a blessed woman.'

Then the jailer took her into his ward, and led her home into his own house, and put her in a fair chamber, shutting the door with a key, and commending his wife the key to keep.

Nevertheless, he let her go to church when she would, and let her eat at his own table and made her right good cheer for Our Lord's sake, thanked be Almighty God thereof.

CHAPTER 47

THEN the steward of Leicester, a seemly man, sent for the said creature to the jailer's wife, and she — for her husband was not at home — would not let her go to any man, steward or otherwise. When the jailer knew thereof he came himself, and brought her before the steward. The steward anon, as he saw her, spake Latin unto her, many priests standing about to hear what she would say. She said to the steward: —

'Speak English if ye please, for I understand not what ye say.'

The steward said to her: — 'Thou liest falsely, in plain English.'

Then she said to him again: — 'Sir, ask what question ye will in English, and by the grace of My Lord Jesus Christ I will answer you reasonably thereto.'

Then asked he many questions, to which she answered so readily and reasonably that he could get no cause against her.

Then the steward took her by the hand, and led her into his chamber and spoke many foul bawdy words unto her, purposing and desiring, as it seemed to her, to oppress her and ravish her. And then she had much dread and much sorrow, crying him for mercy. 55a

She said: — 'Sir, for the reverence of Almighty God, spare me, for I am a man's wife.'

Then said the steward: — 'Thou shalt tell me whether

thou hast this speech of God or the devil, or else thou shalt
go to prison.'

'Sir,' she said, 'to go to prison, I am not afraid for My
Lord's love, Who suffered much more for my love than I
may for His. I pray you do as ye think best.'

The steward, seeing her boldness in that she dreaded
no prisoning, struggled with her, shewing unclean tokens
and ungoodly countenance, wherethrough he scared her
so much that she told him how she had her speech and
her dalliance of the Holy Ghost and not of her own
cunning.

Then he, all astonished at her words, left his business
and his lewdness, saying to her, as many a man had done
before: —

'Either thou art a right good woman, or else a right
wicked one,' and delivered her again to her jailer, and he
led her home again with him. Afterwards they took two
of her fellows that went with her on pilgrimage. One was
Thomas Marchale, aforesaid, the other, a man of Wis-
bech, and put them both in prison, for cause of her. Then
was she grieved and sorry for their distress, and prayed
to God for their deliverance.

Then Our Merciful Lord said to His creature: —

'Daughter, I shall, for thy love, so dispose for them,
that the people will be right fain to let them go, and not
long keep them.'

On the next day following, Our Lord sent such weather
of lightning, thunder and rain, continuing so that all the
people in the town were so afraid that they did not know
what to do. They dreaded them it was because they had
put the pilgrims in prison.

Then the governors of the town went in great haste

and took out both two pilgrims who had lain in prison all the night before, leading them to the Guild Hall, there to be examined before the Mayor and the worshipful men of the town, compelling them to swear if the aforesaid creature were a woman of right faith and right belief, continent and clean of her body, or not.

As far as they knew, they swore, as clearly as God should help them at the Day of Doom, that she was a good woman, of right faith and right belief, clean and chaste in all her behaviour, as far as they could know, in demeanour and bearing, in word and in work.   55b

Then the Mayor let them go whither they would.

And anon, the tempest ceased and it was fair weather, worshipped be Our Lord God.

The pilgrims were glad that they were delivered and durst no longer abide in Leicester, but went ten miles thence, and abode there, that they might have knowledge what should be done with the said creature, for, when they both were put in prison, they had told her themselves that they supposed, if the Mayor might have his will, he would have her burnt.

CHAPTER 48

O<small>N</small> a Wednesday, the said creature was brought into a church of All Hallows[1] in Leicester, in which place, before the High Altar, was set the Abbot of Leicester with some of his canons, the Dean of Leicester, a worthy clerk. There were also many friars and priests; also the Mayor of the same town with many others of the lay people. There were so many people that they stood on stools to behold her and wonder at her.

The said creature lay on her knees, making her prayers to Almighty God, that she might have grace, wit, and wisdom, so to answer that day as might be most pleasure and worship to Him, most profit to her soul, and best example to the people.

Then there came a priest to her, and took her by the hand and brought her before the Abbot and his assessors sitting at the altar, who made her swear on a book that she should answer truly to the Articles of the Faith, as she felt in them.

And first they explained the Blissful Sacrament of the Altar, charging her to say right as she believed there-in.

Then she said: — 'Sirs, I believe in the Sacrament of the Altar in this wise; that whatever man hath taken the order of priesthood, be he ever so vicious a man in his living, if he say duly those words over the bread, that Our Lord

[1] *See* Note O.

Jesus Christ said when He made His Maundy among His disciples, where He sat at the Supper, I believe that it is His very Flesh and His Blood, and no material bread; and never may it be unsaid, be it once said.'

And so she answered forth to all the Articles, as many as they would ask her, so that they were well pleased.

The Mayor, who was her deadly enemy, said: — 'In faith, she meaneth not in her heart what she sayeth with her mouth.'

And the clerks said to him: — 'Sir, she answereth right well to us.' 56a

Then the Mayor strongly rebuked her and said many reprehensible words and ungoodly, which are more expedient to be concealed than expressed.

'Sir,' she said, 'I take witness of My Lord Jesus Christ, Whose Body is here present in the Sacrament of the Altar, that I never had part of man's body in this world in actual deed by way of sin, but of my husband's body, to whom I am bounden by the law of matrimony, and by whom I have borne fourteen children. For I would have you to know, Sir, that there is no man in this world that I love so much as God, for I love Him above all things, and, Sir, I tell you truly, I love all men in God, and for God.'

Also furthermore, she said plainly to his own person: —

'Sir, ye are not worthy to be a Mayor, and that shall I prove by Holy Writ, for Our Lord said Himself, ere He would take vengeance on the cities: — "I shall come down and see," and yet He knew all things. And that was for nothing else, Sir, but to shew men such as ye be, that ye should do no execution in punishing, unless ye had knowledge beforehand that it were worthy so to be done. And, Sir, ye have done all the contrary to me this day, for, Sir, ye have caused me much despite for a thing that I am not guilty in. I pray God forgive you it.'

Then the Mayor said to her: — 'I will know why thou go-est in white clothes, for I trow thou art come hither to have away our wives from us, and lead them with thee.'

'Sir,' she said, 'ye shall not know from my mouth, why I go in white clothes; ye are not worthy to know it. But, Sir, I will tell it to these worthy clerks, with good will, in the manner of confession. Ask them if they will tell it you!'

Then the clerks prayed the Mayor to go down from them with the other people. And when they were gone, she knelt on her knees before the Abbot, and the Dean of Leicester and a Preaching Friar, a worshipful clerk, and told these three clerks how Our Lord, by revelation, warned her and bade her wear white clothes, ere she came to Jerusalem.

'And so have I told my ghostly fathers. And therefore they have charged me that I should go thus, for they dare not act against my feelings, for dread of God; and if they durst, they would, full gladly. Therefore, sirs, if the Mayor will learn why I go in white, ye may say, if ye like, that my ghostly fathers bid me go so; and then shall ye tell no lies, and he shall not know the truth.'

56b

So the clerks called up the Mayor again, and told him in council that her ghostly fathers had charged her to wear white clothes, and she had bound herself to their obedience.

Then the Mayor called her to him, saying: — 'I will not let thee go hence for anything that thou canst say, unless thou wilt go to my lord of Lincoln for a letter, inasmuch as thou art in his jurisdiction, saying that I may be discharged of thee.'

She said: — 'I dare speak to my lord of Lincoln right well, for I have had of him right good cheer before this time.'

Then other men asked her if she were in charity with the Mayor, and she said: —

'Yea, and with all creatures.'

Then she, bowing to the Mayor, prayed him to be in charity with her, with weeping tears, and forgive her anything in which she had displeased him.

And he gave her goodly words for a while, so that she thought all was well, and he was her good friend, but afterwards she well knew it was not so.

And thus she had leave of the Mayor to go to my lord of Lincoln, and fetch a letter by which the Mayor should be excused.

CHAPTER 49

So she went first into the Abbey of Leicester,[1] into the church, and as soon as the Abbot spied her, he, of his goodness, with many of his brethren, came to welcome her.

When she saw them coming, anon in her soul, she beheld Our Lord coming with His Apostles, and she was so ravished into contemplation with sweetness and devotion, that she could not stand till they came, as courtesy demanded, but leant herself to a pillar in the church and held herself strongly thereby, for dread of falling, for she would have stood but might not, for excess of devotion which was the cause that she cried and wept full sore.

When her crying was overcome, the Abbot prayed his brethren to have her in with them and comfort her, and so they gave her right good wine and made her right good cheer.

Then she got a letter of the Abbot to my lord of Lincoln to record what conversation she had had, during the time she was in Leicester; and the Dean of Leicester was ready to record and witness with her also, for he had 57a great confidence that Our Lord loved her, and therefore he cheered her full highly in his own place.

And so she took leave of her said son, purposing forth Lincoln-ward with a man called Patrick who had been with her at Saint James beforetime. And this time he was

[1] *See* Note N.

sent by Thomas Marchale, beforesaid, from Melton Mowbray to Leicester, to inquire and see how it stood with the same creature.

For the aforesaid Thomas Marchale feared she would have been burnt, and therefore he sent this man Patrick to prove the truth.

So she and Patrick, with many good folk of Leicester coming to cheer her, thanking God Who had preserved her, and given her the victory over her enemies, went forth out of the town's end and made her right good cheer, promising her that if ever she came again, she should have better cheer amongst them than she had before.

Then had she forgotten and left in the town a staff of Moses' rod which she had brought from Jerusalem, and she would not have lost it for forty shillings.

Then went Patrick again into the town for her staff and her scrip and happed to meet with the Mayor, and the Mayor would have put him in prison, so that, at the last, he hardly escaped, and left there her scrip.

The aforesaid creature awaited this man in a blind woman's house in great gloom, dreading what had befallen him, because he was so long. At last this man came riding by where she was.

When she saw him, she cried: — 'Patrick, son, where have ye been so long away from me?'

'Yea, yea, mother,' said he, 'I have been in great peril for you. I was on the point of being put in prison for you, and the Mayor hath greatly tormented me for you, and he hath taken away your scrip from me.'

'Ah! Good Patrick,' said she, 'be not displeased, for I shall pray for you, and God shall reward your labour right well; it is all for the best.'

Then Patrick set her upon his horse and brought her home into Melton Mowbray, into his own house, where was Thomas Marchale, before written, who took her down from the horse, highly thanking God that she was not burnt. So they rejoiced in Our Lord all that night.

Afterwards, she went forth to the Bishop of Lincoln, where he lay at that time.

She, not knowing verily where he was, met a worshipful man with a furred hood, a worthy officer of the Bishop's, who said unto her: —

'Damsel, knowest thou not me?'

'No, sir,' she said, 'forsooth.'

'And yet thou wert beholden,' he said, 'for I have sometimes made thee good cheer.'

'Sir, I trust that what ye did, ye did for God's love, and therefore I hope that He shall right well reward you. And I pray you hold me excused, for I take little heed of a man's beauty, or his face, and therefore I forget him much the sooner.'

Then he told her kindly where she would find the Bishop.

So she got her letter from the Bishop to the Mayor of Leicester, admonishing him that he should not vex her, nor hinder her coming and going when she would.

Then there fell great thunder and lightning and many rains, so that the people deemed it was for vengeance on the said creature, greatly desiring that she had been out of that country.

And she would in no wise go thence till she had her scrip again.

When the said Mayor received the aforesaid letter, he sent her her scrip and let her go in safety, where she would. Three weeks she was delayed on her journey by the Mayor of Leicester, ere he would let her go out of that district.

Then she hired the aforesaid man Patrick to go with her in the country, and so they went forth to York.

Wʜᴇɴ she was come into York, she went to an anchoress who had loved her well ere she went to Jerusalem, to have knowledge of her ghostly increase, also desiring, for more ghostly communication, to eat with the anchoress that day nothing else but bread and water, for it was on Our Lady's Eve.

And the anchoress would not receive her, because she had heard so much evil told of her, so she went forth to other friendly folk, and they made her right good cheer for Our Lord's love.

On a day, as she sat in a church in York, Our Lord Jesus Christ said to her soul: — 'Daughter, there is much tribulation thee-ward.'

She was somewhat gloomy and abashed there-of, and therefore she, sitting still, answered not. Then said Our Blessed Lord again: —

'What! Daughter, art thou evil paid to suffer more tribulation for My love? If thou wilt suffer no more, I shall take it away from thee.'

Then she answered: —

58a   'Nay, Good Lord, let me be at Thy will, and make me mighty and strong to suffer all that ever Thou wilt that I suffer, and grant me meekness and patience there-with.'

So, from that time forward, as she knew that it was Our Lord's will that she should suffer more tribulation, she received it goodly when Our Lord would send it, and thanked Him highly there-of, being right glad and merry the day that she suffered any discomfort. And in process of time, that day on which she suffered no tribulation, she was not merry nor glad as the day on which she suffered tribulation.

Afterwards, as she was in the Minster of York aforesaid, a clerk came to her, saying: —

'Damsel, how long will ye abide here?'

'Sir, I propose to abide these fourteen days.' And so she did.

In that time many good men and women prayed her to meat, and made her right good cheer, and were right glad to hear her dalliance, having great marvel of her speech, for it was fruitful.

Also she had many enemies who slandered her, scorned her, and despised her, of whom one priest came to her while she was in the said Minster, and taking her by the collar of her gown, said to her: —

'Thou wolf! What is this cloth that thou hast on?'

She stood still and would not answer in her own cause. Children of the monastery going beside, said to the priest: —

'Sir, it is wool.'

The priest was annoyed because she would not answer, and began to swear many great oaths. Then she began to speak for God's cause; she was not afraid. She said: —

'Sir, ye should keep the commandments of God, and not swear as negligently as ye do.'

The priest asked her who kept the commandments. She said: —

'Sir, they that keep them.'

Then said he: — 'Keepest thou them?'

She answered: — 'Sir, it is my will to keep them, for I am bound there-to, and so are ye, and every man that will be saved at the last.'

When he had long jangled with her, he went away privily ere she was aware, so that she knew not where he went.

CHAPTER 51

Another time, there came a great clerk unto her asking these words, how they should be understood: —

'Crescite et multiplicamini.'

She answering said: — 'Sir, these words be not understood only of begetting of children bodily, but also of the purchasing of virtue, which is ghostly fruit, such as the hearing of the words of God, by giving good example, by meekness and patience, charity and chastity, and such other, for patience is more worthy than miracle-working.' [58b]

And she, through the grace of God, answered so that clerk that he was well pleased; and Our Lord, of His mercy, ever made some men to love her and support her.

In this city of York, there was a doctor of divinity, Master John Aclom, also a Canon of the Minster, Sir John Kendale, and another priest who sang by the bishop's grave. These were her good friends of the spirituality.

So she dwelt still in that city, fourteen days, as she had said before, and some deal more, and on the Sundays she was houselled in the Minster with great weeping, boisterous sobbing and loud crying, so that many men marvelled what ailed her.

Afterwards there came a priest, a worshipful clerk, he seemed, and said unto her: —

'Damsel, thou saidest when thou first came hither that thou wouldst abide here but fourteen days.'

'Yes, sir, with your leave, I said that I would abide

here fourteen days, but I said not that I should abide here neither more nor less. But now, sir, I tell you truly, I go not yet.'

Then he set her a day, commanding her to appear before him in the Chapter-house.

And she said that she would obey his admonition with good will.

She went then to Master John Aclom, the aforesaid doctor, praying him to be there on her part. And so he was, and he took great favour amongst them all.

Also, another master of divinity had promised her to have been there with her, but he drew back till he knew how the cause should go, whether with her or against her.

There were many people that day in the Chapter-house of the Minster, to hear and see what should be said or done to the aforesaid creature.

When the day came she was all ready in the Minster to come to her answer. Then came her friends to her and bade her be of good cheer. She, thanking them, said, so she should.

And immediately came a priest full goodly, and took her by the arm to help her through the press of the people, and brought her before a worshipful doctor, who had admonished her before to appear before him in the Chapter-house on this day in York Minster.

With this doctor sat many other clerks, full reverend and worshipful, of which clerks, some loved the said creature right well.

Then said the worshipful doctor to her: — 'Woman, what dost thou here in this country?'

'Sir, I come on a pilgrimage to offer here to Saint William.'

Then said he again: — 'Hast thou a husband?'
She said: — 'Yea.'
'Hast thou any letter of record?'
'Sir,' she said, 'my husband gave me leave with his own mouth. Why fare ye thus with me, more than ye do with other pilgrims that be here, who have no letter any more than I have? Sir, them ye let go in peace and quiet and in rest, and I no rest may have amongst you. And sir, if there be any clerk amongst you all who can prove that I have said any word other than I ought to do, I am ready to amend it with good will. I will neither maintain error nor heresy, for it is my full will to hold as Holy Church holdeth, and fully to please God.'

Then the clerks examined her in the Articles of the Faith and in many other points, as they liked, to which she answered well and truly, so that they could have no occasion in her words to distress her, thanked be God.

And then the doctor who sat there as a judge, summoned her to appear before the Archbishop of York, and told her what day, at a town called Cawood,[1] commanding her to be kept in prison till the day of her appearing came.

Then the secular people answered for her, and said she should not go to prison, for they would themselves undertake for her and go to the Archbishop with her. So the clerks said no more to her at that time, for they rose up and went where they would, and let her go where she would, worship be to Jesus.

Soon after there came a clerk to her — one of the same that had sat against her — and said: —

'Damsel, I pray thee be not displeased with me, though

[1] *See* Note M.

I sat with the doctor against thee; he cried so upon me that I durst not otherwise do.'

And she said: — 'I am not displeased with you therefor.'

Then said he: — 'I pray you, then, pray for me.'

'Sir,' she said, 'I will, right readily.'

THERE was a monk preaching in York, who heard 59b much slander and much evil language of the said creature. And when he would preach, there was a great multitude of people to hear him, and she present with them. So, when he was at his sermon, he repeated many matters so openly that the people conceived well that it was for cause of her, wherefore her friends, that loved her well, were fully sorry and grieved thereof.

And she was much the more merry, for she had matter to prove her patience and her charity, wherethrough she trusted to please Our Lord Jesus Christ.

When the sermon was done, a doctor of divinity who loved her well, with many others also, came to her and said: —

'Margery, how have ye done this day?'

'Sir,' she said, 'right well. I have cause to be right merry and glad in my soul that I may suffer anything for His love, for He suffered much more for me.'

Anon, afterward, there came a man, who loved her right well, of good will with his wife and many others, and led her seven miles thence, to the Archbishop of York, and brought her into a fair chamber, where came a good clerk, saying to the good man who had brought her thither: —

'Sir, why have ye and your wife brought this woman hither? She will steal away from you, and then shall ye have a villainy of her.'

The good man said: — 'I dare well say she will abide and be at her answer with good will.'

On the next day she was brought into the Archbishop's Chapel, and there came many of the Archbishop's retinue, despising her, calling her 'Lollard' and 'heretic' and swearing many a horrible oath that she should be burnt.

And she, through the strength of Jesus, spoke back to them: —

'Sirs, I dread ye shall be burnt in Hell without end, unless ye amend in your swearing of oaths, for ye keep not the Commandments of God. I would not swear as ye do for all the money in this world.'

Then they went away, as if they had been shamed. She then, making her prayer in her mind, asked grace so to be demeaned that day as was most pleasure to God, and profit to her own soul, and good example to her fellow Christians.

Our Lord, answering her, said it should be right well. At the last, the said Archbishop came into the chapel with his clerks, and sharply he said to her: —

60a

'Why goest thou in white? Art thou a maiden?'

She, kneeling on her knees before him, said: —

'Nay, sir, I am no maiden. I am a wife.'

He commanded his retinue to fetch a pair of fetters and said she should be fettered, for she was a false heretic.

Then she said: — 'I am no heretic, nor shall ye prove me one.'

The Archbishop went away and left her standing alone. Then she made her prayers to Our Lord God Almighty to help her and succour her against all her enemies, ghostly and bodily, a long while, and her flesh trembled and quaked wonderfully, so that she was fain to put her hands under her clothes, so that it should not be espied.

Afterwards the Archbishop came again into the Chapel with many clerks, amongst whom was the same doctor who had examined her before, and the monk that had preached against her a little time before in York. Some of the people asked whether she were a Christian woman or a Jew; some said she was a good woman; some said 'Nay'.

Then the Archbishop took his seat and his clerks also, each of them in this degree, many people being present.

And during the time while the people were gathering together and the Archbishop taking his seat, the said creature stood all behind, making her prayers for help and succour against her enemies with high devotion, so long that she melted all into tears.

And at the last she cried aloud therewith, so that the Archbishop and his clerks and many people had great wonder of her, for they had not heard such crying before. When her crying was passed, she came before the Archbishop and fell down on her knees, the Archbishop saying full boisterously unto her: —

'Why weepest thou, woman?'

She, answering, said: — 'Sir, ye shall wish some day that ye had wept as sore as I.'

Then anon, the Archbishop put to her the Articles of our Faith, to which God gave her grace to answer well and truly and readily without any great study, so that he might not blame her. Then he said to the clerks: —

'She knoweth her Faith well enough. What shall I do with her?'

The clerks said: — 'We know well that she can say the Articles of the Faith, but we will not suffer her to

dwell amongst us, for the people hath great faith in her
60b dalliance, and, peradventure, she might pervert some of
them.'

Then the Archbishop said to her:—

'I am evil informed of thee. I hear it said that thou
art a right wicked woman.'

And she answered back: — 'I also hear it said that ye
are a wicked man. And if ye be as wicked as men say,
ye shall never come to Heaven, unless ye amend whilst ye
be here.'

Then he said full boisterously: —

'Why, thou (wretch), what say men of me?'

She answered: — 'Other men, sir, can tell you well
enough.'

Then said a great clerk with a furred hood: —

'Peace! Speak of thyself, and let him be.'

Afterwards, the Archbishop said to her: —

'Lay thy hand on the book here before me, and swear
that thou wilt go out of my diocese as soon as thou canst.'

'Nay, sir,' she said, 'I pray you give me leave to go
again into York to take leave of my friends.'

Then he gave her leave for a day or two. She thought
it was too short a time. Therefore she said again: —

'Sir, I may not go out of this diocese so hastily, for I
must tarry and speak with good men ere I go, and I must,
sir, with your leave, go to Bridlington, and speak with
my confessor, a good man, who was the good Prior's[1]
confessor, that is now canonized.'

Then said the Archbishop to her: — 'Thou shalt swear

---

[1] St. John of Bridlington, canonized by Pope Boniface IX in 1401, and the
last English saint to be canonized before St. Thomas More and St. John Fisher
in 1935.

that thou wilt neither teach nor challenge the people in my diocese.'

'Nay, sir, I shall not swear,' she said, 'for I shall speak of God, and rebuke those that swear great oaths wheresoever I go, unto the time that the Pope and Holy Church hath ordained that no man shall be so bold as to speak of God, for God Almighty forbiddeth not, sir, that we shall speak of Him. And also the Gospel maketh mention that, when the woman had heard Our Lord preach, she came before Him with a loud voice and said: — "Blessed be the womb that bore Thee, and the teats that gave Thee suck." Then Our Lord again said to her, "Forsooth, so are they blessed that hear the word of God and keep it." And therefore, sir, methinketh that the Gospel giveth me leave to speak of God.'

'Ah! Sir,' said the clerks, 'here wot we well that she hath a devil within her, for she speaketh of the Gospel.'

As quickly as possible, a great clerk brought forth a book and laid Saint Paul, for his part, against her, that no woman should preach.

She answering thereto said: — 'I preach not, sir; I come into no pulpit. I use but communication and good words, and that I will do while I live.'   61a

Then said a doctor who had examined her before: — 'Sir, she told me the worst tales of priests that ever I heard.'

The Bishop commanded her to tell that tale.

'Sir, with reverence to you, I spoke but of one priest in the manner of example, who, as I have learnt, went astray in a wood through the sufferance of God, for the profit of his soul, till the night came upon him. He, destitute of shelter, found a fair arbour in which he rested that night, having a fair pear tree in the midst, all flourished with flowers and embellished, and blooms full delectable to his sight. There came a bear, great and boisterous, huge to behold, shaking the pear tree and felling down the flowers. Greedily this grievous beast ate and devoured those fair flowers; and when he had eaten them, turning his tail-end in the priest's presence, voided them out again at the hinder part.

'The priest, having great abomination of that loathly sight, and feeling great grief for doubt what it might mean, on the next day wandered forth on his way all glum and pensive, when he chanced to meet with a seemly aged man, like a palmer or a pilgrim, who asked the priest the cause of his gloom. The priest, repeating the matter before written, said he conceived great dread and grief when he beheld that loathly beast fouling and devouring such fair flowers and blooms, and afterwards so horribly devoiding them before him at his tail-end, and he did not understand what this might mean. Then the palmer, shewing himself to be the messenger of God, reasoned thus: —

' "Priest, thou thyself art the pear tree, to some extent flourishing and flowering, through thy service-saying, and the sacraments ministering, though thou dost so un-devoutly, for thou takest full little heed how thou sayest thy Matins and thy Service, so long as it be blabbered to an end. Then goest thou to thy Mass without devotion, and for thy sin hast thou full little contrition. Thou receivest there the fruit of everlasting life, the Sacrament of the Altar, in full feeble disposition. Then, all the day after, thou mispendest thy time. Thou givest thyself to buying and selling, chopping and changing; as it were, a

man of the world. Thou sittest at the ale, giving thyself to   61b
gluttony and excess, to lust of thy body, through lechery
and uncleanness. Thou breakest the Commandments of
God through swearing, lying, detraction and backbiting,
and such other sins using.

' "Thus by thy misbehaviour, like unto the loathly
bear, thou devourest and destroyest the flowers and
blooms of virtuous living to thine endless damnation,
and many a man's hindrance, unless thou hast grace of
repentance and amendment." '

Then the Archbishop liked well the tale, and commended it, saying it was a good tale, and the clerk who
had examined her before in the absence of the Archbishop,
said: —

'Sir, this tale smiteth me to the heart.'

The aforesaid creature said to the clerk: —

'A worshipful doctor, sir, in the place where I mostly
dwell, is a worthy clerk, a good preacher, who speaketh
boldly against the misbehaviour of the people, and will
flatter no man. He said many times in the pulpit: — "If
any man be evil-pleased with my preaching, note him well,
for he is guilty." And right so, sir,' said she to the clerk,
'fare ye by me, God forgive you.'

The clerk did not well know what he might say to her.
Afterwards the same clerk came to her and prayed her for
forgiveness that he had been so against her. Also he
prayed her specially to pray for him.

Then anon, the Archbishop said: —

'Where shall I get a man who might lead this woman
away from me?'

Immediately there started up many young men, and
every one of them said: —

'My lord, I will go with her.'

The Archbishop answered: — 'Ye be too young. I will not have you.'

Then a good man of the Archbishop's household asked his lord what he would give him, if he should lead her. The Archbishop proffered him five shillings, and the man asked a noble. The Archbishop answering said: —

'I will not spend so much on her body.'

'Yes! Good sir,' said the said creature. 'Our Lord shall reward you right well in return.'

Then the Archbishop said to the man: —

'See, here is five shillings, and lead her fast out of this country.'

62a   She, kneeling down on her knees, asked his blessing. He, praying her to pray for him, blessed her and let her go.

Then she, going again to York, was received by many people and full worthy clerks, who rejoiced in Our Lord, Who had given her, unlettered, wit and wisdom to answer so many learned men without disgrace or blame, thanks be to God.

CHAPTER 53

LATER on, that good man who was her leader, brought her out of the town, and they went forth to Bridlington to her confessor, who was called Sleytham, and spoke with him, and with many other good men who had cheered her before and done much for her. Then she would not abide there, but took her leave to walk forth on her journey. Her confessor asked her if she durst not abide on account of the Archbishop of York, and she said:—

'No, forsooth!'

Then the good man gave her silver, beseeching her to pray for him, and so she set forth to Hull.

There, upon a time, as they went in procession, a great woman much despised her, and she said no word thereto. Many other folk said she should be put in prison, and made great threats. Notwithstanding all their malice, yet a good man came and prayed her to meat, and made her right good cheer.

Then the malicious people, who had despised her before, came to this good man, and bade him he should do her no good, for they held she was no good woman. On the next day, at morn, her host led her out to the town's end, for he durst no longer keep her.

So she went to Hessle and would have gone over the water at the Humber. Then she happened to find there two Preaching Friars, and two yeomen of the Duke of Bedford's. The Friars told the yeomen what woman she was, and they arrested her, as she would have taken her boat, and arrested a man who was going with her also.

62b   'For our lord,' they said, 'the Duke of Bedford, hath sent for thee, and thou art held the greatest Lollard in all this country, or about London either; and we have sought thee in many a country, and we shall have a hundred pounds for bringing thee before our lord.'

She said to them: —

'With good will, sirs, I shall go with you where ye will lead me.'

Then they brought her again into Hessle, and there men called her 'Lollard', and women came running out of their houses with their distaffs, crying to the people: —

'Burn this false heretic!'

So, as she went forth Beverley-ward with the said yeomen and the friars aforesaid, they met many times with men of the country who said to her: —

'Damsel, forsake this life that thou hast, and go spin and card, as other women do, and suffer not so much shame and so much woe. We would not suffer so much for any money on earth.'

Then she said to them: —

'I suffer not as much sorrow as I would for Our Lord's love, for I suffer but cruel words, and Our Merciful Lord Jesus Christ, worshipped be His Name, suffered hard strokes, bitter scourgings, and shameful death at the last for me and all mankind, blessed may He be. And therefore it is right nothing that I suffer, in regard to what He suffered.'

And so, as she went with the aforesaid men, she told them good tales, till one of the Duke's men who had arrested her, said unto her: —

'I have had doubts since I met with thee, for it seemeth to me that thou sayest right good words.'

She said to him: — 'Sir, doubt not nor repent that ye met with me. Do your lord's will, and I trust all shall be for the best, for I am right well pleased that ye met with me.'

He said again: — 'Damsel, if ever thou be a saint in Heaven, pray for me.'

She answered, saying to him: —

'Sir, I hope ye will be a saint yourself, and every man that shall come to Heaven.'

So they set forth till they came into Beverley, where dwelt one of the men's wives, who had arrested her, and thither they led her and took away from her her purse and her ring. They provided her with a fair chamber and an honest bed there-in, with the necessaries, locking the door with the key, and bearing away the key with them.

63a

Afterwards they took the man, whom they arrested with her, and who was the Archbishop of York's man, and put him in prison. And soon after, the same day, came tidings that the Archbishop was coming into the town where his man was put in prison. It was told to the Archbishop of his man's prisoning, and anon he had him let out. Then that man went to the said creature, with an angry face, saying: —

'Alas! that I ever knew thee. I have been imprisoned for thee.'

She, comforting him, answered: — 'Have meekness and patience, and ye shall have great reward in Heaven therefor.'

So he went away from her.

Then stood she looking out of a window, telling many good tales to them that would hear her, insomuch that women wept sore, and said with great grief in their hearts: —

'Alas! woman, why shalt thou be burnt?'

Then she prayed the good wife of the house to give her drink, for she was sick with thirst, and the good wife said her husband had borne away the key, wherefore she could not come to her, nor give her drink. Then the women took a ladder and set it up to the window, and gave her a pint of wine in a pot, and took her a cup, beseeching her to set away the pot privily, and the cup, so that, when the good man came, he might not espy it.

CHAPTER 54

The said creature, lying in her bed the next night following, heard with her bodily ears a loud voice, calling
'Margery'. At that voice she woke, greatly afraid, and,
lying still in silence, she made her prayers as devoutly as
she could for the time. And soon Our Merciful Lord over
all became present, and comforting His unworthy servant,
said unto her:—

'Daughter, it is more pleasing to Me that thou sufferest
despites and scorns, shames and reproofs, wrongs and dis-
comforts, than if thine head were smitten off three times a
day every day for seven years. And therefore daughter,
fear thee nothing that any man can say to thee; but in My
goodness, and in thy sorrows that thou hast suffered there-
in, hast thou great cause to rejoice, for when thou comest
home to Heaven, then shall every sorrow be turned for
thee to joy.'

63b

On the next day she was brought into the Chapter-
house of Beverley, and there was the Archbishop of York
and many great clerks with him, priests, canons, and
secular men.

Then said the Archbishop to the said creature:—

'What, woman! art thou come again? I would fain be
delivered of thee!'

Then a priest brought her forth before him, and the
Archbishop said, all that were present hearing:—

'Sirs, I had this woman before me at Cawood, and there

197

I, with my clerks, examined her in her Faith, and found no default in her. Furthermore, sirs, I have since that time, spoken with good men who hold her a perfect woman, and a good woman. Notwithstanding all this, I gave one of my men five shillings to lead her out of this country for the quieting of the people. And, as they were going on their journey, they were taken and arrested, my man put in prison for her, also her gold and her silver was taken away from her, with her beads and her ring, and she is brought here again before me. Is there any man here that can say anything against her?'

Then other men said: — 'Here is a friar who knows many things against her.'

The friar came forth and said she depraved all men of Holy Church, and much ill language he uttered at that time of her. Also he said she would have been burnt at Lynne, had his order, the Preaching Friars, not been there. 'And sir, she sayeth that she can weep and have contrition when she will.'

Then came those two men who had arrested her, saying with the friar that she was Cobham's[1] daughter, and was sent to bear letters about the country. And they said she had not been at Jerusalem, nor in the Holy Land, nor on other pilgrimages, as she had been in truth. They denied all truth, and maintained the wrong, as many others had
64a done before. When they had said enough a great while, and for a long time, they were in peace. Then said the Archbishop to her: —

'Woman, what sayest thou hereto?'

[1] In MS., 'Combomis dowtyr'. Probably meant for 'Cobham's daughter', i.e. the spiritual (heretical) daughter of Sir John Oldcastle, the Arch-Lollard, who bore the title of 'Lord Cobham' by right of his wife. The first 'm' is an erroneous anticipation of the other.

She said: — 'My lord, save your reverence, they are lies, all the words that they say.'

Then said the Archbishop to the friar: —

'Friar, the words are not heresy; they are slanderous words and erroneous.'

'My lord,' said the friar, 'she knows her Faith well enough. Nevertheless, my lord of Bedford is wroth with her and he will have her.'

'Well, friar,' said the Archbishop, 'and thou shalt lead her to him.'

'Nay, sir,' said the friar, 'it falleth not for a friar to lead a woman about.'

'And I will not,' said the Archbishop, 'that the Duke of Bedford be wroth with me, for her.'

Then said the Archbishop to his men: —

'Take heed to the friar, till I will have him back,' and commanded another man to keep the said creature also till he would have her back another time, when he liked.

The said creature prayed him, of his lordship, that she should not be put amongst men, for she was a man's wife.

And the Archbishop said:— 'Nay, thou shalt no harm have.'

Then he that was charged with her took her by the hand and led her home to his house, and made her sit with him at meat and drink, showing her goodly cheer.

Thither came many priests and other men soon after to see her and speak with her, and many people had great compassion that she was so evil fared with.

In a short time after, the Archbishop sent for her and she came into his hall. His household was at meat, and she was led into his chamber, even to his bedside. Then she, bowing, thanked him for his gracious lordship which he had shewn to her beforetime.

'Yea, yea,' said the Archbishop, 'I am worse informed of thee, than ever I was before.'

She said: — 'My lord, if ye like to examine me, I shall then know the truth, and if I be found guilty, I will abide by your correction.'

64b Then came forth a Preaching Friar, who was Suffragan with the Archbishop, to whom the Archbishop said: —

'Now, sir, as ye said to me when she was not present, say now while she is present.'

'Shall I so?' said the Suffragan.

'Yea,' said the Archbishop.

Then said the Suffragan to the said creature: —

'Damsel, thou wert at my Lady Westmoreland's?'[1]

'When, sir?' said she.

'At Easter,' said the Suffragan.

She, not replying, said, 'Well, sir?'

Then said he: — 'My lady, her own person, was well pleased with thee, and liked well thy words, but thou counselled my Lady Greystoke to forsake her husband, she that is a baron's wife, and daughter to my Lady of Westmoreland, and now thou hast said enough to be burnt for.'

And so he multiplied many shrewd words before the Archbishop — it is not expedient to repeat them.

At the last, she said to the Archbishop: — 'My lord, if it be your will, I saw not my Lady Westmoreland these two years and more. Sir, she sent for me before I went to Jerusalem, and if it please you, I will go again to her for record that I moved no such matter.'

[1] Joan, daughter of John of Gaunt and sister to Cardinal Beaufort. She was aunt to the Duke of Bedford.

'Nay,' said they that stood about, 'let her be put in prison, and we will send a letter to the worshipful lady, and, if it be truth that she sayeth, let her go quit without danger.'

And she said she was right well satisfied that it should be so.

Then said a great clerk who stood a little to one side of the Archbishop: —

'Put her forty days in prison, and she shall love God the better when she leaveth.'

The Archbishop asked her what tale it was that she told the Lady of Westmoreland, when she spake with her.

She said: — 'I told her a good tale of a lady that was damned because she would not love her enemies, and of a bailiff that was saved because he loved his enemies, and forgave them that had trespassed against him; and yet he was held an evil man.'

The Archbishop said it was a good tale.

Then said his steward and many more with him, crying with a loud voice, to the Archbishop: —

'Lord, we pray you, let her go hence at this time, and if ever she comes back, we will burn her ourselves.' 65a

The Archbishop said: —

'I believe there was never a woman in England so fared with as she is, and hath been.'

Then he said to the said creature: —

'I wot not what I shall do with thee.'

She said: — 'My lord, I pray you, let me have your letter and your seal in record that I have excused myself against my enemies, and that nothing is held against me, neither error nor heresy having been proved, either one, against me, and John, your man, again to bring me over the water.'

The Archbishop full kindly granted her all her desire —
Our Lord reward his deserts — and delivered her purse,
with her ring and her beads, which the Duke's men of
Bedford had taken from her before. The Archbishop had
great marvel whence she had money to go with, about the
country, and she said good men gave to her, that she
should pray for them.

Then she, kneeling down, received his blessing, and
took her leave with right glad cheer, going out of his
chamber.

And the Archbishop's household prayed her to pray for
them, but the steward was wroth, because she laughed and
made good cheer, saying to her: —

'Holy folk should not laugh.'

She said: — 'Sir, I have great cause to laugh, for the
more shame I suffer, and despite, the merrier I may be in
Our Lord Jesus Christ.'

Then she came down into the hall, and there stood the
Preaching Friar, that had caused her all that woe.

So she passed forth with a man of the Archbishop's,
bearing the letter which the Archbishop had granted her
for a record, and he brought her to the Water of Humber,
and there he took his leave of her, returning to his lord,
and bearing the said letter with him again, so she was left
alone without knowledge of the people.

All the aforesaid trouble fell on her on a Friday,
thanked be God for all.

CHAPTER 55

W HEN she had passed the Water of Humber, anon she was arrested as a Lollard, and led prison-ward. There happened to be a person who had seen her before the Archbishop of York, who got her leave to go where she would, and excused her against the bailiff, and undertook for her that she was no Lollard. And so she escaped away in the Name of Jesus. 65b

Then met she with a man of London, and his wife with him, and so she went forth with them till she came to Lincoln; and there she suffered much scorn and many hurtful words, answering back in God's cause, without any hindrance, wisely and discreetly. There, many men marvelled at her knowledge. There were men of law who said unto her: —

'We have gone to school many years, and yet are we not sufficient to answer as thou dost. Of whom hast thou this knowledge?'

And she said: — 'Of the Holy Ghost.'

Then asked they:— 'Hast thou the Holy Ghost?'

'Yea, sirs,' said she, 'no man may say a good word without the gift of the Holy Ghost, for Our Lord Jesus Christ said to His disciples, "Study not what ye shall say, for it shall not be your spirit that shall speak in you, but it shall be the spirit of the Holy Ghost!" '

And thus Our Lord gave her grace to answer them, worshipped may He be.

203

Another time, there came a great lord's men to her, and they swore many great oaths, saying: —

'We are given to know that thou canst tell us whether we will be saved or damned.'

She said: — 'Yea, forsooth can I; for as long as ye swear such horrible oaths and break the commandments of God wittingly as ye do, and will not leave your sin, I dare well say ye will be damned. And, if ye will be contrite, and shriven of your sin, willingly do penance, and leave it whilst ye may, in will no more to turn again thereto, I dare well say ye shall be saved.'

'What! Canst thou not tell us otherwise than this?'

'Sirs,' she said, 'this is right good, methinketh.'

And then they went away from her.

66a After this she went homeward again till she came to West Lynne. When she was there, she sent after her husband into Lynne Bishop, after Master Robert, her confessor, and after Master Aleyn, a doctor of divinity, and told them, in part, of her tribulation.

And then she told them that she might not come home to Lynne Bishop till she had been to the Archbishop of Canterbury for his letter and his seal.

'For, when I was before the Archbishop of York,' she said, 'he would give no credence to my words, inasmuch as I had not my lord's letter and seal of Canterbury. And so I promised him that I should not come into Lynne Bishop till I had my lord's letter and the seal of Canterbury.'

Then she took her leave of the said clerks, asking their blessing, and passed forth with her husband to London.

When she came there, she was anon successful about her letter from the Archbishop of Canterbury.

And so she dwelt in the city of London a long time, and had right good cheer of many worthy men.

Then she came Ely-ward on her way home to Lynne, and when she was three miles from Ely, there came a man riding after them at great speed, and arrested her husband and her, purposing to lead them both into prison. He cruelly rebuked them and greatly reviled them, speaking many wicked words.

At the last, she prayed her husband to shew him my lord's letter, of Canterbury. When the man had read the letter, he spoke fair and kindly unto them, saying: —

'Why shewed ye not your letter to me before?'

And so they parted away from him, and then came into Ely and from thence home into Lynne, where she suffered much despite, much reproof, many a scorn, many a slander, many a banning and many a cursing.

And on a time, a reckless man, little caring for his own shame, with will and with purpose cast a bowlful of water on her head as she was coming along the street. She, in no way moved, said: — 'God make you a good man,' highly thanking God thereof, as she did many other times.

66b

Afterwards God punished her with many great and divers sicknesses. She had the flux a long time, until she was anointed, expecting to be dead. She was so feeble that she could not hold a spoon in her hand. Then Our Lord Jesus Christ spoke to her soul and said she should not die yet. Then she recovered again a little while.

And anon afterwards she had a great sickness in her head, and later, in her back, so that she feared to have lost her wits therethrough.

Afterwards, when she was recovered of all these sicknesses, in a short time there followed another sickness, which was set in her right side, lasting the time of eight years, less eight weeks, at divers times. Sometimes she had it once a week, continuing for thirty hours, sometimes twenty, sometimes ten, sometimes eight, sometimes four and sometimes two, so hard and so sharp that she must void what was in her stomach, as bitter as if it were gall, neither eating nor drinking while the sickness endured, but ever groaning till it was gone.

Then she would say to Our Lord: — 'Ah! Blissful Lord, why wouldst Thou become Man, and suffer so much pain for my sins, and for all men's sins, that shall be saved; and we so unkind, O Lord, to Thee; and I, most unworthy, cannot suffer this little pain. Ah! Lord, because of Thy great pain, have mercy on my little pain.

'For the great pain that Thou suffered, give me not so much as I am worthy, for I may not bear as much as I am worthy. And if Thou wilt, Lord, that I bear it, send me patience, or else I may not suffer it.

'Ah! Blissful Lord, I would rather suffer all the cruel words that men might say of me, and all clerks to preach against me, for Thy love, so that it were no hindrance to any man's soul, than this pain that I have. For cruel words to suffer for Thy love, hurts me right nothing, Lord; and the world may take nothing from me but worship and worldly goods, and by the worship of the world, I set right nothing.

'All manner of goods and worships, and all manner of loves on earth, I pray Thee, Lord, forbid me, especially all those loves and possessions of earthly things which would decrease my love of Thee, or lessen my merit in Heaven.

'And all manner of loves and goods which Thou knowest in Thy Godhead should increase my love of Thee, I pray Thee grant me for Thy mercy to Thine everlasting worship.'

Sometimes, notwithstanding that the said creature had great bodily sickness, yet the Passion of Our Merciful Lord Jesus Christ so wrought in her soul, that for the time she felt not her sickness but wept and sobbed in memory of Our Lord's Passion, as though she had seen Him with her bodily eye, suffering pain and passion before her.

Later, when eight years were passed, her sickness abated so that it came not week by week. But then increased her cries and her weepings, insomuch that priests dare not housel her openly in the church, but privily in

67a

the Prior's Chapel at Lynne, away from the people's hearing.

And in that chapel she had such high contemplation and so much dalliance with Our Lord, inasmuch as she was put out of church for His love, that she cried at the time she was houselled as if her soul and her body would be parted asunder, so that two men held her in their arms till her crying had ceased; for she could not bear the abundance of love that she felt in the Precious Sacrament, which she steadfastly believed was very God and man in the form of bread.

Then Our Blissful Lord said to her mind: —

'Daughter, I will not have My grace hidden, that I give thee, for the busier the people are to hinder and prevent it, the more will I spread it and make it known to all the world.'

CHAPTER 57

THEN, it happed, there came another monk to Lynne
at the time of Removing¹ — as the custom was
amongst them — who loved not the said creature, and
would not allow her to come into their chapel, as she had
done before he came thither.

Then the Prior of Lynne, Dom Thomas Hevyngham,
meeting with the said creature and Master Robert Spryn-
golde, who was her confessor at that time, prayed them to
hold him excused if she were no more houselled in his
Chapel, 'for there is coming', he said, 'a new brother of
mine, who will not come into our chapel as long as she is
therein, and therefore provide yourselves with another
place, I pray you.'

Master Robert answered: — 'Sir, we must then housel
her in the church; we may not choose, for she hath my
lord of Canterbury's letter, and his seal, in which we are
commanded, by virtue of obedience, to hear her confession
and administer to her the Sacrament, as often as we be
required.'

Then was she houselled after this time at the high
altar in Saint Margaret's Church, and Our Lord visited
her with such great grace, when she would be houselled,
that she cried so loud that it could be heard all about the
church, and outside the church, as if she would have died

¹ In some parts of the country, it was then, as now, the custom for all persons
changing their dwellings, to move on the same day.

therewith, so that she could not receive the Sacrament from the priest's hands, the priest turning himself again to the High Altar with the Precious Sacrament till her crying had ceased.

Then he, turning again to her, would administer the Sacrament to her, as he had to do.

And thus it happened many a time when she would be houselled. Sometimes she would weep fully softly and stilly, in receiving the Sacrament without any boisterousness, as Our Lord should visit her with His grace.

68a

On a Good Friday, as the said creature beheld priests kneeling on their knees and other worshipful men with torches burning in their hands before the Sepulchre, devoutly representing the lamentable death and doleful burying of Our Lord Jesus Christ after the good custom of Holy Church, the memory of Our Lady's Sorrows, which she suffered when she beheld His Precious Body hanging on the Cross, and then buried before her sight, suddenly occupied the heart of this creature drawing her mind wholly into the Passion of Our Lord Christ Jesus, Whom she beheld in her ghostly eyes in the sight of her soul as verily as though she had seen His Precious Body beaten, scourged and crucified with her bodily eyes, which sight and ghostly beholding wrought by grace so fervently in her soul, wounding her with pity and compassion, so that she sobbed, moaned and cried, and spreading her arms abroad, said with a loud voice, 'I die! I die!' so that many men wondered and marvelled what ailed her.

And the more she tried to keep herself from crying, the louder she cried, for it was not in her power to take it or leave it, but as God would send it.

Then a priest took her in his arms and bore her into the Prior's Cloister to let her take the air, supposing she would not otherwise have endured it, her labour was so great. Then she waxed all livid like lead, and sweated full sore.

This manner of crying lasted ten years, as has been written before, and every Good Friday in all the aforesaid years she was weeping and sobbing five or six hours together, and therewith cried full loud many times, so that she could not restrain herself therefrom, and this made her full feeble and weak in her bodily might.

Sometimes she wept on Good Friday an hour for the sins of the people, having more sorrow for their sins than for her own, inasmuch as Our Lord forgave her her own sins, ere she went to Jerusalem.

Nevertheless, she wept for her own sins full plenteously when it pleased Our Lord to visit her with His grace. Sometimes she wept another hour for the souls in Purgatory; another hour for them that were in mischief, in poverty or in any dis-ease; another hour for Jews, Saracens, and all false heretics, that God in His great goodness should put away their blindness, so that, through His grace, they might be turned to the Faith of Holy Church and be children of salvation.

68b

Many times, when this creature would make her prayers, Our Lord said unto her: —

'Daughter, ask what thou wilt and thou shalt have it.'

She said: — 'I ask right nothing, Lord, but what Thou mayest well give me, and that is the mercy which I ask for the people's sins. Thou sayest oftentimes in the year to me that Thou hast forgiven me my sins. Therefore I ask now mercy for the sin of the people, as I would do for my own; for, Lord, Thou art all charity, and charity brought

Thee into this wretched world, and caused Thee to suffer full hard pains for our sins.

'Why should I not, then, have charity for the people and desire forgiveness of their sins?

'Blessed Lord, methinketh that Thou hast shewn right great charity to me, an unworthy wretch. Thou art as gracious to me as though I were as clean a maiden as any in this world, and as though I had never sinned.

'Therefore, Lord, I would I had a well of tears to constrain Thee with, so that Thou shouldst not take utter vengeance on man's soul, to part him from Thee without end. For it is a hard thing, to think that any earthly man should ever do any sin through which he would be parted from Thy glorious face, without end.

'If I, Lord, could as well give the people contrition and weeping as Thou givest it me for my own sins and other mens' sins also, and as well as I could give a penny out of my purse, soon should I full fill men's hearts with contrition, so that they might cease from their sins. I have great marvel in my heart, Lord, that I, who have been so sinful a woman, and the most unworthy creature that ever Thou shewed Thy mercy unto, in all this world, should have such great charity to my fellow Christians' souls. Methinketh that, though they had ordained for me the most shameful death that ever might any man or woman suffer on earth, yet I would forgive them it for Thy love, Lord, and have their souls saved from everlasting damnation.

'Therefore Lord, I shall not cease, when I may weep, to weep for them plenteously, prosper if I may. And if Thou wilt, Lord, that I cease from weeping, I pray Thee, take me out of this world.

69a

'What should I do therein, unless I might profit? For, though it were possible that all this world might be saved through the tears of mine eyes, I were not thankworthy. Therefore all praise, all honour, all worship be to Thee, Lord. If it were Thy will, Lord, I would for Thy love, and for the magnifying of Thy Name, be hewn as small as flesh for the pot.'

CHAPTER 58

On a time, as the aforesaid creature was in her contemplation, she hungered right sore after God's word, and said: —

'Alas! Lord, that, however many clerks Thou hast in this world, Thou wouldst not send me one of them who might fill my soul with Thy word and with reading of Holy Scripture. For all the clerks that preach could not fill it full. For, methinketh, my soul is ever so hungry that, if I had gold enough, I would give every day a noble to have every day a sermon, for Thy word is worth more to me than all the world.

'Therefore, Blessed Lord, have pity on me, for Thou hast taken away the anchorite from me, who was to me a singular solace and comfort, and many times refreshed me with Thy holy word.'

Then answered Our Lord Jesus Christ to her soul saying: —

'There shall come one from afar, who shall fulfil thy desire.'

So, many days after this answer, there came a priest, new to Lynne, who had never known her before, and, when he saw her going in the streets, he was greatly moved to speak with her, and inquired of other folk what manner of woman she was.

They said they trusted God she was a right good woman.

Afterwards, the priest sent for her, praying her to come and speak with him and his mother, for he had hired a chamber for his mother and himself, and so they dwelt together. 69b

The said creature went to learn his will, and spoke with his mother and him and had right good cheer from them both.

Then the priest took a book and read therein how Our Lord, seeing the city of Jerusalem, wept there-upon, forseeing the mischiefs and sorrows that would come thereto, for she knew not the time of her visitation.

When the said creature heard read how Our Lord wept, then wept she sore and cried aloud, neither the priest nor his mother knowing the cause of her weeping.

When her crying and weeping had ceased, they rejoiced and were right merry in Our Lord. Afterwards she took her leave and parted from them at that time.

When she was gone, the priest said to his mother:—

'I marvel much of this woman, why she weepeth and crieth so. Nevertheless, methinketh she is a good woman, and I desire greatly to speak more with her.'

His mother was well pleased, and counselled that he should do so.

Afterwards the same priest loved her and trusted her full much, and blessed the time that ever he knew her, for he found great ghostly comfort in her, and she caused him to look up much good scripture, and many a good doctor, which he would not have done at that time, had she not been there.

He read to her many a good book of high contemplation, and other books, such as the Bible, with doctors' views there-on, Saint Bride's book, Hylton's book, Bonaventure, Stimulus Amoris, Incendium Amoris, and such others. And then knew she that it was a spirit sent by God, which said to her, as is written a little before, when she complained of lack of reading, these words: — 'There shall come one from afar that shall fulfill thy desire.' And thus she knew by experience that it was a right true spirit.

70a The aforesaid priest read her books for the most part of seven or eight years, to the great increase of his knowledge and his merit, and he suffered many an evil word for her love, inasmuch as he read her so many books, and supported her in her weeping and crying. Afterwards he waxed beneficed and had a great cure of souls, and then it pleased him full well that he had read so much beforehand.

CHAPTER 59

THUS, through hearing holy books and holy sermons, she ever increased in contemplation and holy meditation. It is in a manner impossible to write all the holy thoughts, holy speeches and high revelations which Our Lord shewed unto her, both of herself and other men and women, and also of many souls, some to be saved and some to be damned.

And it was to her a great punishment and a sharp chastisement to know of those that should be saved. She was full glad and joyful, for she desired, as much as she durst, all men to be saved, and when Our Lord shewed to her any that should be damned, she had great pain. She would not hear or believe that it was God who shewed her such things, and put it out of her mind as much as she might. Our Lord blamed her therefor, and bade her believe that it was His high mercy and His goodness to shew her His privy counsels, saying to her mind: —

'Daughter, thou must as well hear of the damned as of the saved.'

She would give no credence to the counsel of God, but rather believed it was some evil spirit deceiving her.

Then for her frowardness and her unbelief, Our Lord withdrew from her all good thoughts and all good remembrance of holy speeches and dalliance, and the high contemplation which she had been used to before, and suffered her to have as many evil thoughts as she before had good ones.

70b And this vexation endured for twelve days; and just as, before, she had four hours of the forenoon in holy speeches and dalliance with Our Lord, so now she had as many hours of foul thoughts and foul memories of lechery and all uncleanness, as though she had been common to all manner of people.

And so the devil deluded her, dallying unto her with cursed thoughts, as Our Lord dallied to her before with holy thoughts.

And, as she before had many glorious visions and high contemplation in the Manhood of Our Lord, in Our Lady and in many other holy saints, even right so had she now horrible sights and abominable, for aught she could do, of beholding men's members, and such other abominations.

She saw, as she thought verily, divers men of religion, priests and many others, both heathen and Christian, coming before her sight, so that she might not eschew them or put them out of her sight, shewing their bare members unto her.

And therewith the devil bade her, in her mind, choose whom she would have first of them all, and she must be common to them all.

And he said she liked better some one of them than all the others.

She thought that he said truth; she could not say nay; and she must needs do his bidding, and yet she would not have done it for all this world.

Yet she thought it should be done, and she thought these horrible sights and cursed memories were delectable to her, against her will.

Wherever she went, or whatever she did, these cursed

memories remained with her. When she should see the Sacrament, make her prayers, or do any other good deed, ever such cursedness was put into her mind.

She was shriven, and did all that she might, but she found no release, until she was near at despair. It cannot be written what pain she felt, and what sorrow she was in.

Then she said: — 'Alas! Lord, Thou hast said before that Thou shouldst never forsake me. Where now is the truth of Thy word?'

And anon, came her good angel unto her, saying: —

'Daughter, God hath not forsaken thee, and never shall forsake thee, as He hath promised thee; but, because thou believest not that it is the spirit of God that speaketh in thy soul, and sheweth thee His privy counsels, of some that shall be saved and some that shall be damned, therefore God chastiseth thee in this wise and manner. And this chastising shall endure twelve days, until thou wilt believe that it is God Who speaketh to thee, and no devil.'

71a

Then she said to her angel: — 'Ah! I pray thee, pray for me to My Lord Jesus Christ that He will vouchsafe to take from me these cursed thoughts, and speak to me as He did before time, and I shall make a promise to God that I shall believe it is God Who hath spoken to me beforetime, for I may no longer endure this great pain.'

Her angel said again to her: —

'Daughter, My Lord Jesus will not take it away from thee till thou hast suffered it twelve days, for He will that thou know thereby whether it is better that God speak to thee, or the devil. And My Lord Jesus Christ is never the wrother with thee, though He suffer thee to feel this pain.'

So she suffered that pain till twelve days were passed, and then had she as holy thoughts, as holy memories and as holy desires, as holy speeches and dalliance with Our Lord Jesus Christ as ever she had before, Our Lord saying to her: —

'Daughter, believe now well that I am no devil.'

Then she was filled with joy, for she heard Our Lord speaking to her as He was wont to do.

Therefore she said: — 'I shall believe that every good thought is the speech of God, blessed may Thou, Lord, be, that Thou deign to comfort me again. I would not, Lord, for all this world, suffer such another pain as I have suffered these twelve days, for methought I was in Hell, blessed may Thou be that it is past.

'Therefore, Lord, now will I lie still and be obedient to Thy will. I pray Thee, Lord, speak in me what is most pleasing to Thee.'

CHAPTER 60

THE good priest, of whom it is written before, who was her reader, fell into great sickness and she was stirred in her soul to keep him, in God's stead; and when she lacked such as was needful for him, she went about to good men and good women and got such things as were necessary unto him.

He was so sick that men trusted nothing to his life, and his sickness was long continuing.

Then, at one time, when she was in church hearing her Mass, and praying for the same priest, Our Lord said to her that he should live and fare right well.

Then she was stirred to go to Norwich, to Saint Stephen's Church, where is buried the good Vicar who died but little before that time, for whom God shewed high mercy to his people, to thank Him for the recovery of this priest.

She took leave of her confessor, going forth to Norwich. When she came into the churchyard of Saint Stephen's, she cried, she roared, she wept, she fell to the ground, so fervently the fire of love burned in her heart.

Afterwards, she rose up again and went forth weeping into the church to the High Altar, and there she fell down with boisterous sobbings, weepings, and loud cries beside the grave of the good vicar, all ravished with ghostly comfort in the goodness of Our Lord, Who wrought such great grace for His servant who had been her confessor, and many times heard her confession of all her life, and administered to her the Precious Sacrament of the Altar at divers times.

And in so much was her devotion the more increased, as she saw Our Lord working such special grace for such a creature as she had been conversant with, in his life time.

She had such holy thoughts and memories that she could not measure her weeping or her crying; and therefore the people had great marvel of her, supposing that she had wept for some fleshly or earthly affection, and said unto her: —

'What aileth thee, woman? Why farest thus with thyself? We knew him as well as thou.'

Then there were priests in the same place who knew her manner of working, and they full charitably led her to a tavern and gave her drink, and made her full high and goodly cheer.

Also there was a lady who desired to have the said creature to meat, and therefore, as honesty would, she went to the church where the lady heard her service, in which this creature saw a fair image of Our Lady called a 'pieta', and, through beholding that sorrow, her mind was all wholly occupied in the Passion of Our Lord Jesus Christ, and in the compassion of Our Lady, Saint Mary, by which she was compelled to cry full loud and to weep full sore, as if she should have died.

Then came to her the lady's priest, saying: —

'Damsel, Jesus is dead long since.'

When her crying ceased, she said to the priest: —

'Sir, His death is as fresh to me as if He had died this same day, and so, methinketh, it ought to be to you and to all Christian people. We ought ever to have mind of His kindness and ever think of the doleful death He died for us.'

Then the good lady, hearing her communication, said: —

'Sir, it is a good example to me, and to other men also, the grace that God worketh in her soul.'

And so the good lady was her advocate and answered for her.

Afterwards she had her home with her to meat, and shewed her full glad and goodly cheer, as long as she would abide there. And soon after, she came home again to Lynne, and the aforesaid priest, for whom she went most specially to Norwich, who had read to her for about seven years, recovered and went about where he liked, thanked be Almighty God for His goodness.

THEN came a friar to Lynne who was held a holy man and a good preacher. His name and his perfection in preaching spread, and sprung wonder wide.

Then came good men to the said creature in good charity and said: —

'Margery, now shall ye have preaching enough, for there is coming one of the most famous friars in England to this town, to be here in residence.'

Then was she merry and glad and thanked God with all her heart that so good a man was coming to dwell amongst them. In a short time after, he said a sermon in a chapel of Saint James in Lynne, where many people were gathered to hear the sermon; and ere the friar went to the pulpit, the parish priest of the same place where he would preach, went to him and said: —

'Sir, I pray you be not displeased. Here will come a woman to your sermon, who oftentimes, when she heareth of the Passion of Our Lord, or of any high devotion, weepeth, sobbeth, and crieth, but it lasts not long. Therefore, good sir, if she makes any noise at your sermon, suffer it patiently and be not abashed thereof.'

The good friar went forth to say the sermon and preached full holily and devoutly, and spoke much of Our Lord's Passion, so that the said creature could no longer bear it. She kept herself from crying as long as she might, and then at last she burst out with a great cry, and cried wondrous sore.

72b

The good friar suffered it patiently and said no word thereto, at that time.

In a short time after, he preached again in the same place, the said creature being present, and, beholding how fast the people came running to hear the sermon, she had great joy in her soul, thinking in her mind: —

'Ah! Lord Jesus, I trow, if Thou wert here to preach in Thine own Person, the people would have great joy to hear Thee. I pray Thee, Lord, make Thy holy word settle in their souls as I would it should do in mine, and that as many may be turned by his voice, as would be by Thy voice, if Thou preachedest Thyself.'

And with such holy thoughts and holy mind, she asked grace for the people at that time and afterwards; and what with the sermon, and what with her own meditation, the grace of devotion wrought so sore in her mind that she fell into boisterous weeping.

Then said the good friar: — 'I would this woman were out of the church; she annoyeth the people.'

Some that were her friends, answered him: — 'Sir, hold her excused. She cannot withstand it.'

Then many people turned against her and were full glad that the good friar held against her. Then said some men that she had a devil within her, and so had they said 73a many times before, but now they were more bold, for they thought that their opinion was well strengthened or fortified by this good friar. Nor would he suffer her at his sermon unless she would leave off her sobbing and her crying.

There was then a good priest who had read to her much good scripture and who knew the cause of her crying. He spake to another good priest, who had known her many years, and told him his idea; how he proposed to go to the good friar, and try if he might meeken his heart.

The other good priest said he would, with good will, go with him, to get grace, if he might. So they went, both priests together, and prayed the good friar as entirely as they could, that he would allow the said creature quietly to come to his sermon, and suffer her patiently if she happened to sob or cry as other good men had suffered her before.

He answered shortly, that if she came into any church where he should preach, and made any noise as she was wont to do, he would speak sharply against her; he would not suffer her to cry, in no wise.

Afterwards, a worshipful doctor of divinity, a White Friar, a solemn clerk and elder doctor, and well approved, who had known the said creature many years of her life, and believed the grace that God wrought in her, took with him a worthy man, a bachelor of law, a well grounded man in scripture, and long exercised, who was confessor to the said creature, and went to the said friar as the good priests did before, and sent for wine to cheer him with, praying him of his charity to favour the works of Our Lord in the said creature, and grant her his benevolence in supporting her, if she happened to cry or sob whilst he was at his sermon.

These worthy clerks told him that it was a gift of God and she could not have it, but when God would give it. Nor might she withstand it when God sent it, and God would withdraw it when He willed; for that she had by revelation, and that was unknown to the friar.

Then he, neither giving credence to the doctor's words nor to the bachelor's, trusting much in the favour of the

73b

people, said he would not favour her in her crying for aught any man might say or do, for he would not believe it was a gift of God.

But, he said, if she could not withstand it when it came, he believed it was a cardiac ailment, or some other sickness, and if she would so acknowledge, he would have compassion on her, and stir the people to pray for her, and, on this condition, he would have patience with her and suffer her to cry enough, so that she could say it was a natural sickness.

And she herself knew well by revelation, and experience of the working, that it was no sickness, and therefore she would not, for all this world, say otherwise than she felt; and therefore they could not agree.

Then the worshipful doctor and her confessor counselled her that she should not go to his sermon, and that was, to her, great pain.

Then went another man, a worshipful burgess, who a few years afterwards was Mayor of Lynne, and prayed him as the worshipful clerks had done before, and he was answered as they were.

Then was she charged by her confessor that she should not go where he preached, but when he preached in one church, she should go into another. She had so much sorrow that she knew not what she might do, for she was put from the sermon which was to her the highest comfort on earth, when she might hear it, and, right so, the contrary was to her the greatest pain on earth, when she might not hear it. When she was alone by herself in one church, and he preaching to the people in another, she had as loud and marvellous cries as when she was amongst the people.

It was years that she could not be suffered to go to his sermon, because she cried so when it pleased Our Lord to give her remembrance and the very beholding of His bitter Passion.

74a

But she was not excluded from any other clerks preaching but only from the good friar's, as is said before; notwithstanding that, in the meantime, there preached many worshipful doctors and other worthy clerks, both religious and secular, at whose sermons she cried full loud and sobbed full boisterously many times and oft.

And yet they suffered it full patiently, and some who had spoken with her before, and had knowledge of her manner of living, excused her to the people when they heard any rumour or grutching against her.

CHAPTER 62

Afterwards, on Saint James' Day, the good friar
preached in Saint James' Chapel-yard[1] at Lynne — he
was at that time neither bachelor nor doctor of divinity —
where were many people and a great audience, for he had
a holy name and great favour with the people, insomuch
that some men, if they thought he would preach in the
country, they would go with him or else follow him from
town to town, such great delight had they to hear him;
and so, blessed may God be, he preached fully holily and
full devoutly.

Nevertheless, on this day he preached much against the
said creature, not expressing her name, but so exploiting
his conceits that men understood well that he meant her.

Then there was much discussion amongst the people,
for many men and many women trusted her, and loved
her right well, and were right grieved and sorrowful because he spoke as much against her as he did, desiring
that they had not heard him that day.

When he heard the murmur and grutching of the
people, supposing to be gainsaid another day by them
that were her friends, he, smiting his hand on the pulpit,
said: —

'If I hear these matters repeated any more, I shall so
smite the nail on the head,' he said, 'that it shall shame all
her maintainers.'

[1] *See* Note G.

229

And then many of them that pretended friendship to her, turned a-back, for a little vain dread that they had of his words, and durst not well speak with her. Of whom the same priest was one, that afterwards wrote this book, and who was in purpose never to have believed in her feelings afterwards.

And yet Our Lord drew him back in a short time, blessed may He be, so that he loved her more and trusted more to her weeping and her crying than ever he did before. For afterwards he read of a woman called Maria de Oegines,[1] and of her manner of living, of the wonderful compassion that she had in thinking of His Passion, and of the plenteous tears that she wept, which made her so feeble and so weak that she could not endure to behold the Cross, or hear Our Lord's Passion rehearsed, without being dissolved in tears of pity and compassion.

Of the plenteous grace of her tears, he treateth specially in the book before written, the 18th Chapter that begins, 'Bonus est domine, sperantibus in te', and also in the 19th Chapter where he telleth how she, at the request of a priest that he should not be troubled or distraught in his Mass with her weeping and her sobbing, went out of the church door, with a loud voice crying that she could not restrain herself therefrom.

And Our Lord also visited the priest, when at Mass, with such grace and such devotion when he would read the Holy Gospel, that he wept wonderfully, so that he wetted his vestment and the ornaments of the altar, and might not measure his weeping and his sobbing, it was so abundant; nor might he restrain it, or well stand therewith at the Altar.

[1] St. Mary of Oignies.

Then he believed well that the good woman, whom he before had little affection for, could not restrain her weeping, her sobbing or her crying, and who felt more plenty of grace than ever did he, without any comparison. Then he knew well that God gave His grace to whom He would.

Then the priest who wrote this treatise, through stirring of a worshipful clerk, a bachelor of divinity, had seen and read the matter before written much more 75a seriously and expressly than it is written in this treatise, for here is but a little of the effect thereof, for he had not right clear mind of the said matter when he wrote this treatise, and therefore he wrote the less thereof.

Then he drew toward and inclined more seriously to the said creature, whom he had fled and eschewed through the friar's preaching, as is before written.

Also the same priest read afterwards in a treatise that is called the 'Prick of Love', the 2nd Chapter, that Bonaventure wrote of himself, these words following: — 'Ah, Lord why shall I more call and cry! Thou delayest, and Thou comest not, and I, weary and overcome by desire begin to madden, for love governeth me, and not reason. I run with hasty course wherever Thou wilt. I submit, Lord. They that see me, trouble and rue not, knowing me drunken with Thy love. Lord, they say: — "Lo! yon madman crieth in the streets," but how much is the desire of my heart they perceive not.'

He read also of Richard Hampol, hermit, in Incendio Amoris, like matter that moved him to give credence to the said creature.

Also Elizabeth of Hungary cried with a loud voice, as is written in her treatise.

231

And many others, who had forsaken her through the friar's preaching, repented and turned again to her in process of time, notwithstanding that the friar kept his opinion, and would always in his sermon, have a part against her, whether she were there or not, and caused many people to deem full evil of her, many a day and long.

For some said that she had a devil within her, and some said to her own mouth that the friar should have driven those devils out of her. Thus was she slandered, eaten and gnawed by the people, for the grace that God wrought in her, of contrition, devotion, and compassion, through the gift of which graces she wept, sobbed and cried full sore against her will. She might not choose, for she would rather have wept softly and privily, than openly, if it had been in her power.

THEN some of her friends came to her and said it were 75b
more ease to her to go out of the town than abide
therein, so many people were against her. And she said
she would abide there as long as God willed, 'For here,'
she said, 'in this town have I sinned. Therefore it is
worthy that I should suffer sorrow in this town, there-
against. And yet have I not so much sorrow or shame as I
have deserved, for I have trespassed against God. I thank
Almighty God for whatever He sendeth me, and I pray
God that all manner of wickedness that any man shall say
of me in this world, may stand unto remission of my sins,
and any goodness that any man shall say of the grace that
God worketh in me, may turn God to worship and praise,
and to the magnifying of His Holy Name without end.
For all manner of worship belongeth to Him, and all
despite, shame, and reproof belongeth to me, and that
have I well deserved.'

Another time, her confessor came to her in a chapel of
Our Lady, called the Jesyne,[1] saying: —

'Margery, what shall ye now do? There are no more
against you but the moon and seven stars!! Scarcely
is there any man that holdeth with you but I alone.'

She said to her confessor: — 'Sir, be of good comfort,
for it shall be right well at the last. And I tell you truly

---

[1] Old French 'gesine', meaning 'confinement' or 'lying-in'. The chapel was
probably so called because the Nativity was specially honoured and depicted
there.

that My Lord Jesus Christ giveth me great comfort in my soul, or else I should fall into despair. My Blissful Lord Christ Jesus will not let me despair for any holy name that the good friar hath, for My Lord telleth me that He is wroth with him, and He saith to me that it were better he never were born, for he despiseth His works in me.'

Also, Our Lord said to her: — 'Daughter, if he be a priest that despiseth thee, knowing well wherefore thou weepest and cryest, he is accursed.'

And, on a time, as she was in the Prior's Cloister and durst not abide in the church, for disturbing the people with her crying, Our Lord said unto her, being in great grief: —

'Daughter, I bid thee go again into Church, for I shall take away from thee thy crying, so that thou shalt no more cry so loud, nor in the manner as thou hast done before, even though thou wouldst.'

76a She did the commandment of Our Lord and told her confessor just how she felt, and it fell in truth as she felt. She cried no more afterwards so loudly, nor in that manner as she had done before, but she sobbed wonderfully afterwards, and wept as sore as ever she did before, sometimes loudly and sometimes quietly, as God would measure it Himself.

Then many people believed that she durst no longer cry, because the good friar preached so against her, and would not suffer her in any way.

Then they held him a holy man, and her a false feigned hypocrite; and as some spoke evil of her before because she cried, so now some spoke evil of her because she cried not.

And so slander and bodily anguish fell to her on every side, and all was an increase of her ghostly comfort.

Then Our Merciful Lord said unto His unworthy servant: —

'Daughter, I must needs comfort thee, for now thou hast the right way to Heaven. By this way, came I to Heaven and all My disciples, for now thou shalt know the better what sorrow and shame I suffered for thy love, and thou shalt have the more compassion when thou thinkest on My Passion. Daughter, I have told thee many times that the friar should say evil of thee. Therefore I warn thee that thou tell him not of the private counsel which I have shewn to thee, for I will not that he heareth it from thy mouth. And daughter, I tell thee forsooth that he shall be chastised sharply. As his name is now, it shall be thrown down, and thine shall be raised up; and I shall make as many men to love thee for My love as have despised thee for My love. Daughter, thou shalt be in church when he shall be without. In this church, thou has suffered much shame and reproof for the gifts that I have given thee, and for the grace and goodness that I have wrought in thee, and therefore in this church and in this place I shall be worshipped in thee.

'Many a man and woman shall say: — "It is well seen that God loved her well." Daughter, I shall work so much grace for thee, that all the world shall wonder and marvel at My goodness.'

Then the said creature said unto Our Lord with great reverence: —

'I am not worthy that Thou shouldst shew such grace for me, Lord. It is enough for me that Thou save my soul from eternal damnation, by Thy great mercy.' 76b

'It is My worship, daughter, that I shall do and therefore I will that thou hast no will but My will. The less price thou settest on thyself, the more price I set on thee, and the better will I love thee, daughter. Look thou hast no sorrow for earthly goods. I have tried thee in poverty, and I have chastised thee as I would Myself, both within thy soul and without, through the slander of the people. Lo! daughter, I have granted thee thine own desire — that thou shouldst no other Purgatory have, than in this world only.

'Daughter, thou sayest often to Me in thy mind that rich men have great cause to love Me well, and thou sayest right true, for thou sayest that I have given them much money, wherewith they may serve Me and love Me. But, good daughter, I pray thee, love thou Me with all thine heart, and I shall give thee money enough to love Me with, for Heaven and earth should rather fail, than I should fail thee. And if other men fail, thou shalt not fail. And though all thy friends forsake thee, I shall never forsake thee. Thou madest Me once steward of thy household, and executor of all thy good works, and I shall be a true steward and a true executor unto the fulfilling of all thy will and all thy desire. And I shall ordain for thee, daughter, as for Mine Own Mother and as for Mine Own wife.'

[*Here follow Chapters* 64, 65 *and* 66]

CHAPTER 67

On a time, there happed to be a great fire in Lynne Bishop, which fire burnt up the Guild Hall[1] of the Trinity, and in the same town, a hideous fire and grievous, full likely to have burnt the parish church dedicated in honour of Saint Margaret, a stately place and richly honoured, and all the town as well, had there been no grace or miracle.

The said creature being there present, and seeing the peril and mischief of all the town, cried full loud many times that day and wept full abundantly, praying for grace and mercy to all the people.

And, notwithstanding at other times they could not endure her to cry and weep for the plenteous grace that God wrought in her, this day, for the eschewing of their bodily peril, they could suffer her to cry and weep as much as ever she would, and no man would bid her cease but rather prayed her to continue, fully trusting and believing that through her crying and weeping, Our Lord would take them to mercy.

Then came her confessor to her, and asked if it were best to bear the Sacrament to the fire or not. She said: — 'Yes, sir, yes! For Our Lord Jesus Christ told me, it shall be right well.'

So her confessor, parish priest of Saint Margaret's Church, took the Precious Sacrament and went before

79b

the fire as devoutly as he could, and then brought It in again to the church. And the sparks of the fire flew about the church.

The said creature, desiring to follow the Precious Sacrament to the fire, went out of the church door, and, as soon as she beheld the hideous flame of the fire, anon she cried with a loud voice: —

'Good Lord! Make it well.'

These words wrought in her mind, inasmuch as Our Lord had said to her before that He should make it well. And therefore she cried: —

'Good Lord! Make it well and send down some rain, or some weather that may, through Thy mercy, quench this fire and ease my heart.'

Later on, she went again into the church, and then she beheld how the sparks came into the choir through the lantern of the church.

Then she had a new sorrow, and cried full loud again for grace and mercy, with great plenty of tears.

Soon after, there came in to her three worshipful men with white snow on their clothes, saying unto her: —

'Lo! Margery, God hath wrought great grace for us, and sent us a fair snow to quench the fire with. Be now of good cheer, and thank God therefor.'

And with a great cry, she gave praise and thanks to God for His great mercy, and His goodness, and specially because He had said to her before, that it should be right well, when it was full unlikely to be well, save only through a miracle and special grace.

And now that she saw it was well indeed, she thought that she had great cause to thank Our Lord. Then her ghostly father came to her and said he believed that God granted them, for her prayers, to be delivered out of their great perils; for it might not be, without devout prayers, that the air, being bright and clear, should be so soon changed into clouds and darkness, and send down great flakes of snow, by which the fire was stopped, through His kindly work, blessed may Our Lord be.

80a

Notwithstanding the grace that He shewed for her, yet, when the perils were ceased, some men slandered her because she cried, and some said Our Lady never cried.

'Why cry ye in this manner?' and she said, because she could not otherwise do.

Then she fled the people, so that she should give them no occasion, into the Prior's Cloister.

When she was there, she had such great mind of Our Lord's Passion, and of His precious Wounds, and how dearly He bought her, that she cried and roared wonderfully, so that she might be heard a great way, and could not restrain herself therefrom.

Then had she great wonder how Our Lady could suffer or bear to see His Precious Body being scourged and hanged on the Cross. Also it came to her mind how men had said to her before, that Our Lady, Christ's Own Mother, cried not as she did, and that caused her to say in her crying:—

'Lord, I am not Thy Mother. Take away this pain from me, for I may not bear it. Thy Passion will slay me.'

So there came a worshipful clerk near her, a doctor of divinity, and said: —

'I would, rather than twenty pounds, that I might have such sorrow for Our Lord's Passion.'

Then the said doctor sent for her where he was, to come and speak with him, and she, with good will, went to him with weeping tears to his chamber. The worthy and worshipful clerk gave her drink, and made her right good cheer. Later, he led her to an altar and asked her what was the reason that she cried and wept so sore. Then she told him many great causes of her weeping, and yet she told him of no revelations.

And he said she was much bounden to love Our Lord for the tokens of love that He shewed her in divers ways. Afterwards there came a parson, who had taken a degree in school, who would preach both at noon and afternoon. And as he preached full holily and devoutly, the said creature was moved to devotion by his sermon and at last she burst out with a cry. The people began to grutch at her crying, for it was at the time that the good friar preached against her, as is written before, and also, ere Our Lord took her crying from her.

For, though the matter be written before this, nevertheless it fell after this.

Then the parson ceased a little in his preaching and said to the people: —

'Friends, be still and grutch not at this woman, for each of you may sin mortally in her, and she is not the cause, but your own judgment, for, though this manner of working may seem both good and ill, yet ought ye to judge the best in your own hearts, and I doubt not it is right well. Also I dare well say it is a right gracious gift of God, blessed may He be.'

Then the people blessed him for his goodly words, and were the more stirred to believe in his holy works.

Afterwards when the sermon was ended, a good friend

of the said creature met with the friar who had preached so sore against her, and asked him what he thought of her.

The friar, answering sharply back, said: —

'She hath a devil within her,' nothing moved from his opinion, but rather defending his error.

Soon after there was, at Lynne, held the Chapter of the Preaching Friars, and thither came many worshipful clerks of that holy order, of whom it behove one to say a sermon in the parish church.

And there was come, amongst others to the said Chapter, a worshipful doctor, named Master Custawns, and he had known the aforesaid creature many years before. When the creature heard say that he had come thither, she went to him and shewed him why she cried and wept so sore, to learn if he could find any default in her crying or in her weeping. The worshipful doctor said to her: —

81a 'Margery, I have read of a holy woman whom God had given the great grace of weeping and crying as He hath done unto you. In the church where she dwelt, was a priest who had no conceit in her weeping and caused her, through his stirring, to go out of the church. When she was in the church-yard, she prayed God that the priest might have feeling of the grace that she felt, so as to know that it lay not in her power to cry or weep but when God would. And so, suddenly, Our Lord sent him such devotion at his Mass, that he could not control himself, and then would he no more despise her after that, but rather, comfort her.'

Thus the said doctor, confirming her crying and weeping, said it was a gracious and special gift of God, and God was highly to be magnified in His gift.

And then the same doctor went to another doctor of divinity who was assigned to preach in the parish church before all the people, praying him that, if the said creature cried or wept at his sermon, he would suffer it meekly, and not be abashed thereof or speak there-against. So afterwards, when the worshipful doctor should preach, and worthily was brought to the pulpit, as he began to preach full holily and devoutly of Our Lady's Assumption, the said creature, lifted up in her mind by high sweetness and devotion, burst out with a loud voice and cried full loud, and wept full sore.

The worshipful doctor stood still, and suffered all full meekly till it ceased, and then said forth his sermon to an end.

At afternoon, he sent for the same creature to the place where he was, and made her right glad cheer. Then she thanked him for his meekness and his charity that he shewed in support of her crying and her weeping before noon at his sermon. The worshipful doctor answered her: —

'Margery, I would not have spoken against you, though ye had cried till evening. If ye will come to Norwich, ye shall be right welcome and have such cheer as I can make you.'   81b

Thus God sent her good mastership of this worthy doctor, to strengthen her against her detractors, worshipped be His Name.

Afterwards in Lent, preached a good clerk, an Austin Friar,[1] in his own house at Lynne, and had a great audience, where, that time, was the said creature present. And God, of His goodness, inspired the Friar to preach

[1] *See* Note K.

much of His Passion, so compassionately and so devoutly, that she could not bear it. Then she fell down crying and weeping so sore that many of the people wondered on her, and banned and cursed her full sore, supposing that she might have left off her crying if she would, inasmuch as the good friar had so preached there-against, as is before written. Then this good man that preached now at this time, said to the people: —

'Friends, be still, ye wot full little what she feeleth.'

And so the people ceased and were still and heard out the sermon, with quiet and rest of body and soul.

CHAPTER 69

Also, on a Good Friday at Saint Margaret's Church, the Prior of the same place, and the same town, would preach, and he took as his theme: — 'Jesus is dead.'

Then the said creature, all wounded with pity and compassion, cried and wept as if she had seen Our Lord dead with her bodily eye. The worshipful Prior and doctor of divinity suffered her full meekly and in no way moved against her.

Another time, Bishop Wakeryng, Bishop of Norwich, preached at Lynne in the said church of Saint Margaret, and the aforesaid creature cried and wept full boisterously at the time of his sermon, and he suffered it full meekly and patiently, and so did many a worthy clerk, both regular and secular, for there was never clerk preached openly against her crying but the Grey Friar, as is written before.

So Our Lord of His mercy, just as He had promised the said creature that He should ever provide for her, stirring the spirit of two good clerks, who long and many years had known her conversation and all her perfection, made them mighty and bold to speak for His part in excusing the said creature, both in the pulpit and besides, 82a where they heard anything moved against her, strengthening her reasoning by authority of Holy Scripture sufficiently.

Of these clerks, one was a White Friar, a doctor of

divinity; the other clerk was a bachelor-of-law canon, a well laboured man in Scripture.

And then some envious persons complained to the Provincial of the White Friars that the said doctor was too conversant with the said creature, forasmuch as he supported her in her weeping and in her crying, and also informed her in questions of Scripture, when she would ask him any.

Then was he admonished, by virtue of obedience, that he should no more speak with her, nor inform her in any texts of Scripture, and that was, to him, full painful, for, as he said to some persons, he would rather have lost a hundred pounds, if he had had it, than her communication; it was so ghostly and fruitful.

When her confessor perceived how the worthy doctor was charged by obedience that he should not speak or commune with her, then he, to exclude all occasion, warned her also, by virtue of obedience, that she should no more go to the friars, nor speak with the said doctor, nor ask him any questions as she had done before.

And then thought she full great grief and gloom, for she was put from much ghostly comfort. She would rather have lost any earthly possession than his communication, for it was to her great increase of virtue.

Then long afterwards, she happened, as she was going in the street, to meet with the said doctor and neither of them spake one word to the other; and then she had a great cry, with many tears. Afterwards, when she came to her meditation, she said in her mind to Our Lord Jesus Christ: —

'Alas! Lord, why may I no comfort have of this worshipful clerk, who hath known me so many years, and oftentimes strengthened me in Thy love? Now hast Thou, Lord, taken from me the anchorite — I trust to Thy mercy — the most special and singular comfort that ever I had on earth, for he ever loved me for Thy love, and would never forsake me for aught any man could do or say, whilst he lived.

'And Master Aleyn is put from me, and I from him. Sir Thomas Andrew and Sir John Amy are beneficed and out of town. Master Robert dare scarcely speak with me. Now have I, in a manner, no comfort either of man or child.'

Our Merciful Lord, answering to her mind, said: —

'Daughter, I am more worthy to thy soul than ever was the anchorite and all those whom thou hast repeated, or all the world, may be, and I shall comfort thee Myself, for I would speak to thee oftener than thou wilt let Me. And, daughter, I want thee to know that thou shalt speak to Master Aleyn again, as thou hast done before.'

And then Our Lord sent, by provision of the Prior of Lynne, a priest to be keeper of a chapel of Our Lady, called the Jesyne, within the church of Saint Margaret, which priest many times heard her confession in the absence of her principal confessor. And to this priest she shewed all her life, as near as she could, from her young age, both her sins, her labours, her vexations, her contemplations and also her revelations, and such grace as God wrought in her, through His mercy; and so that priest trusted right well that God wrought right great grace in her.

CHAPTER 70

ON a time, God visited the aforesaid doctor, Master Aleyn, with great sickness, so that no man promised him life, who saw him. And so it was told the said creature of his sickness. Then she was full grieved for him, and specially forasmuch as she had by revelation that she should speak with him again, as she had done before; and, if he had died of this sickness, her feeling would not have been true.

Therefore she ran into the choir at Saint Margaret's Church, kneeling down before the Sacrament, and saying in this wise: —

'Ah! Lord, I pray Thee, for all goodness that Thou hast shewn to me, and as truly as Thou lovest me, let this worthy clerk never die till I may speak with him, as Thou hast promised me that I should do; and thou, Glorious Queen of Mercy, have mind what he was wont to say of thee in his sermons. He was wont to say, Lady, that he was well blessed that had you for his friend, for, when ye prayed, all the company of Heaven prayed with you. Now, for the blissful love that ye had for your Son, let him live till the time that he hath leave to speak with me, and I with him, for now we are put asunder by obedience.'

Then she had answer in her soul that he should not die before the time that she had leave to speak with him, and he with her, as they had done years before.

And, as Our Lord willed, in a short time after, the worthy clerk recovered and went about hale and whole, and had leave of his sovereign to speak with the said creature, and she had leave of her confessor to speak with him.

So it happened that the aforesaid doctor should dine in town with a worshipful woman, who had taken the mantle and the ring, and he sent for the said creature to come and speak with him. She, having great marvel thereof, took leave and went to him. When she came into the place where he was, she could not speak for weeping, and for joy that she had in Our Lord, inasmuch as she found her feeling true, and not deceivable, that he had leave to speak to her and she to him.

Then the worshipful doctor said to her: — 'Margery, ye are welcome to me, for I have long been kept from you, and now hath Our Lord sent you hither that I may speak with you, blessed may He be.'

There was a dinner of great joy and gladness, much more ghostly than bodily, for it was sauced and savoured with tales of Holy Scripture. And then he gave the said creature a pair of knives, in token that he would stand with her in God's cause, as he had done beforetime.

On a day, there came a priest to the said creature, who had great trust in her feelings and in her revelations — desiring to prove them in divers times — and prayed her to pray to Our Lord that she might have understanding if the Prior of Lynne, who was a good master to the said priest, should be removed or not, and, as she felt, make him true account. She prayed for the aforesaid matter,

83b and, when she had answer there-of, she told the priest that the Prior of Lynne, his master, should be called home to Norwich, and another of his brethren should be sent to Lynne in his stead. And so it was indeed.

But he, that was sent to Lynne, abode there but a little while, ere he was called home to Norwich again, and he, that had been Prior of Lynne before, was sent again to Lynne, and dwelt there just about four years till he died.

In the meantime, the said creature had often feeling that he, who was last called home to Norwich and abode but a little while at Lynne, should yet be Prior of Lynne again. She would give no credence thereto, inasmuch as he had been there and was, in a little time, called home again.

Then as she went one time in the White Friars' church at Lynne, up and down, she felt a wondrous sweet savour and a heavenly, so that she thought she might have lived thereby without meat or drink, if it would have continued.

And, at that time, Our Lord said unto her: — 'By this sweet smell, thou mayest well know that there shall, in a short time, be a new Prior in Lynne, and it shall be he who was last removed hence.'

And soon after, the old Prior died, and then Our Lord said to her, as she lay in her bed: —

'Daughter, loath as thou art to believe my stirring, yet shalt thou see him, of whom I shewed thee before, Prior of Lynne ere this day sennight.'

And so Our Lord repeated to her this matter each day of the sennight, till she saw it was so indeed, and then she was full glad and joyful that her feeling was true.

Afterwards, when this worshipful man was come to Lynne and had dwelt there but a little while, and who was a full worshipful clerk, a doctor of divinity, he was appointed to go over the sea to the King,[1] into France, and other clerks also, of the worthiest in England.

Then a priest, that had an office under the said Prior, came to the aforesaid creature and beseeched her to have this matter in mind when God would minister his holy dalliance to her soul, and find out, in this matter, whether the Prior should go over the sea or not.

And so she prayed to have understanding of this matter, and she had answer that he should not go. Nevertheless 84a he expected himself to have gone, and was all provided therefor, and, with great grief, had taken leave of his friends, supposing never to come back again, for he was a full weak man and a feeble, in constitution.

In the meantime, the King died, and the Prior stayed at home; and so her feeling was true, without any deceit.

Also it was voiced that the Bishop of Winchester was

[1] King Henry V, who died in France in 1422.

251

dead, and, notwithstanding, she had a feeling he lived, and so it was, in truth.

And so had she feeling of many more than be written, which Our Lord, of His mercy, revealed to her understanding, though she were unworthy of her merits.

CHAPTER 72

So, by process of time, her mind and her thought was so joined to God that she never forgot Him, but continually had mind of Him and beheld Him in all creatures. And ever the more that she increased in love and in devotion, the more she increased in sorrow and contrition, in lowliness, in meekness and in the holy dread of Our Lord, and in knowledge of her own frailty, so that, if she saw a creature being punished or sharply chastised, she would think that she had been more worthy to be chastised than the creature was, for her unkindness against God.

Then would she cry, weep and sob for her own sin, and for the compassion of the creature that she saw being so punished and sharply chastised.

If she saw a prince, a prelate, or a worthy man of state and degree, whom men worshipped and reverenced with lowliness and meekness, anon her mind was refreshed unto Our Lord, thinking what joy, what bliss, what worship and reverence He had in Heaven amongst His blessed saints, since a mortal man had such great worship on earth.

And most of all, when she saw the Precious Sacrament borne about the town with lights and reverence, the people kneeling on their knees, then had she many holy thoughts and meditations, and then oftentimes would she cry and roar, as though she would have burst, for the faith and the trust that she had in the Precious Sacrament.

Also the said creature was desired by many people to be with them at their dying, and to pray for them, for, though they loved not her weeping or her crying in their lifetime, they desired that she should both weep and cry when they should die, and so she did.

When she saw folk anointed, she had many holy thoughts, many holy meditations, and, if she saw them dying, she thought she saw Our Lord dying.

And sometimes Our Lady, like Our Lord God, would illuminate her ghostly sight with understanding. Then would she cry, weep, and sob full wonderfully, as if she beheld Our Lord in His dying, or Our Lady in her dying. And she thought, in her mind, that God took many out of this world who would full fain have lived; 'and I, Lord' thought she 'would full fain come to Thee, and after me Thou hast no yearning'; and such thoughts increased her weeping and her sobbing.

On a time, a worshipful lady sent for her, for cause of communing, and, as they were in their communication, the lady gave to her some manner of worship and praise, and it was, to her, great pain to have any praise. Nevertheless, anon she offered it up to Our Lord, for she desired no praising but His only, with a great cry and many devout tears.

So there was no worship or praise, love or defect, shame or despite that might draw her love from God, but, after the sentence of Saint Paul; 'To them that love God, all things turneth into goodness'. So it fared with her.

Whatever she saw or heard, always her love and her ghostly affection increased Our Lord-ward, blessed may He be, that wrought such grace in her for men's profit.

Another time, there sent for her another worshipful lady, who had a large retinue about her, and great worship and great reverence was done unto her. When the said creature beheld all her retinue about her, and the great reverence and worship that was done unto her, she fell to great weeping and cried therewith right sadly. There was a priest who heard how she cried and how she wept — and he was a man savouring ghostly things — who banned her full fast, saying unto her: —

'What devil aileth thee? Why weepest thou so? God give thee sorrow.'

She sat still and answered no word.

Then the lady had her into a garden by themselves alone, and prayed her to tell why she cried so sore, and then she, supposing it was expedient so to do, told her, in part, of the cause. Then the lady was ill-pleased with her priest, who had so spoken against her, and loved her right well, desiring and praying her to abide still with her. Then she excused herself and said she might not accord with the array and the behaviour that she saw there amongst her retinue.

85a

CHAPTER 73

On the Holy Thursday, as the said creature went in procession with other people, she saw in her soul Our Lady, Saint Mary Magdalene, and the twelve Apostles. And then she beheld with her ghostly eye, how Our Lady took her leave of her blessed Son, Christ Jesus, how He kissed her and all his Apostles, and also His true lover, Mary Magdalene.

She thought it was a sorrowful parting, and also a joyful parting. When she beheld this sight in her soul, she fell down in the field amongst the people. She cried, she roared, she wept as though she would have burst therewith. She could not control herself, nor rule herself, but cried and roared so that many men wondered at her, but she took no heed what any man said or did, for her mind was occupied in Our Lord.

She felt many a holy thought in that time, which she knew never after. She had forgotten all earthly things and only attended to ghostly things. She thought that all her joy was gone. She saw her Lord ascend up into Heaven. Because she could not do without Him on earth, therefore she desired to have gone with Him, for all her joy and all her bliss was in Him, and she knew well that she should never have joy or bliss till she came to Him.

Such holy thoughts and such holy desires caused her to weep, and the people knew not what ailed her.

Another time, the said creature beheld how Our Lady

was, as she thought, dying, and all the Apostles kneeling before her and asking grace. Then she cried and wept sore. The Apostles commanded her to cease and be still. The creature answered to the Apostles: —

'Would ye I should see the Mother of God dying, and I not weep? It may not be, for I am so full of sorrow that I may not withstand it. I must needs cry and weep.'

And then she said in her soul to Our Lady: —   85b

'Ah! Blessed Lady, pray for me to your Son, that I may come to you, and be no longer tarried from you; for, Lady, this is all too great a sorrow, to be both at your Son's death and at your death, and not to die with you, but to live still alone and no comfort have with myself.'

Then Our Gracious Lady answered to her soul, promising her to pray for her to her Son and said: —

'Daughter, all these sorrows that thou hast had for me and for my Blessed Son shall turn thee to great joy and bliss in Heaven without end. And doubt thee not, daughter, that thou shalt come to us right well, and be right welcome when thou comest. But thou mayest not come yet, for thou shalt come in right good time. And, daughter, wot thee well, thou shalt find me a very mother to thee, to help thee and succour thee, as a mother ought to do her daughter, and purchase to thee grace and virtue and the same pardon that was granted thee beforetime. It was confirmed on Saint Nicholas' Day — that is to say, plenary remission — and it is not only granted to thee, but to all those that believe, and to all those that shall believe unto the world's end, that God loveth thee, and shall thank God for thee, if they will forsake their sin and be in full will, no more to turn again thereto, but be sorry and grieved for what they have done, and will do due penance therefor. They shall have the same pardon that is granted to thyself; and that is all the pardon that is in Jerusalem, as was granted to thee when thou wert at Pafnys,[1] as is before written.'

[1] *See* Note R. Evidently a clerical error for 'Rafnys' on the part of the scribe.

CHAPTER 74

THE said creature one day, hearing her Mass and revolving in her mind the time of her death, sore sighing and sorrowing because it was so long delayed, said in this manner: —

'Alas! Lord, how long shall I thus weep and mourn for Thy love, and for desire of Thy presence?'

Our Lord answered in her soul and said: —

'All these fifteen years.'

Then said she: — 'Ah! Lord, I shall think it many thousand years.'

Our Lord answered to her: — 'Daughter, thou must bethink thyself of My blessed Mother, who lived after Me on earth fifteen years; also Saint John the Evangelist, and Mary Magdalene, who loved Me right highly.'

'Ah! Blissful Lord,' said she, 'I would I were as worthy to be secure of Thy love, as Mary Magdalene was.'

Then said Our Lord: — 'Truly, daughter, I love thee as well, and the same peace that I gave to her, the same peace I give to thee. For, daughter, there is no saint in Heaven displeased, though I love a creature on earth as much as I do them. Therefore they will not otherwise than I will.'

Thus Our Merciful Lord Christ Jesus drew His creature unto His love, and to mind of His Passion, so that she could not endure to behold a leper or other sick

86a

man, especially if he had any wounds appearing on him.

So she cried, and so she wept, as if she had seen Our Lord Jesus Christ with His wounds bleeding. And so she did, in the sight of her soul, for, through the beholding of the sick man, her mind was all taken over to Our Lord Jesus Christ.

Then had she great mourning and sorrowing because she might not kiss the lepers when she saw them, or met with them, in the streets, for the love of Jesus.

Now began she to love what she had most hated beforetime, for there was nothing more loathsome or more abominable to her, while she was in those years of worldly prosperity, than to see or behold a leper, whom now, through Our Lord's mercy, she desired to embrace and kiss for the love of Jesus, when she had time and place convenient.

Then she told her confessor what great desire she had to kiss lepers, and he warned her that she should kiss no men, but if she would anyhow kiss, she should kiss women. Then was she glad, because she had leave to kiss the sick women, and went to a place where sick women dwelt who were right full of the sickness, and fell down on her knees before them, praying them that she might kiss their mouths for the love of Jesus. So she kissed there two sick women with many a holy thought and many a devout tear, and when she had kissed them, she told them full many good words and stirred them to meekness and patience, so that they would not grutch at their sickness, but highly thank God therefor, and they should have great bliss in Heaven through the mercy of Our Lord Jesus Christ.

86b

Then one woman had so many temptations that she

260

knew not how she might best be governed. She was so laboured with her ghostly enemy that she durst not bless herself, or do any worship to God, for dread that the devil should slay her; and she was laboured with many foul and horrible thoughts, many more than she could tell. And, as she said, she was a maid.

Therefore the said creature went to her many times to comfort her, and prayed for her also full specially, that God should strengthen her against her enemy. And it is to be believed that He did so, blessed may He be.

CHAPTER 75

As the said creature was in a church of Saint Margaret to say her devotions, there came a man kneeling at her back, wringing his hands and shewing tokens of great grief. She, perceiving his grief, asked him what ailed him. He said it stood right hard with him, for his wife was newly delivered of a child, and she was out of her mind.

'And, dame,' he said, 'she knoweth not me or any of her neighbours. She roareth and crieth so that she maketh folk evil afeared. She will both smite and bite, and therefore is she manacled on her wrists.'

Then asked she the man if he would that she went with him and saw her, and he said: —

'Yea, dame, for God's love.'

So she went forth with him to see the woman; and when she came into the house, as soon as the sick woman, who was alienated from her wits, saw her, she spake to her soberly and kindly and said she was right welcome to her, and she was right glad of her coming, and greatly comforted by her presence, 'For ye are,' she said, 'a right good woman, and I behold many fair angels about you, and therefore, I pray you, go not from me, for I am greatly comforted by you.'

And when other folk came to her, she cried and gaped as if she would have eaten them, and said that she saw many devils about them. She would not suffer them to

262

touch her, by her own good will. She roared and cried so, both night and day, for the most part, that men would not suffer her to dwell amongst them, she was so tedious to them.

Then was she taken to the furthest end of the town, into a chamber, so that the people should not hear her crying, and there was she bound, hand and foot, with chains of iron, so that she should smite nobody. 87a

And the said creature went to her each day, once or twice at least; and whilst she was with her, she was meek enough, and heard her speak and chat with good will, without any roaring or crying.

And the said creature prayed for this woman every day, that God should, if it were His will, restore her to her wits again, and Our Lord answered in her soul and said she should fare right well.

Then was she more bold to pray for her curing than she was before, and each day, weeping and sorrowing, prayed for her recovery, till God gave her her wits and her mind again. And then was she brought to church and purified as other women are, blessed may God be.

It was, as they thought that knew it, a right great miracle, for he that wrote this book had never, before that time, seen man or woman, as he thought, so far out of herself as this woman was, nor so evil to rule or to manage.

And later, he saw her sad and sober enough, worship and praise be to Our Lord without end, for His high mercy and His goodness, Who ever helpeth at need.

CHAPTER 76

IT happened, on a time, that the husband of the said creature, a man in great age, passing three score years, as he would have come down from his chamber bare-foot and bare-legged, he slithered, or else failed of his footing, and fell down to the ground from the stairs, his head under him grievously broken and bruised, insomuch that he had in his head five linen plugs[1] for many days, whilst his head was healing.

And, as God willed, it was known to some of his neighbours how he had fallen down from the stairs, peradventure through the din and the rush of his fall. So they came to him and found him lying with his head under him, half alive, all streaked with blood, and never likely to have spoken with priest or clerk, but through high grace and a miracle.

87b   Then the said creature, his wife, was sent for and so she came to him. Then was he taken up and his head sewn, and he was sick a long time after, so that men thought he should have been dead.

Then the people said, if he died, his wife was worthy to be hanged for his death, forasmuch as she might have kept him and did not. They dwelt not together nor lay together, for, as is written before, they both with one assent and with the free will of each, had vowed to live chaste. Therefore, to avoid all perils, they dwelt and

---

[1] In MS. 'teyntys'; the old method of draining a suppurating wound.

264

sojourned in divers places where no suspicion could be had of their incontinence. For, at first, they dwelt together after they had made their vow, and then people slandered them, and said they used their lust and their pleasure, as they did before making their vow. And when they went out on pilgrimage, or to see and speak with other ghostly creatures, many evil folk, whose tongues were their own, failing the dread and love of Our Lord Jesus Christ, deemed and said they went rather to woods, groves, and valleys, to use the lust of their bodies, so that people would not espy it or know it.

Having knowledge how prone people were to deem ill of them, and desiring to avoid all occasion for it as much as they rightly might, they, of their own free will and common consent, parted asunder, as touching their board and their chambers, and went to board in divers places. And this was the cause that she was not with him; and also that she should not be hindered from her contemplation. And therefore when he had fallen, and grievously was hurt, as is said before, the people said, if he died, it was worthy that she should answer for his death. Then she prayed to Our Lord that her husband might live a year, and she be delivered out of slander, if it were His pleasure.

Our Lord said to her mind: — 'Daughter, thou shalt have thy boon, for he shall live, and I have wrought a great miracle for thee in that he was not dead, and I bid thee take him home and keep him for My love.'

She said: — 'Nay, good Lord, for I shall then not attend to Thee as I do now.'

'Yes, daughter,' said Our Lord, 'thou shalt have as much reward for keeping him and helping him in his

88a

265

need at home, as if thou wert in church, making thy prayers. Thou hast said many times thou wouldst fain keep Me. I pray thee now keep him for the love of Me, for he hath some time fulfilled thy will and My will, both. And he hath made thy body free to Me, so that thou shouldst serve Me, and live chaste and clean, and I will that thou be free to help him at his need in My name.'

'Ah! Lord,' said she, 'for Thy mercy grant me grace to obey and fulfil Thy will, and let never my ghostly enemies have any power to hinder me from fulfilling Thy will.'

Then she took home her husband with her and kept him years after, as long as he lived, and had full much labour with him; for in his last days he turned childish again, and lacked reason, so that he could not do his own easement by going to a seat, or else he would not, but, as a child, voided his natural digestion in his linen clothes, where he sat by the fire or at the table, whichever it were; he would spare no place.

And therefore was her labour much the more in washing and wringing, and her costage in firing; and it hindered her full much from her contemplation, so that many times she would have loathed her labour, save she bethought herself how she, in her young age, had full many delectable thoughts, fleshly lusts, and inordinate loves to his person.

And therefore she was glad to be punished with the same person, and took it much the more easily, and served him, and helped him, as she thought, as she would have done Christ Himself.

[Here follows Chapter 77]

For many years, on Palm Sunday, as this creature was at the Passion with other good people in the church-yard, and beheld how the priests did their observance, how they knelt to the Sacrament, and the people also, it seemed to her ghostly sight as if she had been then in Jerusalem, and seen Our Lord in His Manhood received by the people, as He was whilst He went here on earth.

Then had she so much sweetness and devotion that she might not bear it, but cried, wept and sobbed full boisterously. She had many a holy thought of Our Lord's Passion, and beheld Him in her ghostly sight, as verily as if He had been before her in her bodily sight. There-fore might she not withstand weeping and sobbing, but she must needs weep, cry, and sob, when she beheld her Saviour suffer such great pain for her love.

Then would she pray for all the people that were living on earth, that they might do Our Lord due worship and reverence at those times and all times, and that they might be worthy to hear and understand the holy words and laws of God, and meekly obey and truly fulfil them according to their power.

And it was the custom of the place where she was dwelling to have a sermon on that day and then, as a worshipful doctor of divinity was in the pulpit and said the sermon, he repeated oftentimes these words — 'Our Lord Jesus languoreth for love'. Those words wrought so in

90a

her mind, when she heard tell of the perfect love that Our Lord Jesus Christ had for mankind, and how dear He bought us with His bitter Passion, shedding His heart's blood for our redemption, and suffered so shameful a death for our salvation, that she could no longer keep the fire of love in her breast, but, whether she would or not, there appeared without, what was enclosed within.

And so she cried full loud, and wept and sobbed full sore, as though she would have burst for the pity and compassion that she had for Our Lord's Passion.

And sometimes she was all of a sweat with the labour of the crying, it was so loud and so boisterous, and many people wondered on her and banned her full fast, supposing that she had feigned to cry.

And soon after, Our Lord said unto her: — 'Daughter, this pleaseth Me right well, for the more shame and more despite that thou hast for My love, the more joy shalt thou have with Me in Heaven, and it is rightful that it be so.'

Sometimes she heard great sounds and great melodies with her bodily ears, and then she thought it was full merry in Heaven, and had full great languoring and full great longing thitherward with many a silent mourning. And then, many times, Our Lord Jesus Christ would say unto her: —

'Daughter, here is, this day, a fair people, and many of them shall be dead ere this day twelve month,' — and told her before when pestilence should fall.

90b And she found it indeed as she had felt before, and that strengthened her much in the love of God.

Our Lord would say also: — 'Daughter, they that will not believe the goodness and the grace that I shew unto thee in this life, I shall make them know the truth when they are dead, and out of this world. Daughter, thou hast a good zeal of charity, in that thou wouldst all men were saved and so would I. And they say that so would they; but thou mayest well see that they will not themselves be saved, for all they will sometimes hear the word of God; but they will not always do there-after, and they will not sorrow themselves for their sins, nor will they suffer any others to suffer for them.

'Nevertheless, daughter, I have ordained thee to be a mirror amongst them, to have great sorrow, so that they should take example by thee, and have some little sorrow in their hearts for their sins, so that they might there-through be saved; but they love not to hear of sorrow or contrition. But good daughter, do thou thy duty, and pray for them whilst thou art in this world, and thou shalt have the same meed and reward in Heaven, as if all the world were saved by thy good will and thy prayer.

'Daughter, I have many times said to thee, that many thousand souls shall be saved through thy prayers; and some that lie at point of death shall have grace through thy merit and thy prayers, for thy tears and thy prayers are full sweet and acceptable unto Me.'

Then she said in her mind to Our Lord Jesus Christ: —

'Ah! Jesus, blessed may Thou be without end, for I have many a great cause to Thank Thee and love Thee with all my heart, for it seemeth to me Lord, that Thou art all charity, to the profit and health of man's soul. Ah! Lord, I believe that he shall be right wicked, that shall be parted from Thee without end. He shall neither will good, nor do good, nor desire good.

'And therefore, Lord, I thank Thee for all the goodness that Thou hast shewn unto me, right unworthy wretch.'

Then, on the same Sunday, when the priest took the cross-staff and smote on the church door, the door opened before him, and then the priest entered with the Sacrament and all the people followed into the church.

91a Then thought she that Our Lord spake to the devil and opened Hell's gates, confounding him and all his host, and what grace and goodness He shewed to the souls, delivering them from everlasting prison, in spite of the devil and all his.

She had many a holy thought and many a holy desire which she could never tell or repeat, nor ever might her tongue express the abundance of grace that she felt, blessed be Our Lord for all His gifts.

When they were come into the church, she beheld the priests kneeling before the crucifix, and as they sang, the priest who executed the service that day drew up a cloth before the crucifix three times, each time higher than the others, so that the people should see the crucifix. Then was her mind all wholly taken out of all earthly things and set all in ghostly things, praying and desiring that she might, at the last, have full sight of Him in Heaven, Who is both God and Man in one Person.

And then would she all the Mass-time after, weep and sob full plenteously and sometimes, amongst it, cry right fervently, for she thought that she saw Our Lord Christ Jesus as verily in her soul with her ghostly eye, as she had seen, before, the crucifix with her bodily eye.

THEN she beheld, in the sight of her soul, Our Blissful Lord Christ Jesus coming to His Passion-ward, and, ere He went, He knelt down and took His Mother's blessing.

Then she saw His Mother falling down in a swoon before Her Son, saying unto Him: —

'Alas! My dear Son, how shall I suffer this sorrow, who have no joy in this world but Thee alone. Ah! Dear Son, if Thou wilt, in any case, die, let me die before Thee, and let me never suffer this day of sorrow, for I may never bear this sorrow that I shall have for Thy death. I would, Son, that I might suffer death for Thee, so that Thou shouldst not die, if men's souls might so be saved. Now, dear Son, if Thou hast no ruth for Thyself, have ruth for Thy Mother, for Thou knowest full well that no man can, in all this world, comfort me but Thou alone.'

Then Our Lord took up His Mother in His arms and kissed her full sweetly, and said to her: — 91b

'Ah! Blessed Mother, be of good cheer and of good comfort, for I have told you full often that I must needs suffer death, else no man should be saved, or ever come into bliss. And, Mother, it is My Father's will that it be so, and therefore I pray you, let it be your will also, for My death shall turn Me to great worship, and you and all mankind to great joy and profit, who trust in My Passion and work there-after.

'And therefore, blessed Mother, ye must abide here

after Me, for, in you, shall rest all the faith of Holy Church, and, by your faith, Holy Church shall increase in her faith. Therefore, I pray you, dearworthy Mother, cease of your sorrowing, for I shall not leave you comfortless. I shall leave here with you John, my cousin, to comfort you instead of Me; I shall send My holy angels to comfort you on earth, and I shall comfort you in your soul Mine Own Self; for, Mother, ye wot well that I have promised you the bliss of Heaven, and that ye are secure thereof.

'Ah! dearworthy Mother, what would ye better than, where I am King, ye to be Queen, and all angels and saints shall be obedient to your will. And what grace ye ask Me, I shall not deny your desire. I shall give you power over the devils, so that they shall be afraid of you, and ye, not of them. And also, My blessed Mother, I have said to you beforetime, that I shall come for you Mine own Self, when ye shall pass out of this world, with all My angels and all My saints that are in Heaven, and bring you before My Father with all manner of music, melody, and joy.

'There shall I set you in great peace and rest without end. And there shall ye be crowned as Queen of Heaven, as Lady of all the world, and as Empress of Hell.

'And therefore, My dearworthy Mother, I pray you bless Me and let Me go and do My Father's will, for therefor I came into this world, and took flesh and blood of you.'

When the said creature beheld this glorious sight in her soul, and saw how He blessed His Mother, and His Mother Him, and then how His blessed Mother could not speak one word more to Him, but fell down on the ground, and so they parted asunder, His Mother lying

92a

still as if she had been dead, then the said creature thought she took Our Lord Jesus Christ by the clothes, and fell down at His feet, praying Him to bless her.

And therewith she cried full loud, and wept right sore, saying in her mind: —

'Ah! Lord, where shall I be come? I had well rather that Thou wouldst slay me than let me abide in the world without Thee, for without Thee, I may not abide here, Lord.'

Then answered Our Lord to her: —

'Be still, daughter, and rest with My Mother here, and comfort thyself in her, for she, that is Mine Own Mother, must suffer this sorrow. But I shall come again, daughter, to My Mother and comfort her and thee, both, and turn all your sorrow into joy.'

And then she thought Our Lord went forth on His way, and she went to Our Lady and said: —

'Ah! Blessed Lady, rise up and let us follow your blessed Son, as long as we may see Him, that I may look enough upon Him, ere He dies. Ah! dear Lady, how can your heart last, and see your blissful Son see all this woe? Lady, I may not endure it, and yet am I not His Mother.'

Then Our Lady answered and said: — 'Daughter, thou hearest well that it will not otherwise be, and therefore I must needs suffer it for my Son's love.'

And then she thought that they followed forth after Our Lord, and saw how He made His prayers to His Father on the Mount of Olivet, and heard the goodly answer that came from His Father, and the goodly answer that He gave His Father again.

Then she saw how Our Lord went to His disciples and bade them waken, His enemies were near. And then came a great multitude of people with many lights, and many armed men, with staves, swords, and pole-axes, to seek Our Lord Jesus Christ, Our Merciful Lord, meek as a lamb, saying unto them: —

'Whom seek ye?' They answered with a sharp spirit: —
'Jesus of Nazareth.' Our Lord answered: —
'Ego sum.'

And then she saw the Jews falling down on the ground — they could not stand for dread — but anon, they rose again, and sought as they had done before. And Our Lord asked: —

'Whom seek ye?' And they said again: —
'Jesus of Nazareth.' Our Lord answered: —
'I it am.'

92b And then anon, she saw Judas come and kiss Our Lord, and the Jews laid hands upon Him full violently.

Then had Our Lady and she much sorrow and great pain to see the Lamb of Innocence so contemptibly hauled and dragged by His own people, that He was specially sent unto.

And immediately the said creature beheld, with her ghostly eye, the Jews putting a cloth before Our Lord's eyes, beating Him and buffeting Him on the head and jogging Him on His sweet mouth, crying full cruelly unto Him: —

'Tell us now, who smote thee?'

They spared not to spit in His face, in the most shameful way that they could. And then Our Lady and she, her unworthy handmaiden for the time, wept and sighed full sore, because the Jews fared so foul and so venomously with her Blissful Lord. And they would not spare to lug His blissful ears, and drag the hair of His beard.

274

And anon, she saw them drag off His clothes and make Him all naked, and then pull Him forth before them as if He had been the greatest malefactor in all the world. And He went forth full meekly before them, all mother-naked as He was born, to a pillar of stone, and spake no word against them, but let them do and say what they would. And there they bound Him to the pillar as tight as they could, and beat Him on His fair white Body with rods, with whips and with scourges.

Then she thought Our Lady wept wondrous sore, and therefore the said creature must needs weep and cry when she saw such ghostly sights in her soul as clearly and as verily as if it had been done indeed in her bodily sight; and she thought that Our Lady and she were always together to see Our Lord's pains.

Such ghostly sights had she every Palm Sunday and every Good Friday, and in many other ways as well, many years together.

And therefore cried she and wept full sore, and suffered full much despite and reproof in many a country.

Then Our Lord said, in her soul: —

'Daughter, these sorrows, and many more, suffered I for thy love, and divers pains, more than any man can tell on earth. Therefore, daughter, thou hast great cause to love Me right well, for I have bought thy love full dear.'

('True it is, blessed Lord.')

93a ANOTHER time, she saw, in her contemplation, Our Lord Jesus Christ bound to a pillar, and His hands were bound above His head. And then she saw sixteen men with sixteen scourges, and each scourge had eight pellets of lead on the end, and every pellet was full of sharp prickles as if it had been the rowel of a spur. And those men with the scourges made covenant that each of them should give Our Lord forty strokes.

When she saw this piteous sight, she wept and cried right loud, as if she would have burst, for sorrow and pain.

And when Our Lord was all beaten and scourged, the Jews loosed Him from the pillar, and gave Him His Cross to bear to the Mount on His shoulder. Then she thought that Our Lady and she went by another way to meet with Him; and, when they met with Him, they saw Him bearing the heavy Cross with great pain; it was so heavy and so unwieldy that He hardly might bear it.

Then Our Lady said unto Him:—'Ah! My sweet Son, let me help to bear that heavy Cross.'

And she was so weak that she could not, but fell down and swooned and lay still, as if she had been a dead woman. Then the creature saw Our Lord fall down by His Mother and comfort her, as He might, with many sweet words.

When she heard the words and saw the compassion that the Mother had of the Son, and the Son of His Mother, then she wept, sobbed and cried as though she would have died, for the pity and compassion that she had of that piteous sight, and the holy thoughts that she had in the meantime, which were so subtle and heavenly that she could never tell them after, as she had them in feeling.

Later, she went forth in contemplation, through the mercy of Our Lord Jesus Christ, to the place where He was nailed to the Cross. And then she saw the Jews, with great violence, rend off Our Lord's Precious Body a cloth of silk, which had cleaved and hardened so firmly and straitly to Our Lord's Body with His Precious Blood, that it drew away all the hide and all the skin off His Blessed Body, and renewed His Precious wounds, and made the blood run down all about on every side.

Then that Precious Body appeared to her sight as raw as a thing that was newly flayed out of the skin, full 93b piteous and rueful to behold. And so had she a new sorrow, so that she wept and cried right sore.

And anon, afterwards, she beheld how the cruel Jews laid His Precious Body on the Cross, and then took a long nail, rough and coarse, and set it on one hand, and, with great violence and cruelty, they drove it through His hand. His Blissful Mother beholding — and this creature — how His Precious Body shrank and drew together with all the sinews and veins in that Precious Body for the pain that It suffered and felt, they sorrowed and mourned and sighed full sore.

Then saw she, with her ghostly eye, how the Jews fastened ropes on the other hand — for the sinews and veins were so shrunken with pain that it might not come to the hole that they had bored for it — and pulled there-on to make it meet with the hole. And so her pain and her sorrow ever increased. And then they dragged His blissful feet in the same manner.

And then she thought, in her soul, that she heard Our Lady say to the Jews: —

'Alas, ye cruel Jews, why fare ye so with my sweet Son, Who never did ye any harm? Ye fill my heart full of sorrow.'

And then she thought the Jews spoke again boisterously to Our Lady, and put her away from her Son.

Then the aforesaid creature thought she cried out to the Jews, and said: —

'Ye cursed Jews, why slay ye my Lord Jesus Christ? Slay me rather, and let Him go.'

And then she wept and cried passing sore, so that many of the people in the church wondered on her body.

And anon she saw them take up the cross with Our Lord's Body hanging there-on, and make great noise and great cries, and lift it up from the earth a certain distance, and then let the Cross fall down into the mortise. Then Our Lord's Body shook and shuddered, and all the joints of that Blissful Body burst and went asunder, and His precious wounds ran down with rivers of blood on every side; and so she had ever more cause of more weeping and sorrowing.

And then she heard Our Lord, hanging on the Cross, say these words to His Mother: —

'Woman, see thy son, Saint John the Evangelist.'

Then she thought Our Lady fell down and swooned, 94ᵃ and Saint John took her up in his arms and comforted her with sweet words, as well as he could or might.

The creature said then to Our Lord, as it seemed to her: —

'Alas! Lord, Thou leavest here a care-full Mother.

278

What shall we now do, and how shall we bear this great sorrow, that we shall have for Thy love?'

And then she heard the two thieves speaking to Our Lord, and Our Lord said to one thief: —

'This day shalt thou be with Me in Paradise.'

Then was she glad of that answer, and prayed Our Lord, of His mercy, that He would be as gracious to her soul when she should pass out of this world, as He was to the thief, for she was worse, she thought, than any thief.

And then she thought Our Lord commended His spirit into His Father's hands, and therewith He died.

Then she thought she saw Our Lady swoon and fall down and lie still, as if she had been dead. Then the creature thought that she ran all about the place, as if she had been a mad woman, crying and roaring. And later she came to Our Lady, and fell down on her knees before her, saying to her: —

'I pray you, Lady, cease from your sorrowing, for your Son is dead and out of pain, for me-thinketh ye have sorrowed enough. And, Lady, I will sorrow for you, for your sorrow is my sorrow.'

Then she thought she saw Joseph of Arimathea take down Our Lord's Body from the Cross, and lay It before Our Lady on a marble stone. Our Lady had then a manner of joy, when her dear Son was taken down from the Cross and laid on the stone before her.

And then Our Blissful Lady bowed down to her Son's Body, and kissed his mouth, and wept so plenteously, over His blissful face, that she washed away the blood from His face with the tears of her eyes.

And then the creature thought she heard Mary Magdalene saying to Our Lady: —

'I pray you, Lady, give me leave to handle and kiss His feet, for at these get I grace.'

Anon, Our Lady gave leave to her and all those that were about, to do what worship and reverence they would to that Precious Body.

And anon Mary Magdalene took Our Lord's feet, and Our Lady's sisters took His hands, one sister one hand and the other sister the other hand, and wept full sore in 94b kissing those hands and those precious feet. And the said creature thought that she ran ever to and fro, as if she had been a woman without reason, greatly desiring to have had the Precious Body by herself alone, so that she might have wept enough in the presence of that Precious Body, for she thought that she would have died with weeping and mourning on His death, for the love that she had for Him.

And at once she saw Saint John the Evangelist, Joseph of Arimathea and other friends of Our Lord come, and want to bury Our Lord's Body, and pray Our Lady that she would suffer them to bury that Precious Body.

Our Lady said to them: —

'Sirs, would ye take away from me my Son's Body? I might never look upon Him enough while He lived. I pray you let me have Him, now He is dead, and part not me and my Son asunder. And if ye will anyhow bury Him, I pray you, bury me with Him, for I may not live without Him.'

And the creature thought that they prayed Our Lady so fair, till at the last Our Lady let them bury her dear Son with great worship and great reverence, as was fitting for them to do.

CHAPTER 81

W<small>HEN</small> Our Lord was buried, Our Lady fell down in a swoon as she would have come from the grave, and Saint John took her up in his arms, and Mary Magdalene went on the other side to support and comfort Our Lady, as much as they could or might. Then the said creature, desiring to abide still by the grace of Our Lord, mourned, wept, and sorrowed with loud crying for the tenderness and compassion that she had of Our Lord's death, and many a lamentable desire that God put into her mind for the time. Wherefore the people wondered on her, having great marvel what ailed her, for they knew full little the cause. She thought she would never have departed thence, but desired to have died there, and been buried with Our Lord. Later the creature thought she saw Our Lady go homeward again, and as she went, there came many good women to her and said: —

'Lady, woe are we that your Son is dead, and that our people have done Him so much despite.'

And then Our Lady bowing her head, thanked them full meekly with cheer and countenance, for she could not speak; her heart was so full of grief.

Then the creature thought, when Our Lady was come 95a home and was laid down on a bed, that she made for Our Lady a good caudle, and brought it her to comfort her, and then Our Lady said unto her: —

'Take it away, daughter. Give me no food, but mine own Child.' The creature answered: —

'Ah! Blessed Lady, ye must needs comfort yourself and cease of your sorrowing.'

'Ah! Daughter, where should I go, or where should I dwell without sorrow? I tell thee, certainly was there never woman on earth who had such great cause to sorrow as I have, for there was never a woman in this world who bore a better Child, or a meeker to His mother, than my Son was to me.'

And she thought she heard Our Lady crying anon with a lamentable voice, and saying: —

'John, where is my Son Jesus Christ?'

And Saint John answered back and said: —

'Dear Lady, ye know well that He is dead.'

'Ah! John,' she said, 'that is to me a care-full counsel.'

The creature heard as clearly this answer in the understanding of her soul, as she would understand one man speaking to another. And anon, the creature heard Saint Peter knocking at the door, and Saint John asked who was there. Peter answered: —

'I, sinful Peter, who hath forsaken my Lord Jesus Christ.'

Saint John would have made him come in, but Peter would not, till Our Lady bade him come in. Then Peter said: —

'Lady, I am not worthy to come in to you,' and was still, outside the door.

Then Saint John went to Our Lady and told her that Peter was so abashed that he durst not come in. Our Lady bade Saint John go again quickly to Saint Peter and bid him come in to her. And then the creature, in her ghostly sight, beheld Saint Peter come before Our Lady and fall down on his knees, with great weeping and sobbing, and say: —

'Lady, I cry you mercy, for I have forsaken your dear-worthy Son and my sweet Master, Who hath loved me full well, and therefore, Lady, I am never worthy to look on Him, or you either, but by your great mercy.'

'Ah! Peter,' said Our Lady, 'dread thee not, for, though thou hast forsaken my sweet Son, He forsook never thee, Peter, and He shall come again and comfort us all right well; for He promised me, Peter, that He would come again on the third day and comfort me. Ah! Peter,' said Our Lady, 'full long time shall I think it, till that day cometh that I may see His blessed face.' 95b

Then Our Lady lay still on her bed, and heard how the friends of Jesus made their complaint of the sorrow that they had. And ever Our Lady lay still, mourning and weeping with sorrowing face, and at the last, Mary Magdalene and Our Lady's sisters took their leave of Our Lady, to go and buy ointment, that they might anoint therewith Our Lord's Body.

Then the creature was left still with Our Lady and thought it a thousand years till the third day came; and that day, she was with Our Lady in a chapel where Our Lord Jesus Christ appeared unto her, and said: —

'Salve, sancta parens.'

And then the creature thought, in her soul, that Our Lady said: —

'Thou art my sweet Son, Jesus?'

And He said: —

'Yea, blessed Mother, I am your own Son, Jesus.'

Then He took up His blessed Mother and kissed her full sweetly.

And then the creature thought that she saw Our Lady feeling and tasting Our Lord's Body all over, and His hands and His feet, to see if there was any soreness or any pain. And she heard Our Lord say to His Mother:—

'Dear Mother, My pain is all gone, and now shall I live for evermore. And Mother, so shall your pain and your sorrow be turned into full great joy. Mother, ask what ye will, and I shall tell you.'

And when He had suffered His Mother to ask what she would, and had answered to her questions, then He said:—

'Mother, by your leave, I must go and speak with Mary Magdalene.'

Our Lady said:— 'It is well done, for, Son, she hath full much sorrow for Your absence. And I pray You, be not long from me.'

These ghostly sights and understandings caused the creature to weep, to sob, and to cry full loud, so that she might not control herself or restrain herself there-from, on Easter Day and other days, when Our Lord would visit her with His grace, blessed and worshipped may He be.

And anon afterwards, the creature was, in her contemplation, with Mary Magdalene, mourning and seeking Our Lord at the grave, and heard and saw how Our Lord Jesus Christ appeared to her in the likeness of a gardener, saying:—

'Woman, why weepest thou?'

Mary, not knowing who He was, all inflamed with the fire of love, answered Him:—

96a 'Sir, if thou hast taken away my Lord, tell me, and I shall take Him back again.'

Our Merciful Lord, having pity and compassion on her, said:—

'Mary.'

With that word, she, knowing Our Lord, fell down at His feet, and would have kissed His feet, saying: —

'Master.'

Our Lord said to her: — 'Touch Me not.'

Then the creature thought that Mary Magdalene said to Our Lord: —

'Ah! Lord, I see well Ye will not that I be so homely with You as I have been before,' and made a grieving look.

'Yes, Mary,' said Our Lord, 'I shall never forsake thee, but I shall ever be with thee without end.'

And then Our Lord said to Mary Magdalene: —

'Go! Tell My brethren and Peter that I am up-risen.'

And then the creature thought that Mary went forth with great joy, and it was great marvel to her that Mary rejoiced, for if Our Lord had spoken to her as He did to Mary, she thought that she could never have been merry. That was when she would have kissed His feet, and He said:—'Touch Me not.'

The creature had such great grief and misery in that word that, whenever she heard it in any sermon, as she did many times, she wept, sorrowed and cried, as if she would have died, for the love and desire that she had to be with Our Lord.

CHAPTER 82

O N the Purification Day, or otherwise Candlemas Day, when the said creature beheld the people with their candles in church, her mind was ravished into beholding Our Lady offering her Blissful Son to the priest Simeon in the Temple, as verily to her ghostly understanding as if she had been there in her bodily presence to have offered with Our Lady's own person. Then was she so comforted by the contemplation in her soul, that she had in the beholding of Our Lord Jesus Christ and of His Blessed Mother, of Simeon the priest, of Joseph and of other persons that were there when Our Lady was purified, and of the heavenly songs that she thought she heard when Our Blissful Lord was offered up to Simeon, that she might full evil bear up her own candle to the priest, as other folk did at the time of offering, but went wavering on each side like a drunken woman, weeping and sobbing so sore, that scarcely could she stand on her feet, for the fervour of love and devotion that God put into her soul through high contemplation.

And sometimes she could not stand, but fell down among the people and cried full loud, so that many men wondered and marvelled what ailed her; for the fervour of the spirit was so great that the body failed, and might not endure it.

She had such holy thoughts and meditations many times when she saw women being purified of their children.

96b

286

She thought in her soul that she saw Our Lady being purified, and had high contemplation in the beholding of the women who came to offer with the women that were purified. Her mind was all drawn from earthly thoughts and earthly sights, and set altogether in ghostly sights, which were so delectable and so devout, that she could not, in the time of fervour, withstand her weeping, her sobbing, or her crying, and therefore suffered she full much wonder, many a jape, and many a scorn.

Also, when she saw weddings, men and women being joined together after the law of the church, anon she had in meditation how Our Lady was joined to holy Joseph, and of the ghostly joining of man's soul to Jesus Christ, praying to Our Lord that her love and her affection might be joined to Him only, without end; and that she might have grace to obey Him, love Him and dread Him, worship and praise Him, and no thing to love but what He loved, nor any thing to want, but what He wanted, and ever to be ready to fulfil His will, both night and day, without grumbling or grief, with all gladness of spirit; and many more holy thoughts than she ever could repeat, for she had them not of her own study or her own wit, but of His gift, Whose wisdom is incomprehensible to all creatures, save only to those that He chooseth and inspireth, more or less, as He will His Own Self, for His will may not be constrained. It is in His Own free disposition.

She had these thoughts and these desires with profound tears, sighings and sobbings, and sometimes with great boisterous cries, as God would send it; and sometimes soft tears and secret, without any noise.

She might neither weep loud nor still but when God would send it, for she was sometimes thus barren of tears 97ª a day or half a day, and had such great pain for the desire she had of them, that she would have given all this world, if it had been hers, for a few tears, or have suffered right great bodily pain, to have got them with.

And then, when she was thus barren, she could find no joy or comfort in meat or drink or conversation, but ever was gloomy in face and behaviour till God would send them to her again, and then she was merry enough.

And so it was that Our Lord withdrew from her sometimes, the abundance of tears; yet He withdrew not from her, holy thoughts and desires for years together, for ever her mind and her desire was to Our Lord.

But she thought that there was no savour or sweetness but when she might weep, for then she thought that she could pray.

CHAPTER 83

T wo priests who had great trust in her manner of crying
and weeping, nevertheless were sometimes in great doubt
whether it were deceitful or not, forasmuch as she cried
and wept in the sight of the people. They had a private
idea, she unwitting, that they would prove whether she
cried because the people would hear her, or not. One day,
the two priests came to her and asked if she would go two
miles from where she dwelt, on pilgrimage to a church
standing in the open, a good long distance from any other
house, which was dedicated in honour of God and Saint
Michael the Archangel.

And she said she would go with them with good will.

They took with them a child or two and went to the
said place, all in company. When they had a while made
their prayers, the said creature had so much sweetness and
devotion, that she could not keep it secret, but burst out
into boisterous weeping and sobbing, and cried as loud,
or louder, than she did when she was amongst the people
at home, and she could not restrain herself therefrom, nor
any person there present.

Then the two priests, and a child or two with them,
marvelled. And then as they came homeward again, they
met women with children in their arms, and the aforesaid
creature asked if there was any man-child amongst them,
and the women said, 'Nay.'

Then was her mind so ravished into the childhood of 97b

289

Christ, for the desire that she had to see Him, that she might not bear it, but fell down and wept and cried so sore that it was a marvel to hear it.

Then the priests had the more trust that it was right well with her, when they heard her crying in a private place as well as in an open one, and in the fields as in the town.

Also there were nuns who desired to have knowledge of the creature, so that they should be the more stirred to devotion. She was in their church at midnight to hear their Matins, and Our Lord sent her such high devotion and such high meditation, and such ghostly comforts, that she was all inflamed with the fire of love, which increased so fast that it burst out with a loud voice and great crying, so that Our Lord's Name was the more magnified amongst His servants, who were good, meek and simple souls, and would believe the goodness of Our Lord Jesus Christ, Who giveth His grace to whom He will, and specially to them that doubt not or mistrust not in their asking.

Her crying greatly profited to the increase of merit and of virtue. To them that little trusted and little believed, peradventure there was little increase of virtue or of merit; but whether the people believed in her crying or not, her grace was never the less, but ever increased.

With equal kindness, Our Lord visited her by night as by day, when He would, and how He would, and where He would, for she lacked no grace except when she doubted or mistrusted the goodness of God, supposing or dreading that it was the wile of her ghostly enemy, informing or teaching her otherwise than was to her ghostly health.

When she supposed thus, or consented to any such thoughts through the work of any man or through any evil spirit in her mind, which would many a time have made her leave her good purpose, had the mighty hand of Our Lord's mercy not withstood his great malice, then lacked she grace and devotion and all good thoughts and all good desires, till she was, through the mercy of Our Lord Jesus Christ, compelled to believe steadfastly, without any doubt, that it was God Who spake in her, and would be magnified in her for His Own goodness and her profit and for the profit of many others.

And when she believed that it was God and no evil spirit that gave her so much grace of devotion, contrition and holy contemplation, then had she so many holy thoughts, holy speeches, and dalliance in her soul, teaching her how she should love God, how she should worship Him and serve Him, that she could never repeat but a few of them.

98a

They were so holy and so high that she was abashed to tell them to any creature, and also they were so high above her bodily wits that she might never express them with her bodily tongue, as she felt them.

She understood them better in her soul than she could utter them.

If one of her confessors came to her when she rose up newly from her contemplation, or else from her meditation, she could have told him many things of the dalliance that Our Lord made with her soul, and in a short time after, she had forgotten the most part thereof, and nigh all of it.

THE Abbess of Denny,[1] a house of nuns, oftentimes sent for the said creature, so that she should come to speak with her and with her sisters. The creature thought she would not go till another year, for she might ill endure the labour.

Then, as she was in her meditation and had great sweetness and devotion, Our Lord commanded her to go to Denny and comfort the ladies that desired to commune with her, saying in this manner to her soul: —

'Daughter, go forth to the house of Denny, in the Name of Jesus, for I will that thou comfort them.'

She was loath to go, for it was pestilence time, and she thought that she would, for no good, have died there.

Our Lord said to her mind again: —

'Daughter, thou shalt go safely and come safely back.'

She went then to a worshipful burgess' wife, who loved her and trusted her right much, whose husband lay in great sickness, and told the worshipful wife that she should go to Denny. The worthy woman would that she should not go, and said: —

'I would not,' she said, 'that my husband died while ye were away, for forty shillings.'

And she answered: —

'If ye would give me a hundred pounds, I would not abide at home.'

[1] *See* Note C.

For when she was bidden in her soul to go, she would in no way withstand it, but anyhow would go forth, whatever befell; and when she was bidden to stay at home, she would not, for anything, go out.

And then Our Lord told her that the aforesaid burgess should not die. Then went she again to the worthy wife   98b
and bade her be of good comfort, for her husband should live and fare right well, and that he should not die yet. The good wife was right glad and said unto her: —

'Now, gospel may it be in your mouth.'

Then the creature would have sped herself forth, as she was commanded, but when she came to the waterside, all the boats were gone Cambridge-ward ere she came.

Then had she much distress, how she would fulfil Our Lord's bidding.

And anon she was bidden in her soul that she should not be sorry or grieved, for she should be provided for well enough, and she should go safely, and come safely back. And it fell so indeed.

[Here follows remainder of Chapter]

O<small>N</small> a time, as the said creature was kneeling before an altar of the Cross and saying an orison, her eyes were ever together-ward as if she would have slept. And at the last, she might not choose; she fell into a little slumber and anon appeared verily to her sight an angel, all clothed in white as if he had been a little child, bearing a huge book before him.

Then said the creature to the child, or otherwise to the angel: —

'Ah!' she said, 'This is the Book of Life.'

And she saw in the book the Trinity, and all in gold.

Then said she to the child: — 'Where is my name?'

The child answered and said: —

'Here is thy name, written at the Trinity's foot,' and therewith he was gone, she knew not how.

And anon, afterwards, Our Lord Jesus Christ spake unto her and said: —

'Daughter, look that thou be now true and steadfast, and have a good faith, for thy name is written in Heaven in the Book of Life; and this was an angel that gave thee comfort. Therefore, daughter, thou must be right merry for I am right busy both forenoon and afternoon to draw 100b thy heart unto My heart, for thou shouldst keep thy mind altogether on Me, and shall greatly increase thy love to God.

'For daughter, if thou wilt follow after God's counsel,

thou mayest not do amiss, for God's counsel is to be meek, patient in charity and in chastity.'.

Another time, as the creature lay in her contemplation in a chapel of Our Lady, her mind was occupied in the Passion of Our Lord Jesus Christ, and she thought verily that she saw Our Lord appear to her ghostly sight in His Manhood, with His wounds bleeding as fresh as though He had been scourged before her.

And then she wept and cried with all the might of her body, for, if her sorrow was great before this ghostly sight, it was much greater after than it was before, and her love was more increased Our Lord-ward.

And then had she great wonder that Our Lord should become Man and suffer such grievous pains for her, who was so unkind a creature to Him.

Another time, as she was in a church of Saint Margaret, in the choir, being in great sweetness and devotion with great plenty of tears, she asked Our Lord Jesus Christ how she might best please Him; and He answered to her soul, saying: —

'Daughter, have mind of thy wickedness and think on My goodness.'

Then she prayed, many times and often, these words: —

'Lord, for Thy great goodness, have mercy on all my wickedness, as surely as I was never so wicked as Thou art good, nor ever may be, though I would; for Thou art so good that Thou mayest no better be. And therefore it is a great wonder that ever any man should be parted from Thee without end.'

Then, as she lay still in the choir, weeping and mourning for her sins, suddenly she was in a kind of sleep. And anon, she saw with her ghostly eye, Our Lord's Body lying before her, and His head, as she thought, close by her, with His blessed face upwards, the seemliest Man that ever might be seen or thought of.

And then came one with a dagger-knife to her sight, and cut that Precious Body all along the breast. And anon she wept wondrous sore, having more memory, pity, and compassion of the Passion of Our Lord Jesus Christ than she had before.

And so every day increased her mind and her love of Our Lord, blessed may He be, and the more than her love increased, the more was her sorrow for the sin of the people.

Another time, the said creature being in a chapel of Our Lady, sore weeping in memory of Our Lord's Passion, and such other graces and goodness as Our Lord ministered to her mind, suddenly, she knew not how soon, she was, in a manner, asleep.

And anon, in the sight of her soul, she saw Our Lord standing right up over her, so near that she thought she took His toes in her hand and felt them, and to her feeling, it was as if they had been very flesh and bone.

And then she thanked God for all, for through these ghostly sights her affection was all drawn into the manhood of Christ and into the memory of His Passion, unto that time that it pleased Our Lord to give her understanding of His inunderstandable Godhead.

As is written before, this manner of visions and feelings she had soon after her conversion, when she was fully set and purposed to serve God with all her heart, according to her power, and had fully left the world, and kept in the church both forenoon and afternoon and most especially in Lent time, when she, with great insistence and much prayer, had leave of her husband to live chaste and clean, and did great bodily penance ere she went to Jerusalem.

But afterwards, when she and her husband, with one assent, had made a vow of chastity, as is before written, and she had been at Rome and Jerusalem, and suffered much despite and reproof for her weeping and her crying, Our Lord of His high mercy, drew her affection into His Godhead, and that was more fervent in love and desire, and more subtle in understanding than was the Manhood.

And nevertheless, the fire of love increased in her, and her understanding was more enlightened and her devotion more fervent than it was before, while she had her meditation and her contemplation only in His Manhood.

Yet had she not that manner of violence in crying as she had before; but it was more subtle and more soft, and more easy for her spirit to bear, and as plenteous in tears, as ever it was before.

Another time, as this creature was in a house of the 101b Preaching Friars, within a chapel of Our Lady, standing at her prayers her eye-lids went a little together in a kind of sleep, and suddenly she saw, she thought, Our Lady in the fairest sight that ever she saw, holding a fair white kerchief in her hand, and saying to her: —

'Daughter, wilt thou see my Son?'

And anon, forthwith she saw Our Lady hold her Blessed Son in her hand and swathe Him full lightly in the white kerchief, so that she might well behold how she did it.

The creature had then a new ghostly joy and a new ghostly comfort, which was so marvellous that she could never tell it as she felt it.

[Here follow Chapters 86, 87 and 88]

Aᴌsᴏ, while the aforesaid creature was occupied about the writing of this treatise, she had many holy tears and weeping, and oftentimes there came a flame of fire about her breast, full hot and delectable; and also he that was her writer could not sometimes keep himself from weeping.

And often in the meantime, when the creature was in church, Our Lord Jesus Christ with His Glorious Mother and many saints also came into her soul and thanked her, saying that they were well pleased with the writing of this book. And also she heard many times a voice of a sweet bird singing in her ear, and oftentimes she heard sweet sounds and melodies that passed her wit to tell of. And she was many times sick while this treatise was in writing, and, as soon as she would go about the writing of this treatise, she was hale and whole suddenly, in a manner; and often she was commanded to make herself ready in all haste.

And, on a time, as she lay in her prayers in the church at the time of Advent before Christmas, she thought in her heart she would that God of His goodness would make Master Aleyn to say a sermon as well as he could; and as quickly as she had thought thus, she heard Our Sovereign Lord Christ Jesus saying in her soul: —

'Daughter, I wot right well what thou thinkest now of Master Aleyn, and I tell thee truly that he shall say a right holy sermon; and look that thou believest steadfastly the words that he shall preach, as though I preached them Myself, for they shall be words of great solace and comfort to thee, for I shall speak in him.'

When she had heard this answer, she went and told it to her confessor and to two other priests that she trusted much on; and when she had told them her feeling, she 106b was full sorry for dread whether he should speak as well as she had felt or not, for revelations be hard sometimes to understand.

And sometimes those that men think were revelations, are deceits and illusions, and therefore it is not expedient to give readily credence to every stirring, but soberly abide, and pray if it be sent of God. Nevertheless, as to this feeling of this creature, it was very truth, shewn in experience, and her dread and her gloom turned into great ghostly comfort and gladness.

Sometimes she was in great gloom for her feelings, when she knew not how they should be understood, for many days together, for dread that she had of deceits and illusions, so that she thought she would that her head had been smitten from her body till God of His goodness declared them to her mind.

For sometimes, what she understood bodily was to be understood ghostly, and the dread that she had of her feelings was the greatest scourge that she had on earth; and especially when she had her first feelings; and that dread made her full meek, for she had no joy in the feeling till she knew by experience whether it was true or not.

But ever blessed may God be, for He made her always more mighty and more strong in His love and in His dread, and gave her increase of virtue with perseverance.

Here endeth this treatise, for God took him to His mercy, that wrote the copy[1] of this book, and, though he wrote it not clearly nor openly to our manner of speaking, he, in his manner of writing and spelling made true sense, which, through the help of God and of herself that had all this treatise in feeling and working, is truly drawn out of the copy into this little book.

[1] By 'copy', Margery means the original ill-written book that they have just finished copying here.

CHAPTER 1

Aᴏ̨ғᴛᴇʀ Our Sovereign Saviour had taken the person 107a
who wrote first the treatise aforesaid, to His manifold
mercy, and the priest, of whom is before written, had
copied the same treatise after his simple cunning, he held
it expedient to the honour of the Blissful Trinity, that His
holy works should be notified and declared to the people,
when it pleased Him, to the worship of His Holy Name.

And then he began to write in the year 1438, on the
feast of Saint Vitalis, Martyr, by such grace as Our Lord
wrought in His simple creature, of the years that she lived
after; not all, but some of them, after her own tongue.

And first, there is a notable matter which is not written
in the aforesaid treatise. It befell soon after the creature
before written had forsaken the occupation of the world,
and was joined in her mind to God as much as frailty
would suffer.

The said creature had a son, a tall young man, dwelling
with a worshipful burgess in Lynne, using merchandise
and sailing over the sea, whom she desired to have drawn
out of the perils of this wretched and unstable world, if
her power might have attained thereto. Nevertheless, she
did as much as was in her, and when she could meet with
him at leisure, many times she counselled him to leave
the world and follow Christ, insomuch that he fled her
company and would not gladly meet with her.

So, on a time, it happed the mother to meet with her

son, though it were against his will and his intent at that time. And, as she had done before time, so now she spake to him again, that he should flee the perils of this world, and not set his study or his business so much thereon, as he did, he not consenting but sharply answering back.

She, some deal moved with sharpness of spirit, said: —

'Now, since thou wilt not leave the world at my counsel, I charge thee to keep thy body clean, at the least, from woman's fellowship, till thou take a wife after the law of the Church. And, if thou dost not, I pray God chastise thee and punish thee therefor.'

They parted asunder, and soon after, the young man passed over the sea, in way of merchandise, and then what
107b through evil enticing of other (company and) persons, and folly of his own behaviour, he fell into the sin of lechery. Soon after, his colour changed, his face waxed full of weals and blubbers as if he were a leper.

Then he came home again into Lynne to his master, with whom he had been dwelling beforetime. His master put him out of his service, for no default that he found with him, but peradventure supposing he had been a leper, as shewn by his visage.

The young man told where he liked, how his mother had banned him, wherethrough, as he supposed, God so grievously punished him. Some persons, having knowledge of his complaint, and compassion for his dis-ease, came to his mother, saying she had done right evil, for through her prayer, God had taken vengeance on her own child.

She, taking little heed of their words, let it pass forth as if she did not care, till he should come and pray for grace himself. So at the last, when he saw no other remedy, he came to his mother, telling her of his misbehaviour, promising he would be obedient to God and to her, and to amend his default, through the help of God eschewing all misbehaviour from that time forward, according to his power.

He prayed his mother for her blessing and specially he prayed her to pray for him, that Our Lord, of His high mercy, would forgive him that he had trespassed, and take away that great sickness for which men fled his company and his fellowship, as for a leper.

For he supposed, by her prayers, Our Lord sent him that punishment and therefore he trusted by her prayers to be delivered there-of, if she would of her charity pray for him. Then she, having trust of his amending, and compassion on his infirmity, with sharp words of correction, promised to fulfil his intent, if God would grant it.

When she came to her meditation, not forgetting the fruit of her womb, she asked forgiveness for his sin and release from the sickness that God had given him, if it were His pleasure, and profit to his soul.

So long she prayed, that he was clean delivered of the sickness and lived many years after, and had a wife and a child, blessed may God be, for he wedded his wife in Pruce[1] in Dewcheland.   108a

When tidings came to his mother from over the sea, that her son had wedded, she was right glad, and thanked God with all her heart, supposing and trusting that he would live clean and chaste, as the law of matrimony asketh.

Later, when God willed, his wife had a child, a fair maid child. Then he sent tidings to his mother into Eng-

[1] Prussia.

303

land of how graciously God had visited him and his wife, his mother being in a chapel of Our Lady, thanking God for the grace and goodness that He shewed to her son, and having desire to see them if she might. Anon, it was answered to her mind that she should see them all, ere she died.

She had wonder at this feeling, how it could be as she felt, inasmuch as they were beyond the sea, and she on this side the sea, never purposing to pass the sea whilst she lived.

Nevertheless, she knew well, to God nothing was impossible, and therefore she trusted it would be as she had feeling, when God willed.

CHAPTER 2

In a few years after this young man had wedded, he came home to England to his father and his mother all changed in his array and his condition, for aforetime his clothes were all slashed and his language all vanity. Now he wore no slashes, and his dalliance was full of virtue.

His mother, having great marvel of this sudden changing, said unto him: —

'Benedicite, son, how is it with thee, that thou art so changed?'

'Mother,' said he, 'I hope that through your prayers, Our Lord hath drawn me and I purpose by the grace of God to follow your counsel more than I have done before.'

Then his mother, seeing this marvellous call of Our Lord, thanked God as she could, taking good heed of his behaviour for dread of simulation.

The longer she beheld his behaviour, the more sober she thought he was, and the more reverent our Lord-ward. When she knew it was the call of Our Lord's mercy, then she was full joyful, thanking God many times for His grace and His goodness.

Later on, so that he should be the more diligent and the more busy to follow Our Lord's call, she opened her heart to him, shewing him and informing him how Our Lord had drawn her through His mercy and by what means; also how much grace He had shewn her, to which he said he was unworthy to hear.

108b

Then he went many pilgrimages to Rome and to many other holy places to purchase his pardon, resorting again to his wife and child as he was bounden to do.

He informed his wife of his mother, insomuch that she would leave her father and her mother and her own country to come to England and see his mother.

He was full glad thereof, and sent word into England to his mother to certify her of his wife's desire, and to know whether his mother would counsel him to come by land or water, for he trusted much in his mother's counsel, believing it was of the Holy Ghost.

His mother, when she had a letter from him, and knew his desire, went to her prayer to know Our Lord's counsel and Our Lord's will. And as she prayed for the said matter, it was answered to her soul, that, whether her son came by land or by water, he should come in safe ward.

Then wrote she letters to him, saying that whether he came by land or by water, he should come in safety by the grace of God.

When he was certified of his mother's counsel, he enquired when ships would come to England, and hired a ship, or else part of a ship, in which he put his property, his wife, his child, and his own self, purposing to all come into England together.

When they were in the ship, there arose such tempests that they durst not take the sea, and so they went on land again, both he, his wife and their child.

Then they left their child in Pruce with their friends, and he and his wife came into England by land way, to his father and mother. When they were come thither, his mother full much rejoiced in Our Lord that her feeling was true, for she had feeling in her soul, as is written before, that whether they came by land or by water, they should come in safety. And so it was indeed, blessed may God be.

They came home on the Saturday in good health, and on the next day, that was the Sunday, while they were at meat at noon with other good friends, he fell into great sickness, so that he rose from the table and laid himself on a bed; which sickness and infirmity occupied him about a month, and then in good life and right belief, he passed to the mercy of Our Lord.

So ghostly and bodily it might well be verified, he shall come home in safety, not only into this land of mortals, but also into the land of living men where death shall never appear.

In a short time after, the father of the said person followed the son the way which every man must go.

Then lived still the mother of the said person, of whom this treatise specially maketh mention, and she that was his wife, a Dewchewoman, dwelling with his mother a year and a half, unto the time that her friends who were in Ducheland, desiring to have her home, wrote letters to her, and stirred her to resort to her own country.

And so she, desiring the benevolence of her friends, uttered her conceit to her mother in law, declaring to her the desire of her friends, praying her for good love and leave that she might resort to her own country.

And so, with her mother-in-law's consent, she arranged to go as soon as any ships went into that land. So they enquired for a ship of that same land and her own country-men to sail thither, and they thought it was good that she should rather sail with them in their ship than with other men.

109a

Then she went to her confessor to be shriven, and whilst she was at the shriving, the said creature, her mother-in-law, went up and down in the choir, thinking in her mind: —

'Lord, if it were Thy will, I would take leave of my confessor, and go with her over the sea.'

Our Lord answered to her thought, saying: —

'Daughter, I know well, if I bade thee go, thou wouldst go readily. Therefore I will that thou speakest no word to him of this matter.'

Then was she right glad and merry, trusting she would not go over the sea, for she had been in great peril on the sea aforetime and was in purpose never to go there-on more, by her own will.

When her daughter-in-law was shriven, the good man who was confessor to them both at that time, came to her and said: —

109b 'Who shall go with your daughter to the sea side till she comes to her ship? It is not proper that she should go so far with a young man alone in a strange country where neither is known.'

For a strange man was come for her, and both were but little known in this country, wherefore her confessor had the more compassion for her. Then the said creature answered: —

'Sir, if ye bid me, I shall go with her myself till she cometh to Ipswich, where lieth the ship and her own countrymen, who shall take her over the sea.'

Her confessor said: — 'How shall ye go with her? Ye hurt but lately your foot, and ye are not yet well, and also ye are an old woman. Ye may not go.'

'Sir,' she said, 'God, as I trust, shall help me right well.'

Then he asked who should go with her and bring her home again. And she said: —

'Sir, there is, belonging to this church, a hermit, a young man. I hope he will, for Our Lord's love, go and come with me, if ye will give me leave.'

So she had leave to bring her daughter to Ipswich and then come back to Lynne. Thus they passed forth on their journey in time of Lent, and when they were five or six miles from Lynne, they came by a church, and so they turned in to hear Mass. And as they were in the church, the aforesaid creature, desiring tears of devotion, could purchase none at that time, but ever was commanded in her heart to go over the sea with her daughter.

She would have put it out of her mind, but ever it came again strongly so that she could have no rest or quiet in her mind, but ever was laboured and commanded to go over the sea. She thought it was hard on her to take such labour upon herself and excused herself to Our Lord in her mind saying: —

'Lord, Thou knowest well I have no leave from my ghostly father, and I am bounden to obedience. Therefore I may not do thus without his will and his consent.'

It was answered again to her thought: —

'I bid thee go in My Name — Jesus — for I am above thy ghostly father, and I shall excuse thee, and lead thee, and bring thee back again in safety.'

She would yet excuse herself if she might in any way, and therefore she said: —

'I am not provided with gold or silver sufficient to go 110a with, as I ought to be; and though I were, and would go, I know well my daughter would rather I were at home,

309

and peradventure the ship-masters would not receive me into their vessel to go with them.'

Our Lord said again: — 'If I be with thee, who shall be against thee? I shall provide for thee, and get thee friends to help thee. Do as I bid thee, and no man of the ship shall say nay to thee.'

The creature saw that there was no help for it, but forth she must go at the command of God. She thought that she would first go to Walsingham,[1] and offer in worship of Our Lady; and, as she was on the way thither-ward, she heard tell that a friar would preach a sermon in a little village, a little out of her way. She turned into the church, where the friar said the sermon, a famous man, who had a great audience at his sermon. And many times he said these words: —

'If God be with us, who shall be against us?' Through which words, she was the more stirred to obey the will of God, and perform her intent. So she went forth to Walsingham, and later to Norwich with her daughter-in-law, and the hermit with them.

When they came to Norwich, she met a Grey Friar, a worshipful clerk, a doctor of divinity, who had heard of her life and her feelings beforetime. The doctor shewed her great cheer, and chatted with her as he had done beforetime. She, many times sighing, was sorrowful in face and in bearing.

The doctor asked what ailed her. 'Sir,' she said, 'when I came out of Lynne with the leave of my confessor, I purposed to lead my daughter to Ipswich, where there is a ship in which she, by the grace of God, shall sail to Deucheland, and I then to turn home again, as soon as I

[1] *See* Note P.

comfortably could, to Lynne with a hermit who came with me with the same intent to lead me home again; and he believed fully that I should do so. And, sir, when I was about six miles out of Lynne, in a church making my prayers, I was commanded in my soul that I should go over the sea with my daughter, and I know well that she would I were at home, and so would I, if I durst. Thus was I moved in my soul and could have no rest in my spirit, nor devotion, till I consented to do as I was moved 110b in my spirit, and this is, to me, great dread and grief.'

The worshipful clerk said unto her: — 'Ye shall obey the will of God, for I believe it is the Holy Ghost that speaketh in you, and therefore follow the moving of your spirit in the Name of Jesus.'

She was much comforted with his words, and took her leave, going forth to the sea side with her fellowship. When they were come thither, the ship was ready to sail. Then she prayed the master that she might sail with them into Ducheland, and he kindly received her, and they that were in the ship said not once 'nay'. There was no one so much against her as her daughter, who ought most to have been with her.

Then she took her leave of the hermit who was come thither with her, rewarding him somewhat for his labour and praying him to excuse her to her confessor and to her other friends, when he came home to Lynne, for it was not her thought or her intent when she parted from them, to have passed the sea ever whilst she lived, 'but', she said, 'I must obey the will of God.'

The hermit parted from her with a sad face, and came home again to Lynne, excusing her to her confessor and to other friends, telling them of their sudden and wonderful parting, and how it was not to his knowledge that they would be parted so suddenly asunder.

The people that heard there-of had great wonder, and spoke as they would. Some said it was a woman's whim, and a great folly, for the love of her daughter-in-law, to put herself, a woman of great age, to the perils of the sea, and to go into a strange country where she had not been before, nor knew how she should come back. Some held it was a deed of great charity, forasmuch as her daughter had beforetime left her friends and her country, and come with her husband to visit her in this country, that she should now help her daughter home again into the country she came from. Others who knew more of the creature's life, supposed and trusted that it was the will and the working of Almighty God to the magnifying of His Own Name.

CHAPTER 3

T<small>HE</small> said creature and her fellowship entered their <small>111a</small> ship on the Thursday in Passion Week, and God sent them fair wind and weather that day and the Friday, but on the Saturday, Our Lord, turning His hand as He pleased, and on the Palm Sunday also, proving their faith and their patience, on these two nights sent them such storms and tempests, that they expected all to have perished.

The tempests were so grievous and hideous that they could not rule or govern the ship. They knew no better safeguard than to commend themselves and their ship to the governance of Our Lord; they left their craft and their cunning, and let Our Lord drive them where He would. The said creature had sorrow and care enough: she thought she had never so much before.

She cried to Our Lord for mercy for the preservation of herself and all her fellowship.

She thought in her mind: — 'Ah! Lord, for thy love I came hither, and Thou hast oftentime promised me that I should never perish either on land or in water, or by any tempest. The people hath many a time banned me, cursed me and sworn at me for the grace Thou hast wrought in me, desiring that I should die in mischief and great distress; and now, Lord it is likely that their banning cometh into effect, and I, unworthy wretch, am deceived and defrauded of the promise that Thou hast made many a time to me, who hath ever trusted in Thy mercy and goodness, unless Thou the sooner withdraw these tempests and shew us mercy. Now may mine enemies rejoice and I may sorrow, if they have their intent and I be deceived. Now, Blissful Jesus, have mind of Thy manifold mercies and fulfil Thy promises that Thou hast made me. Shew Thou art truly God, and no evil spirit that hath brought me hither into the perils of the sea. Whose counsel I have trusted and followed for many years, and shall do, through Thy mercy, if Thou deliver us out of these grievous perils. Help us and succour us, Lord, ere we perish or despair, for we may not long endure this peril that we be in without Thy mercy and succour.'

111b Our Merciful Lord, speaking in her mind, blamed her for her fear, saying: — 'Why dost thou dread? Why art thou so afraid? I am as mighty here on the sea as on the land. Why wilt thou mistrust Me? All that I have promised thee, I shall truly fulfil, and I shall never deceive thee. Suffer patiently awhile and have trust in My mercy. Waver not in thy faith, for without faith, thou mayest not please Me. If thou wouldst verily trust in Me, and nothing doubt, thou mayest have great comfort in thyself, and mightst comfort all thy fellowship, where ye be now, all in great dread and grief.'

With such manner of dalliance, and much more high and holy than ever I could write, Our Lord comforted His creature, blessed may He be. Holy saints whom she prayed unto, dallied to her soul by the sufferance of Our Lord, giving her words of great comfort.

At last came Our Lady, and said: — 'Daughter, be of good comfort. Thou hast ever found my tidings true, and therefore be no longer afraid, for I tell thee truly these winds and tempests shall soon cease, and ye shall have right fair weather.'

And so, blessed may God be, it was, in a short time after. Their ship was driven to the Norway coast, and there they landed on Good Friday, and abode there Easter Eve and Easter Day, and the Monday after Easter. And on that Monday there were houselled within the ship, all that belonged to the ship.

On Easter Day, the master of the ship and the said creature and others, for the most part of the ship's company, went on land and heard their service at the church. After the custom of the country, the Cross was raised on Easter Day about noontime, and she had her meditation and her devotion with weeping and sobbing as well as if she had been at home. God withdrew not His grace from her either in church or in the ship, or on the sea, or in any place that she had come to, for ever she had Him in her soul.

When they had received the Sacrament on Easter Monday, as is written before, Our Lord sent them a fair wind, which brought them out of that country and drove them home into Ducheland, as they desired.

The aforesaid creature found such grace in the master of the ship that he arranged for her meat and drink and all that was necessary unto her as long as she was in the ship, and was as tender to her as if she had been his mother. He covered her in the ship with his own clothes, for otherwise she might have died of cold; she was not provided as the others were. She went at the bidding of Our Lord, and therefore Her Master, Who had bade her go, provided for her, so that she fared as well as any of her fellowship, worship and praise be to Our Lord therefor.

112a

CHAPTER 4

THE said creature abode in Danske[1] in Ducheland about five or six weeks, and had right good cheer of many people for Our Lord's love. There was no one so much against her as was her daughter-in-law, who was most bounden and beholden to have comforted her, if she had been kind.

Then the creature rejoiced in Our Lord that she had such great cheer for His love, and purposed to abide there a longer time. Our Lord, speaking to her thought, admonished her to go out of the country. She was then in great grief and distress as to how she should do the bidding of God, Whom she would in no way withstand, and had neither man nor woman to go with her in fellowship.

By the water would she not go, if she could help it, because she was so afraid on the sea as she came thither, and by land she could not easily go, for there was war in the country she would pass by. So, through one cause and another, she was in great distress, not knowing how she would be relieved. She went into a church and made her prayers to Our Lord, that, as He had commanded her to go, He should send her help and fellowship with whom she could go.

And, suddenly, a man coming to her, asked if she would go on pilgrimage to a country far from thence, to a place

[1] Danzig.

316

called Wilsnak, where is worshipped the Precious Blood of Our Lord Jesus Christ, which by a miracle came from three Hosts, the Sacrament of the Altar. These three Hosts, and the Precious Blood are, to this day, held there in great worship and reverence, and sought from many a country.

She, with glad cheer, said she would go thither if she had good fellowship, and if she knew of any good man 112b who would afterwards bring her to England.

He promised her that he would go on pilgrimage with her to the aforesaid place at his own cost, and afterwards if she would requite his costs into England, he would come with her till she was on the coast of England, so that she might have good fellowship of her nation. He obtained a smack, a little ship in which they should sail towards the holy place. Then could she get no leave to go out of that land, for she was an Englishwoman, and so had she great vexation and much hindrance ere she got leave from one of the lords of Pruce to go hence.

At last, through the guidance of Our Lord, there was a merchant of Lynne who heard tell of it, and he came to her and comforted her, promising her that he would help her from thence, either privily or openly; and this good man, with great labour, got her leave to go where she would.

Then she, with the man who had provided for her, took their vessel, and God sent them calm wind, which wind pleased her right well, for there arose no wave on the water. Her fellowship thought they made no way, and were sad and grutching. She prayed to Our Lord and He sent them wind enough, so that they sailed a great course and the waves rose sore. Her fellowship were glad and merry, and she was sad and sorry for dread of the waves. When she looked upon them, she was ever afraid.

Our Lord, speaking to her spirit, bade her lay down her head so that she would not see the waves, and she did so, but ever she was afraid, and therefore was she oftentimes blamed.

And so they sailed forth to a place which is called Strawissownd.[1] If the names of the places be not right written, let no man marvel, for she studied more about contemplation than the names of the places, and he that wrote them had never seen them and therefore, hold him excused.

[1] Stralsund.

CHAPTER 5

Wʜᴇɴ they were come to Strawissownd, they took the land, and so the said creature with the aforesaid man went towards Wilsnak in great dread, and passed many perils. The man who was her guide was ever afraid and would ever have forsaken her company. Many times she _{113a} spoke as fair to him as she could, so that he should not forsake her in those strange countries and in the midst of her enemies, for there was open war betwixt the English and those countries.

Therefore her dread was much the more, and ever amidst it, Our Lord spoke to her mind: —

'Why dreadest thou? No man shall do harm to thee, or to any one thou go-est with. Therefore comfort thy man and tell him no man shall hurt him or harm him whilst he is in thy company. Daughter, thou knowest well, a woman that hath a fair man and a seemly for her husband, if she love him, she will go with him wherever he will. And, daughter, there is no one so fair and so seemly, or so good as I. Therefore, if thou lovest Me, thou shalt not fear to go with Me wherever I will have thee. Daughter, I brought thee hither and I shall bring thee home again to England, in safe ward. Doubt it not, but believe it right well.'

Such holy dalliance and speech in her soul caused her to sob right boisterously, and weep full plenteously. The more she wept, the more irked was her man of her company, and the more he tried to go from her and leave her alone. He went so fast that she might not follow without great labour and great distress. He said that he was afraid of enemies and of thieves; that they would take her away from him, peradventure, and beat him and rob him there-to. She comforted him as well as she could, and said she durst undertake that no man should either beat them or rob them or say an evil word to them.

And soon after her words, there came a man out of a wood, a tall man, with good weapons and well arrayed to fight, as it seemed to them.

Then her man, being in great dread, said to her: —

'Lo! What sayest thou now?'

She said: — 'Trust in Our Lord, and dread no man.'

The man came by them, and said no evil word with them, so they passed forth Wylsnak-ward with great labour. She could not endure such great journeys as the man might and he had no compassion on her, nor would he abide for her.

113b   And therefore she laboured as long as she might, till she fell in sickness and could go no further. It was a great marvel and miracle that a woman unused to going, and also about three score years of age, should endure daily to keep her journey and her pace with a man eager and lusty to go on.

On Corpus Christi Eve, it lucked them to come to a little hostelry far from any town, and there could they get no bedding but a little straw; and the said creature rested herself there-upon that night and the next day till it was again evening. Our Lord sent lightning, thunder and rain nigh all the time, so that they durst not work outdoors. She was full glad thereof, for she was right sick, and she knew well, if it had been fair weather, the man who went with her would not await her. He would have gone from her. Therefore she thanked God Who gave him the occasion to abide, though it were against his will.

In the meantime, because of her sickness, there was provided a wain and so she was carried forth to the Holy Blood of Wilsnak with great penance and great discomfort.

The women of the country, as they went, having compassion, said many times to the aforesaid man that he was worthy of great blame, because he laboured her so sore. He, desiring to be delivered of her, cared not what they said, nor ever spared her the more.

Thus, what with weal and with woe, through the help of Our Lord, she was brought to Wilsnak and saw that Precious Blood which by a miracle came out of the Blissful Sacrament of the Altar.

CHAPTER 6

THEY abode not long in the said place, but in a short time took their way Akun-ward,[1] riding in wains, till they came to a water where there was much concourse of people, some to Akun-ward, and some to other places, amongst whom was a monk, a full reckless man and ill behaved, and in his company were young chapmen.

The monk and the chapmen knew well the man who was guide to the said creature, and called him by his name, shewing him right glad cheer. When they were past the water and went on the land, the monk with the chapmen and the said creature with her man, all in 114ᵃ fellowship together in wains, they came by a house of Friars Minor. Having much thrift, they then bade the said creature to go in to the friars and get them some wine.

She said: — 'Sirs, ye shall hold me excused, for if it were a house of nuns, I would readily go, but forasmuch as they are men, I shall not go, by your leave.'

So one of the chapmen went, and fetched to them a pottle of wine. Then came friars to them and prayed them that they would come and see the Blissful Sacrament in their church, for it was within the Octave of Corpus Christi, and It stood open in a crystal, that men might see It if they would.

The monk and the men went with the friars to see the Precious Sacrament. The said creature thought she

[1] Aachen.

would see it as well as they, and followed after, as though
it were against her will.

And when she beheld the Precious Sacrament, Our
Lord gave her so much sweetness and devotion that she
wept and sobbed wondrous sore, and could not restrain
herself therefrom. The monk was wroth, and all her
fellowship, because she wept so sore, and when they were
come again to their wains, they chid her and rebuked her,
calling her 'hypocrite', and said many an evil word to her.

She, to excuse herself, laid Scripture against them,
verses of the Psalter: — 'Qui seminant in lacrimis,'
etcetera; 'Euntes ibant et flebant,' etcetera, and such others.

Then were they well more wroth, and said she should
no longer go in their company, and persuaded her man to
forsake her.

She meekly and benignly prayed them that they would,
for God's love, suffer her to go forth in their company,
and not leave her alone where she knew no man, and no
man her, wherever she should go. With great prayer and
insistence, she went forth with them till they came to a
good town, in the Octave of Corpus Christi, and there
they said utterly that not for anything should she any longer
go with them. He that was her guide and had promised
her to bring her to England, forsook her, delivering
her gold and such things as he had of hers in keeping,
and offered to lend her more gold, if she had wanted.

She said to him: — 'John, I desired not your gold; I
had rather your fellowship in these strange countries than
all the money ye have, and I believe ye would more
please God by going with me, as ye promised me at Dansk,
than if ye went to Rome on your feet.'

Thus they put her out of their company and let her go

114b

where she would. She said then to him that had been her
guide: —

'John, ye forsake me for no other cause but that I
weep when I see the Sacrament, and when I think on
Our Lord's Passion. And since I am forsaken for God's
cause, I believe that God will arrange for me and bring
me forth as He would Himself, for He deceived me never,
blessed may He be.'

So they went their way and left her there still. The
night fell, and she was right miserable, for she was alone.
She knew not with whom she might rest that night, nor
with whom she should go on the next day. There came
priests to her, where she was hostelled, of that country.
They called her 'English sterte',[1] and spoke many lewd
words unto her, shewing uncleanly expression and
behaviour, proffering to lead her about if she would.

She had much dread of her chastity, and was in great
misery. Then went she to the good wife of the house,
praying her to get some of her maidens, who might lie
with her that night. The good wife assigned two maidens,
who were with her all that night, yet durst she not sleep
for fear of defilement.

She woke and prayed nigh all that night that she might
be preserved from all uncleanness, and meet with some
good fellowship that might help her forth to Akun.
Suddenly she was commanded in her soul to go to church
betimes on the next day, and there should she meet with
fellowship.

On the next day, betimes, she paid for her lodging,
inquiring of her hosts if they knew of any fellowship to
Akun-ward.

----

[1] 'Tail', a Dutch term of abuse for the English, whom they believed had tails.

They said: — 'Nay.'

She, taking her leave of them, went to the church to feel and prove if her feelings were true or not. When she came there, she saw a company of poor folk. Then went she to one of them, asking whither they were purposed to go.

He said: — 'To Akun.'

She prayed him that he would suffer her to go in their company.

'Why, dame,' he said, 'hast thou no man to go with thee?' 115a

'No,' she said, 'my man is gone from me.'

So she was received into a company of poor folk, and when they came to any town, she bought her meat, and her fellowship went on begging.

When they were outside the towns, her fellowship took off their clothes, and sitting naked, picked themselves. Need compelled her to await them and prolong her journey and be at much more cost than she would otherwise have been.

This creature was ashamed to put off her clothes as her fellows did, and therefore, through her communing, had part of their vermin and was bitten and stung full evil, both day and night, till God sent her other fellowship.

She kept on with her fellowship with great anguish and discomfort and much delay, until they came to Akun.

CHAPTER 7

W HEN they were come to Akun, the said creature met with a monk of England who was to Rome-ward.

Then was she much comforted, inasmuch as she had a man that she could understand.

And so they abode there together ten or else eleven days to see Our Lady's smock and other holy relics which were shewn on Saint Margaret's Day.

And in the meantime that they abode there, it lucked that a worshipful woman came from London, a widow, with much retinue with her, to see and worship the holy relics. The said creature came to this worthy woman, complaining that she had no fellowship to go with her, home into England. The worthy woman granted her all her desire, and made her eat and drink with her and made her right good cheer.

When Saint Margaret's Day was come and gone, and they had seen the holy relics, the worshipful woman sped herself fast out of Akun with all her retinue. The said creature, thinking to have gone with her and thus defrauded of her purpose, was in great grief. She took her leave of the monk who was Rome-ward, as is written before, and afterwards got herself a wain with other pilgrims, and pursued after the aforesaid worthy woman 115b as fast as she could, to see if she could overtake her, but it was not to be.

326

Then she happened to meet with two men of London, going London-ward. She prayed them to go in their company. They said, if she could endure to go as fast as they, she would be welcome, but they could not have any great hindrance; nevertheless they would help her forth in her journey with good will.

So she followed after them with great labour till they came to a good town where they met pilgrims of England, who were coming from the Court of Rome and would go home again to England. She prayed them that she might go with them, and they said shortly that they would not delay their journey for her, for they had been robbed and had but little money to bring them home, wherefore they must needs make the sharper journeys and therefore, if she might endure to go as fast as they, she would be welcome; otherwise not.

She saw no other succour but to abide with them as long as she could and so left those other two men, and abode still with these men.

Then they went to their meat and made merry. The said creature looked a little beside her, and saw a man lying and resting himself on a bench's end. She enquired what man that was. They said he was a friar, one of their fellowship.

'Why eateth he not with you?'

'Because we were robbed as well as he, and therefore each man must help himself as well as he may.'

'Well,' she said, 'he shall have part of such provisions as God sendeth me.'

She trusted well that Our Lord would provide for them both as was needful to them. She made him eat and drink, and comforted him right much.

Afterwards they all went on together. The said creature came soon behind; she was too aged and too weak to hold foot with them. She ran and leapt as fast as she might till her might failed. Then she spake with the poor friar whom she had cheered before, offering to requite his costs till he came to Caleys, if he would abide with her and let her go with him till they came there, and yet give him reward for his labour. He was well content and consented to her desire.

116a So they let their fellowship go forth and they two followed softly, as they could endure.

The friar, being evil for thrift, said to the creature: —

'I know these countries well enough, for I have oftentimes gone thus to Rome-ward and I wot well there is a place of recreation a little hence. Let us go thither and drink.'

She was well pleased and followed him.

When they came there, the good wife of the house, having compassion on the creature's labour, counselled that she should take a wain with other pilgrims and not go so, with a man alone. She said she had intended and fully trusted to have gone with a worshipful woman of London, and she was deceived. By the time they had rested a while and chatted with the good wife of the house, there came a wain by, with pilgrims. The good wife, having knowledge of the pilgrims in the wain, when they were past her house, called them back, beseeching them that this creature might ride with them in their wain for the more speed on her journey. They, kindly consenting, received her into their wain, riding all together till they came to a good town where the said creature perceived the worshipful woman of London, of whom aforesaid.

Then she prayed the pilgrims that were in the wain that they would hold her excused, and let her pay for the time she had been with them, as they liked, for she would go to a worshipful woman of her nation that she perceived was in the town, with whom she had made compact when she was at Akun, to go home with her into England. She had good love and leave, and parted from them.

They rode forth and she went to the worshipful woman expecting to be received with right glad cheer. And it was even right contrary. She found right short cheer, and had right sharp language, the worshipful woman saying to her: —

'What! Thinkest thou to go with me? Nay! I give thee well to know, I will not meddle with thee.'

The creature was so rebuked that she knew not what to do. She knew no man there, and no man knew her. She knew not whither to go. She knew not where the friar was, who should have been her guide, nor whether he would come that way or not. She was in great distress and grief, the greatest, as she thought, that she had suffered since she was come out of England.

Nevertheless, she trusted in Our Lord's promise and abode still in the town till God would send her some comfort.

And when it was nigh evening, she saw the friar coming towards the town. She hied her to speak with him, complaining how she was deceived and refused by the good woman that she had trusted so much to. The friar said they would do as well as God would give them grace, and comforted her according to his power, but said he would not abide in that town that night, for he knew well they were a perilous people.

116b

329

Then went they forth together out of the town again in the evening with great dread and sadness, mourning by the way where they should have harbourage that night. They happed to come under a woodside, busily looking if they might espy any place where-in they might rest. And, as Our Lord willed, they perceived a house or two, and in haste, thither they drew. There dwelt a good man with his wife and two children. Then kept they no hostel and would not receive guests into their dwelling.

The said creature saw a heap of bracken in a house, and with great insistence, she purchased grace to rest herself on the bracken that night. The friar, with great prayer, was laid in a barn, and they thought they were well eased that they had the house over them.

On the next day they made satisfaction for their lodging, taking the way Caleys-ward, going weary and grievous in deep sand, hills and valleys two days ere they came thither, suffering great thirst and great penance, for there were few towns by the way that they went, and full feeble harbourage.

And at nights had she most dread. Oftentimes and peradventure, it was of her ghostly enemy, for she was ever afraid of being ravished or defiled. She durst trust no man; whether she had cause or not, she was ever afraid. She durst full evil sleep any night, for she thought men would have defiled her.

Therefore she went to bed gladly on no night unless she had a woman or two with her. For that grace God sent her. 117a Wheresoever she came, for the most part, maidens would with good cheer lie by her, and that was to her great comfort.

She was so weary and so overcome with labour Caleys-ward, that she thought her spirit would have departed from her body as she went on the way.

Thus with great labours she came to Caleys, and the good friar with her, who full kindly and honestly had behaved towards her, the time they went together, and therefore she gave him such reward as she could attain and he was well pleased and content and they parted asunder.

CHAPTER 8

In Caleys this creature had good cheer of divers persons, both men and women, who had never seen her before. There was a good woman who had her home to her house, and who washed her full cleanly and put her on a new smock and comforted her right much. Other good persons had her to meat and drink. While she was there abiding shipping for three or four days, she met there with divers persons who had known her before, who spoke fair to her and gave her goodly language. Other things they gave her none. These persons awaited shipping as she did.

She, desiring to sail with them to Dover, in nothing would they help her, or let her know what ship they purposed to sail in. She speered and spied as diligently as she could, and ever she had knowledge of their intent, one way or another, till she was shipped with them; and when she had borne her things into the ship where they were, supposing they would have sailed in haste, she knew not how soon, they got themselves another ship ready to sail. What the cause was, she never knew.

Through grace, she, having knowledge of their purpose, how ready they were to sail, left all her things in the vessel that she was in, and went to the ship where they were, and through Our Lord's help, she was received into the ship.

And there was the worshipful woman of London, who

had refused her, as is before written, and so they sailed all together to Dover.

The said creature, perceiving by their faces and manner that they had little affection for her person, prayed to Our Lord that He would grant her grace to hold her head up, and preserve her from voiding unclean matter in their presence,[1] so that she should cause them no abomination.   117b

Her desire was fulfilled, so that, others in the ship voiding and casting full boisterously and uncleanly, she, all of them marvelling, could help them and do what she would.

And specially the woman of London had most of that passion and that infirmity, and whom this creature was most busy to help and comfort for Our Lord's love, and by charity — other cause she had none.

So they sailed forth till they came to Dover, and then each one of the company got himself fellowship to go on with, if he liked, save she only, for she could get no fellow to her ease.

Therefore she took her way Canterbury-ward by herself alone, sorry and sad in manner that she had no fellowship and that she knew not the way. She was up betimes in the morning and came to a poor man's house, knocking at the door. The good poor man, huddled into his clothes, unfastened and unbuttoned, came to the door to know her will. She prayed him, if he had any horse, that he would help her to Canterbury and she would requite his labour. He, desiring to do her pleasure in Our Lord's Name, fulfilled her intent, leading her to Canterbury.

She had great joy in Our Lord, Who sent her help and

[1] The page in the frontispiece begins here.

succour in every need, and thanked Him with many a devout tear, with much sobbing and weeping, almost in every place she came to.

Of all that, it is not written; as well on yon half of the sea as on this half, on water as on land, blessed may God be.

F ROM thence she went to London, clad in a cloth of canvas, as it were a sacken apron, as she had gone beyond the sea.

When she was coming into London, many people took notice of her well enough, inasmuch as she was not clad as she would like to have been, for lack of money. She, desiring to go unknown till such time as she might arrange to borrow some money, bore a kerchief before her face. Notwithstanding that she did so, some dissolute persons, supposing it was Mar. Kempe[1] of Lynne, said, so that she might easily hear, these words of reproof: —

'Ah! thou false flesh, thou shalt no good meat eat.'

She, not answering, passed forth as if she had not 118a heard. The aforesaid words were never of her speaking, either from God or good man, though so it was laid against her, and she, many times and in many places, had great reproof thereby. They were invented by the devil, father of lies, favoured, maintained and born forth of his members, false envious people, having indignation at her virtuous living, powerless to hinder her but through their false tongues.

There was never a man nor woman that ever could prove that she had said such words, but ever they made other liars their authority, saying in excuse of themselves that other men told them so. In this manner were these false words invented through the devil's suggestion.

[1] The only occasion on which her surname occurs anywhere in the book.

Some one person, or else more persons, deceived by their ghostly enemy, contrived this tale not long after the conversion of the said creature, saying that she, sitting at meat on a fish day, at a good man's table, served with divers sorts of fish, such as red herring and good pike, and such others, thus said, as they reported: —

'Ah! thou false flesh, thou wouldst now eat red herring, but thou shalt not have thy will.'

And therewith she set away the red herring and ate the good pike, as they said. And thus it sprang into a manner of proverb against her, so that some said: —

'False flesh, thou shalt eat no herring.'

And some said the words which are before written, and all was false, but yet they were not forgotten; they were repeated in many a place where she was never kid or known.

She went forth to a worshipful widow's house in London where she was kindly received and had great cheer for Our Lord's love, and in many places in London she was highly entertained in Our Lord's Name, God reward them all.

There was one worshipful woman who specially shewed her high charity, both in meat and drink, and in giving other rewards, and in whose place at one time she, being at meat with other divers other persons of divers conditions, she unknown to them and they to her, 118b of whom some were of the Cardinal's[1] house — as she had by information of others — they had a great feast and fared right well.

And, when they were in their mirth, some repeated the words before written, or others like them, that is to say: —

[1] Cardinal Beaufort.

'Thou false flesh, thou shalt not eat of this good meat.' She was still and suffered a good while. Each of them jangled to the other, having great game of the imperfection of that person that these words were said of.

When they had well sported themselves with these words, she asked them if they had any knowledge of the person who should have said these words.

They said: — 'Nay, forsooth, but we have heard tell that there is such a false feigned hypocrite in Lynne, who sayeth such words and, leaving off coarse meats, she eateth the most delectable and delicious meats that come on the table.'

'Lo, Sirs,' she said, 'ye ought to say no worse than ye know, and still not as evil as ye do know. Nevertheless here ye say worse than ye know, God forgive you, for I am that same person to whom these words are attributed, who oftentimes suffers great shame and reproof and am not guilty in this matter, God I take to record.'

When they beheld her unmoved in this matter, in no way reproving them, desiring through the spirit of charity their correction, they were rebuked by their own honour shaming them to make amends.

She spoke boldly and mightily wheresoever she went in London, against swearers, banners, liars, and such other vicious people, against the pompous array, both of men and women.

She spared them not, she flattered them not, either for their gifts or for their meat, or for their drink. Her speaking profited right much in many persons.

Therefore, when she came into church to her contemplation, Our Lord sent her full high devotion, thanking her that she was not afraid to reprove sin in His Name, and because she suffered scorn and reproof for His sake; promising her much grace in this life and, after this life, to have joy and bliss without end.

She was so comforted in the sweet dalliance of Our Lord that she could not control herself or govern her spirit after her own will, or after the discretion of other 119a men, but as Our Lord would lead it and measure it Himself, in sobbing full boisterously and weeping full plenteously.

Wherefore she suffered full much slander and reproof, especially from the curates and priests of the churches in London. They would not suffer her to abide in their churches, and therefore she went from one church to another, so that she should not be tedious unto them.

Many of the common people magnified God in her, having good trust that it was the goodness of God that wrought that high grace in her soul.

From London she went to Sheen, three days before Lammas Day, to purchase her pardon through the mercy of Our Lord. And when she was in the church at Sheen she had great devotion and full high contemplation. She had plenteous tears of compunction and compassion in remembrance of the bitter pains and passions which Our Merciful Lord Jesus Christ suffered in His blessed Manhood.

They that saw her weeping and heard her so boisterously sobbing were taken with great marvel and wonder, what was the occupation of her soul. A young man who beheld her face and manner, moved through the Holy Ghost, went to her, when he could courteously by himself alone, with fervent desire to understand what might be the cause of her weeping.

To whom, he said: — 'Mother, if it please you, I pray you show me the occasion for your weeping, for I have not seen a person so plenteous in tears as ye be, and especially, I have not heard before any person, so boisterous in sobbing as ye be. And, mother, though I be young, My desire is to please My Lord Jesus Christ, and so to follow Him as I can and may. And I intend by the grace of God to take the habit of His holy religion, and therefore I pray you, be not strange unto me. Shew motherly and kindly your conceit unto me as I trust unto you.'

She, benignly and meekly, with gladness of spirit, as she thought it expedient, commended him in his intent, and shewed to him in part that the cause of her weeping and sobbing was her great unkindness towards her Maker, wherethrough she had many times offended His goodness; and the great abomination that she had of her sins caused her to sob and weep.

Also the great, excellent charity of her Redeemer, by whom, through the virtue of His Passion suffering, and His Precious Blood shedding, she was redeemed from everlasting pain, trusting to be an heir of joy and bliss, moved her to sob and weep, as was no marvel.

She told him many good words of ghostly comfort, through which he was stirred to great virtue, and afterwards he ate and drank with her, in the time that she was there, and was full glad to be in her company.

On Lammas Day was the principal day of pardon, and as the said creature went into the church at Sheen, she had a sight of the hermit who led her out of Lynne, when she went sea-ward with her daughter-in-law, as is written before.

Anon, with great joy of spirit, she offered herself to his presence, welcoming him with all the might of her soul, saying unto him: —

'Ah! Reynald, ye are welcome. I trust Our Lord sent you hither, for now I hope, as ye led me out of Lynne, so ye shall bring me home again to Lynne.'

The hermit shewed short cheer, and dismal countenance, neither in will nor in purpose to bring her home to Lynne as she desired.

He, answering full shortly, said: — 'I make you well to know that your confessor hath forsaken you, because ye went over the sea, and would tell him no word thereof. Ye took leave to bring your daughter to the sea side; ye asked no leave any further. There was no friend ye had that knew of your counsel; therefore I suppose ye will find but little friendship when ye come there. I pray you, get your fellowship where ye can, for I was blamed for your fault when I led you last; I will no more.'

She spoke fair and prayed, for God's love, that he would not be displeased, for they that loved her for God, ere she went out, would love her for God when she came home. She proferred him to requite his costs on the way homeward.

So at last he, consenting, brought her again to London 120a and afterwards home to Lynne, to the high worship of God and to the great merit of both their souls.

When she was come home to Lynne, she made obedience to her confessor. He gave her full sharp words, for she was his obedience, and had taken upon herself such a journey without his knowledge. Therefore he was moved the more against her, but Our Lord helped her so that she had as good love of him, and of other friends after, as she had before, worshipped be God. Amen.

[Here follows 'Her Method of Prayer']

APPENDIX

THE PROEM

ERE beginneth a short treatise and a comfortable, for sinful wretches, 1a wherein they may have a great solace and comfort to themselves and understand the high and unspeakable mercy of our Sovereign Saviour Christ Jesus, Whose Name be worshipped and magnified without end; Who now in our days to us unworthy, deigneth to exercise His nobility and goodness. All the works of Our Saviour be for our example and instruction, and what grace that He worketh in any creature is our profit, if lack of charity be not our hindrance.

And therefore, by the leave of our merciful Lord Christ Jesus, to the magnifying of His holy Name, Jesus Christ, this little treatise shall treat somewhat in part of His wonderful works, how mercifully, how benignly and how charitably He moved and stirred a sinful caitiff unto His love, which sinful caitiff many years was in will and purpose, through stirring of the Holy Ghost, to follow the Saviour, making great promises of fasting with many other deeds of penance. And ever she was turned a-back in time of temptation, like unto the reed-spear which boweth with every wind, and never is stable unless no wind bloweth, unto the time that our merciful Lord Christ Jesus, having pity and compassion on His handiwork and His creature, turned health into sickness, prosperity into adversity, worship into reproof, and love into hatred.

Thus everything turning upside down, this creature who for many years had gone astray and ever been unstable, was perfectly drawn and stirred to enter the way of high perfection; which perfect way Christ Our Saviour, in His proper Person, exampled. Earnestly He trod it and duly He went it aforetime.

Then this creature, of whom this treatise through the mercy of Jesus shall shew in part the life, was touched by the hand of Our Lord with great bodily 1b sickness, wherethrough she lost reason and her wits a long time, till Our Lord by grace restored her again, as it shall more openly be shewn afterwards. Her worldly goods which were plenteous and abundant at that date, a little while afterwards were full barren and bare. Then was pomp and pride cast down and laid aside. They that before had worshipped her, afterwards full sharply reproved her; her kindred and they that had been friends were now most her enemies. Then she, considering this wonderful changing, seeking succour under the wings of her Ghostly Mother Holy Church, went and offered obedience to her ghostly father, accusing herself of her misdeeds, and afterwards did great bodily penance, and in a short time Our Merciful Lord visited this creature with plenteous tears of contrition day by day, insomuch that some said she might weep when she would, and slandered the work of God.

She was so used to being slandered and reproved, to being chidden and rebuked by the world for grace and virtue with which she was endued through the strength of the Holy Ghost, that it was to her, in a manner, solace and comfort when she suffered any dis-ease for the love of God and for the grace that God wrought in her. For ever the more slander and reproof that she suffered, the more she increased in grace, and in devotion of holy meditation, of high contemplation, and of wonderful speeches and dalliance which Our Lord spake and conveyed to her soul, teaching her how she should be despised for His love, how she should have patience, setting all her trust, all her love and all her affection in Him only.

She knew and understood many secret and privy things which should befall afterwards, by inspiration of the Holy Ghost. And oftentimes while she was kept 2a by such holy speeches and dalliance, she would so weep and sob that many men were greatly awonder, for they little knew how homely Our Lord was in her soul. She herself could never tell the grace that she felt, it was so heavenly, so high above her reason and her bodily wits, and her body so feeble in time of the presence of grace that she might never express it with her word as she felt it in her soul.

Then had this creature much dread, because of illusions and deceits of her ghostly enemies. Then went she, by the bidding of the Holy Ghost, to many worshipful clerks, both archbishops and bishops, doctors of divinity and bachelors also. She spoke also with many anchorites and showed them her manner of living and such grace as the Holy Ghost, of His goodness, wrought in her mind and in her soul, as her wit would serve her to express it. And all those that she shewed her secrets unto, said she was much bound to love Our Lord for the grace that He shewed unto her, and counselled her to follow her movings and her stirrings and trustingly believe they were of the Holy Ghost, and of no evil spirit.

Some of these worthy and worshipful clerks averred, at the peril of their souls and as they would answer to God, that this creature was inspired with the Holy Ghost, and bade her that she should have them written down and make a book of her feelings and revelations. Some proffered to write her feelings with their own hands, and she would not consent in any way, for she was commanded in her soul that she should not write so soon. And so it was twenty years and more from the time this creature had her first feelings and revelations, ere she did any writing. Afterwards, when it pleased Our Lord, He commanded her 2b and charged her that she should get written her feelings and revelations and the form of her living, that His goodness might be known to all the world.

Then had the creature no writer that would fulfil her desire or give credence to her feelings unto the time that a man dwelling in Dewchland, who was an Englishman in his birth, and afterwards wedded in Dewchland and had there both a wife and a child, having good knowledge of this creature and of her desire, moved, I trust, through the Holy Ghost, came to England with his wife and his goods, and dwelt with the aforesaid creature till he had written as much as she would tell him, for the time they were together. And afterwards he died.

Then was there a priest that this creature had great affection for, and so she communed with him of this matter, and brought him the book to read. The book was so evil-written that he shewed little skill thereon, for it was neither good

English nor Dewch, nor were the letters shaped or formed as other letters were. Therefore the priest believed fully that never could man read it, but by special grace. Nevertheless he promised her that if he could read it, he would copy it out and write it better, with good will. Then there was such evil speaking of this creature and of her weeping, that the priest durst not for cowardice speak with her but seldom, nor would he write as he had promised unto the aforesaid creature. And so he avoided and deferred the writing of this book well on to four years or else more, notwithstanding the creature cried often on him therefor. At the last, he said unto her that he could not read it, wherefore he would not do it. He would not, he said, put himself in peril thereof. Then he counselled her to go to a good man who had been much conversant with him that first wrote the book, supposing that he should know best how to read the book, for he had sometimes read letters of the other man's writing, sent from beyond the sea, whilst he was in 3a Dewchland.

And so she went to that man, praying him to write this book and never to reveal it as long as she lived, granting him a great sum of money for his labour. And this good man wrote about a leaf and yet it was little to the purpose, for he could not well fare therewith, the book was so evil set and so unreasonably written. Then the priest was vexed in his conscience, for he had promised her to write this book if he might come to the reading thereof, and was not doing his part as well as he might, and prayed this creature to get again the book, if she kindly would. And then she got again the book and brought it to the priest with right glad cheer, praying him to do his goodwill, and she would pray to God for him, and purchase him grace to read it and write it also.

The priest, trusting in her prayers, began to read this book and it was much more easy, as he thought, than it was beforetime. And so he read it over before this creature every word, she sometimes helping where any difficulty was. This book is not written in order, each thing after another as it was done, but like as the matter came to the creature in mind when it should be written; for it was so long ere it was written that she had forgotten the time and the order when things befell. And therefore she had nothing written but what she knew right well for very truth.

When the priest began first to write on this book, his eyes failed so that he might not see to make his letters and could not see to mend his pen. Everything else he could see well enough. He set a pair of spectacles on his nose, and then was it well worse than it was before. He complained to the creature of his dis-ease. She said his enemy had envy of his good deed and would hinder him if he might, and bade him do as well as God would give him grace and not give up. When he came again to his book he could see, he thought, as well as ever he did before, by day-light and by candle-light both. And for this cause, when he had written a quire, he added a leaf thereto, and then wrote he this proem, to express more openly than doth the next following, which was written earlier than this. Anno domini 1436.

APPENDIX

CHAPTER 5

T HEN on the Friday before Christmas Day, as this creature was kneeling in a chapel of Saint John, within a Church of St. Margaret in N . . ., weeping wondrous sore, and asking mercy and forgiveness for her sins and trespasses, Our 9a merciful Lord Christ Jesus, blessed may He be, ravished her spirit and said unto her:—

'Daughter, why weepest thou so sore? I am coming to thee, Jesus Christ Who died on the cross, suffering bitter pains and passions for thee. I, the same God, forgive thee thy sins to the uttermost point, and thou shalt never come to Hell or Purgatory, but when thou shalt pass out of this world, within a twinkling of an eye, thou shalt have the bliss of Heaven, for I am the same God that hath brought thy sins to thy mind and made thee be shriven thereof. And I grant thee contrition to thy life's end. Therefore I bid thee and command thee, boldly call me "Jesus Christ, thy love", for I am thy love, and shall be thy love without end. And, daughter, thou hast a haircloth on thy back. I will that thou put it away, and I shall give thee a haircloth in thy heart that shall please Me much better than all the haircloths in the world. Also, My dearworthy daughter, thou must forsake that which thou lovest best in this world, and that is the eating of flesh. Instead of that flesh, thou shalt eat of My flesh and My blood, that is the Very Body of Christ in the Sacrament of the Altar. This is My will, daughter, that thou receive My Body every Sunday, and I shall flow so much grace into thee, that all the world shall marvel thereof. Thou shalt be eaten and gnawed by the people of the world as any rat gnaweth stockfish. Dread thee nought, daughter, for thou shalt have victory over all thine enemies. I shall give thee grace enough to answer every clerk in the love of God. I swear to thee by My Majesty that I will never forsake thee in weel or in woe. I shall help thee and keep thee, so that no devil in Hell shall part thee from Me, nor angel in Heaven, nor man on earth, for devils in Hell may not, and angels in Heaven will not, and man on earth shall not. And daughter, I will thou leave thy bidding of many beads, and think such thoughts as I shall put into thy mind. I shall give thee leave to pray till six of the clock, saying what thou wilt. Then shalt thou be still and speak to Me in thought 9b and I shall give to thee high meditation and very contemplation. I bid thee go to the anchorite at the Preaching Friars and shew him My secrets and My counsels which I shew to thee, and work after his counsel, for My Spirit shall speak in him to thee.'

Then this creature went forth to the anchorite as she was commanded, and shewed him the revelations, as they were revealed to her. Then the anchorite, with great reverence and weeping, thanking God, said:—

'Daughter, ye suck even on Christ's breast, and ye have an earnest-penny of Heaven. I charge you to receive such thoughts as God gives, as meekly and devoutly as ye can, and to come to me and tell me what they are, and I shall, with the leave of Our Lord Jesus Christ, tell you whether they are of the Holy Ghost or of your enemy the devil.'

APPENDIX

CHAPTER 14

T HIS creature thought it was full merry to be reproved for God's love. It was to her great solace and comfort when she was chidden and scolded for the love of Jesus, for reproving sin, for speaking of virtue, and for conversing in Scripture which she had learnt in sermons and in communing with clerks. She imagined to herself what death she might die for Christ's sake. She thought she would like to be slain for God's love, but feared the point of death and therefore imagined for herself the most soft death, as she thought, for fear of impatience, which was to be bound head and foot to a post, and her head to be smitten off with a sharp axe, for God's love.

Then said Our Lord in her mind:—'I thank thee, daughter, that thou wouldst suffer death for My love, for, as often as thou thinkest so, thou shalt have the same reward in Heaven as if thou hadst suffered the same death. And yet shall no man slay thee, nor fire burn thee, nor water drown thee, nor wind harm thee, for I may not forget how thou art written on My hands and My feet. It likes me well, the pains I have suffered for thee. I shall never be wroth with thee, but I shall love thee without end, though all the world be against thee. Dread thee not, for they have no understanding of thee. I swear to thy mind, that if it were possible for Me to suffer pain again as I have done before, I would rather suffer as much pain as ever I did for thy soul alone, rather than thou shouldst part from Me without end. Therefore, daughter, just as thou see-est the priest take the child at the font-stone and dip it in the water and wash it from original sin, right so shall I wash thee in My Precious Blood from all thy sin. 15b

'And though I withdraw sometimes the feeling of grace from thee, either of speech or of weeping, dread thee not thereof, for I am a hidden God in thee, so that thou shouldst have no vainglory, and that thou shouldst know well thou mayest not have tears or such dalliance, except when God will send them to thee, for they are the free gifts of God without thy merit, and He may give them to whom He will, and do thee no wrong.

'Therefore take them meekly and thankfully, when I send them, and suffer patiently when I withdraw them, and seek busily till thou mayest get them, for tears of compunction, devotion, and compassion are the highest and surest gifts that I give on earth.

'And what should I do more for thee unless I took thy soul out of thy body and put it in Heaven, and that I will not do yet. Nevertheless wherever God is, Heaven is, and God is in thy soul, and many an angel is about thy soul, to keep it both night and day, for when thou go-est to church, I go with thee; when thou sittest at thy meat, I sit with thee; when thou go-est to bed, I go with thee: and when thou go-est out of town, I go with thee.

'Daughter, there was never a child so obedient to the father as I will be to thee, to help thee and keep thee. I fare sometimes with My grace to thee, as I do with the sun. Sometimes thou knowest well that the sun shineth all abroad, that many men may see it, and sometimes it is hid under a cloud, that men may not see it, and yet the sun is there, nevertheless, in his heat and in his brightness. And right so fare I with thee and with my chosen souls.

'Though it be that thou weep not always at thy list, My grace is nevertheless in thee. Therefore I prove that thou art a very daughter to Me, and a mother also, a sister, a wife and a spouse, as witness the Gospel where Our Lord saith unto His disciples:—"He that doth the will of My Father in Heaven is both mother, brother and sister unto Me." When thou studyest to please Me, then thou art a very daughter. When thou weepest and mournest for My pain and My Passion, then art thou a very mother having compassion on her child. When thou weepest for other men's sins and adversities, then art thou a very sister. And when thou sorrowest that thou art so long from the bliss of Heaven, then art thou a very spouse and a wife, for it belongeth to the wife to be with her husband, and to have no very joy till she cometh into his presence.

16a

CHAPTER 22

As this creature lay in contemplation for weeping, in her spirit she said to Our Lord Jesus Christ: —

'Ah! Lord, maidens dance now merrily in Heaven. Shall not I do so? For, because I am no maiden, lack of maidenhood is to me now great sorrow; methinketh I would I had been slain when I was taken from the font-stone, so that I should never have displeased Thee, and then shouldst Thou, blessed Lord, have had my maidenhood without end. Ah! dear God, I have not loved Thee all the days of my life and that sore rueth me; I have run away from Thee, and Thou hast run after me; I would fall into despair, and Thou wouldst not suffer me.'

'Ah! Daughter, how often have I told thee that thy sins are forgiven thee, and that we are united (in love) together without end. Thou art to Me a singular love, daughter, and therefore I promise thee thou shalt have a singular grace in Heaven, daughter, and I promise thee that I shall come to thine end at thy dying with My Blessed Mother, and my holy angels and twelve apostles, Saint Katherine, Saint Margaret, Saint Mary Magdalene and many other saints that are in Heaven, who give great worship to Me for the grace that I give to thee, thy God, thy Lord Jesus. Thou needest dread no grievous pains in thy dying, for thou shalt have thy desire, that is to have more mind of My Passion than of thine own pain. Thou shalt not dread the devil of Hell, for he hath no power in thee. He dreadeth thee more than thou dost him. He is wroth with thee because thou tormentest him more with thy weeping than doth all the fire in Hell; thou winnest many souls from him with thy weeping. And I have promised thee that thou shouldst have no other Purgatory than the slander and speech of the world, for I have chastised thee Myself as I would, by many great dreads and torments that thou hast had with evil spirits, both asleep and awake for many years. And there-

25b

fore I shall preserve thee at thine end through My mercy, so that they shall have no power over thee either in body or in soul. It is a great grace and miracle that thou hast thy bodily wits, for the vexation thou hast had with them aforetime.

'I have also, daughter, chastised thee with the dread of My Godhead, and many times have I terrified thee with great tempests of winds, so that thou thoughtst vengeance would have fallen on thee for sin. I have proved thee by many tribulations, many great griefs, and many grievous sicknesses, insomuch that thou hast been anointed for death, and all, through My grace, hast thou escaped. Therefore dread thee naught, daughter, for with Mine own hands which were nailed to the Cross, I will take thy soul from thy body with great mirth and melody, with sweet smells and good odours, and offer it to My Father in Heaven, where thou shalt see Him face to face, living with Him without end.

'Daughter, thou shalt be right welcome to My Father, and My Mother, and to all My saints in Heaven, for thou hast given them drink full many times with the tears of thine eyes. All My holy saints shall rejoice at thy coming home. Thou shalt be full filled with all manner of love that thou covetest. Then shalt thou bless the time that thou wert wrought, and the Body that thee hath (dearly) bought. He shall have joy in thee and thou in Him without end.

'Daughter, I promise thee the same grace that I promised Saint Katherine, Saint Margaret, Saint Barbara, and Saint Paul, insomuch that what creature on earth unto the Day of Doom asketh thee any boon and believeth that God loveth thee, he shall have his boon or else a better thing. Therefore they that believe that God loveth thee, they shall be blessed without end. The souls in Purgatory shall rejoice in thy coming home, for they know well that God loveth thee specially. And men on earth shall rejoice in God for thee, for He shall work much 26a grace for thee and make all the world to know that God loveth thee. Thou hast been despised for My love and therefore thou shalt be worshipped for My love.

'Daughter, when thou art in Heaven, thou shalt be able to ask what thou wilt, and I shall grant thee all thy desire. I have told thee beforetime that thou art a singular lover, and therefore thou shalt have a singular love in Heaven, a singular reward, and a singular worship. And, forasmuch as thou art a maiden in thy soul, I shall take thee by the one hand in Heaven, and My Mother by the other hand, and so shalt thou dance in Heaven with other holy maidens and virgins, for I may call thee dearly bought, and Mine own dearworthy darling. I shall say to thee, Mine own blessed spouse: — "Welcome to Me with all manner of joy and gladness, here to dwell with Me and never to depart from Me without end, but ever to dwell with Me in joy and bliss, which no eye may see, nor ear hear, nor tongue tell, nor heart think, that I have ordained for thee and all My servants who desire to love and please Me as thou dost." '

APPENDIX

CHAPTER 35

As this creature was in the Apostles' Church in Rome on Saint Lateran's Day, the Father of Heaven said to her: —

42b 'Daughter, I am well pleased with thee, inasmuch as thou believest in all the Sacraments of Holy Church and in all faith that belongeth thereto, and especially because thou believest in the manhood of My Son, and for the great compassion thou hast for His bitter Passion.'

Also the Father said to this creature: — 'Daughter, I will have thee wedded to My Godhead because I shall shew thee My secrets and My counsels, for thou shalt live with Me without end.'

Then the creature kept silence in her soul and answered not thereto, for she was full sore afraid of the Godhead; and she had no knowledge of the dalliance of the Godhead, for all her love and all her affection were set in the manhood of Christ, and there-of she had knowledge, and she would not for anything be parted therefrom.

She had so much affection for the manhood of Christ, that when she saw women in Rome bearing children in their arms, if she could ascertain that any were men-children, she would then cry, roar, and weep as if she had seen Christ in His childhood.

And if she might have had her will, oftentimes she would have taken the children out of their mothers' arms and have kissed them in the stead of Christ.

If she saw a seemly man, she had great pain in looking at him, lest she might have seen Him Who was both God and man.

And therefore she cried many times and often when she saw a seemly man, and wept and sobbed full sore on the manhood of Christ, as she went in the streets of Rome, so that they that saw her wondered full much at her, for they knew not the cause.

Therefore it was no wonder if she was still and answered not the Father of Heaven when He told her that she should be wedded to His Godhead.

Then said the Second Person, Christ Jesus, Whose manhood she loved so much, to her: —

'What sayest thou, Margery, daughter, to My Father of these words He spake to thee? Art thou well pleased that it be so?'

And then she would not answer the Second Person, but wept wondrous sore, desiring to have still Himself and in no wise to be parted from Him. Then the Second Person in the Trinity answered to His Father for her, and said: —

'Father, hold her excused, for she is yet but young, and not fully learned how she should answer.'

43a And then the Father took her by the hand, (ghostly) in her soul, before the Son and the Holy Ghost; and the Mother of Jesus and all the twelve Apostles and Saint Katherine and Saint Margaret and many other saints and holy virgins with a great multitude of angels, saying to her soul: —

'I take thee, Margery, for My wedded wife, for fairer, for fouler, for richer, for poorer, so that thou be kindly and gentle to do as I bid thee. For, daughter, there was never a child so gracious to its mother as I shall be to thee, both in weel and in woe, to help thee and comfort thee. And thereto I make thee surety.'

Then the Mother of God, and all the saints that were present in her soul, prayed that they might have much joy together. And then the creature with high devotion with great plenty of tears, thanked God for His ghostly comfort, holding herself, in her own feeling, right unworthy to any such grace as she felt, for she felt many great comforts, both ghostly comforts and bodily ones. Sometimes she felt sweet smells with her nose. They were sweeter, she thought, than ever was any sweet earthly thing that she smelt before, nor could she ever tell how sweet they were, for she thought she might have lived thereby, if they had lasted.

Sometimes she heard with her bodily ears such sounds and melodies that she could not well hear what a man said to her at that time, unless he spoke the louder. These sounds and melodies had she heard nearly every day for the term of twenty-five years, when this book was written, and especially when she was in devout prayer, and also many times while she was at Rome and in England both.

She saw with her bodily eyes many white things flying all about her on every side, as thick, in a manner, as specks in a sunbeam. They were right subtle and comfortable, and the brighter the sun shone, the better might she see them. She saw them many divers times and in many divers places, both in church and in her chamber, at her meat, and at her prayers, in the fields, and in town, both going and sitting. And many times she was afraid what they might be, for she saw them as well at night in darkness, as in daylight. Then, when she was afraid of them, Our Lord said to her: — 43b

'By this token, daughter, believe that it is God Who speaketh in thee, for, wheresoever God is, Heaven is, and where God is, there be many angels, and God is in thee and thou art in Him. And therefore be not afraid, daughter, for these be tokens that there are many angels about thee, to keep thee both day and night so that no devil shall have power over thee, nor evil men to harm thee.'

Then from that time forward, she used to say, when she saw them coming: — 'Benedictus qui venit in nomine Domini.'

Also Our Lord gave her another token which endured about sixteen years, and it increased ever more and more, and that was a flame of fire, wondrous hot and delectable, and right comfortable, not wasting but ever increasing, of love; for though the weather were never so cold, she felt the heat burning in her breast and at her heart, as verily as a man could feel the material fire if he put his hand or his finger therein.

When she first felt the fire of love burning in her breast, she was afraid thereof, and then Our Lord answered to her mind and said: —

'Daughter, be not afraid, for this heat is the heat of the Holy Ghost, which shall burn away all thy sins; for the fire of love quencheth all sins. And thou shalt understand by this token that the Holy Ghost is in thee, and thou knowest well that wherever the Holy Ghost is, there is the Father, and where the Father is, there is the Son, and so thou hast fully in thy soul all the Holy Trinity. Therefore thou hast great cause to love Me right well; and yet thou shalt have greater cause than ever thou hadst to love Me, for thou shalt hear what thou hast never heard, and see what thou hast never seen, and thou shalt feel what thou hast never felt.

'For daughter, thou art as secure in the love of God, as God is God. Thy soul is more certain of the love of God, than of thine own body, for thy soul shall part from thy body, but God shall never part from thy soul, for they are united together without end. Therefore, daughter, thou hast as great cause to be merry as any lady in this world; and if thou knew, daughter, how much thou pleasest Me when thou sufferest Me wilfully to speak in thee, thou wouldst never do otherwise, for this is a holy life, and the time is right well spent. For daughter, this life pleaseth Me more than the wearing of the haburion or the haircloth, or fasting on bread and water; for, if thou saidst every day a thousand Pater Nosters, thou wouldst not please Me so well as thou dost when thou art in silence and sufferest Me to speak in thy soul.'

44a

CHAPTER 36

'Fasting, daughter, is good for young beginners, and discreet penance, especially as their ghostly father giveth them or enjoineth them to do. And to bid many beads is good for those that can do no better, yet it is not perfect. But it is a good way perfection-ward. For I tell thee, daughter, that they who are great fasters, and great doers of penance, they would that it should be held the best life; also they that are given to saying many devotions, they would have that the best life; and they that give much alms, they would that that were held the best life.

'I have oftentimes told thee, daughter, that thinking, weeping, and high contemplation is the best life on earth, and thou shalt have more merit in Heaven for one year of thinking in thy mind than for a hundred years of praying with thy mouth; and yet thou wilt not believe Me, for thou wilt bid many beads whether I will or not. And yet, daughter, I will not be displeased with thee, whether thou think, say, or speak, for I am always well pleased with thee.

'And if I were on earth as bodily as I was before I died on the Cross, I should not be ashamed of thee, as other men be, for I should take thee by the hand amongst the people, and make thee great cheer, so that they should well know that I loved thee right well.

'For it is fitting for the wife to be homely with her husband. Be he ever so great a lord, and she ever so poor a woman when he weddeth her, yet they must lie together and rest together in joy and peace. Right so must it be between thee and Me, for I take no heed what thou hast been, but what thou wouldst be, and oftentimes have I told thee that I have clean forgiven thee all thy sins. Therefore I must needs be homely with thee, and lie in thy bed with thee.

'Daughter, thou desirest greatly to see Me, and thou mayest boldly, when thou art in thy bed, take Me to thee as thy wedded husband, as thy dearworthy

darling, and as thy sweet son, for I will be loved as a son should be loved by the 44b
mother, and I will that thou lovest Me, daughter, as a good wife ought to love
her husband. Therefore thou mayest boldly take Me in the arms of thy soul and
kiss My mouth, My head, and My feet, as sweetly as thou wilt. And as oftentimes as thou thinkest of Me, or wouldst do any good deed to Me, thou shalt have
the same reward in Heaven, as if thou didst it to Mine own Precious Body which
is in Heaven, for I ask no more of thee but thine heart to love Me, Who loveth
thee, for My love is ever ready for thee.'

Then she gave thanks and praise to Our Lord Jesus Christ for the high grace
and mercy that He shewed unto her, unworthy wretch.

This creature had divers tokens in her bodily hearing. One was a sort of sound
as if it were a pair of bellows blowing in her ear. She, being abashed thereby,
was warned in her soul no fear to have, for it was the sound of the Holy Ghost.
And then Our Lord turned that sound into the voice of a dove, and later on, He
turned it into the voice of a little bird which is called a red-breast, that sang full
merrily oftentimes in her right ear. And then she would ever have great grace
after she heard such a token. She had been used to such tokens for about
twenty-five years, at the time of writing this book.

Then said Our Lord Jesus Christ to His creature:—

'By these tokens mayest thou well know that I love thee, for thou art to Me a
very mother, and to all the world, for that great charity which is in thee; and yet
I am the cause of that charity Myself, and thou shalt have great reward therefor
in Heaven.'

CHAPTER 64

T HE creature said unto her Lord Christ Jesus: — 'Ah! Blissful Lord, I would
I knew where-in I might best love Thee and please Thee, and that my love
were as sweet to Thee, as methinketh, Thy love is unto me.'

Then Our Sweet Lord Jesus Christ, answering His creature, said: —

'Daughter, if thou knew how sweet thy love is unto Me, thou shouldst never
do another thing but love Me with all thy heart. And therefore believe well,
daughter, that My love is not so sweet to thee, as thy love is to Me. Daughter,
thou knowest not how much I love thee, for it may not be known in this world
how much it is, nor be felt as it is, for thou wouldst fail and burst and never
endure it, for the joy thou wouldst feel.

'And therefore I measure it as I will, to thy greatest ease and comfort.

'But daughter, thou shalt well know in another world how much I loved thee 77a
on earth, for there thou shalt have great cause to thank Me. There thou shalt
see without end every good day that ever I gave thee on earth of contemplation,
of devotion and of all the great charity that I have given to thee, to the profit of
thy fellow Christian. For this shall be thy reward when thou comest home into

Heaven. There is no clerk in all this world that can, daughter, teach thee better than I can do, and if thou wilt be obedient to My Will, I shall be obedient to thy will. Where is a better token of love than to weep for Thy Lord's love? Thou knowest well, daughter, that the devil hath no charity, for he is full wroth with thee, and he might out-hurt thee, but he shall not harm thee, save a little, in this world, to make thee afraid sometimes, so that thou shouldst pray the mightier to Me for grace, and guide thy charity the more Me-ward. There is no clerk that can speak against the life that I teach thee; and, if he does, he is not God's clerk: he is the devil's clerk. I tell thee right forsooth, that there is no man in this world, if he would suffer as much despite for My love wilfully as thou hast done, and cleave as sore unto Me, not wishing, for anything that may be done or said against him, to forsake Me, but I shall fare right fair with him, both in this world and in the other.'

Then said the creature: — 'Ah! My dearworthy Lord, this life shouldst Thou show to religious men and priests.'

Our Lord said again to her: — 'Nay, nay, daughter, for that thing that I love best, they love not, and that is shame, despite, scorn and reproof from the people, and therefore shall they not have this grace.

'For daughter, I tell thee, he that dreadeth the shames of the world, may not perfectly love God. And, daughter, under the habit of holiness is hidden much wickedness. Daughter, if thou saw the wickedness that is wrought in the world as I do, thou shouldst have great wonder that I take not utter vengeance on them. But, daughter, I spare for thy love.

'Thou weepest so every day for mercy, so that I must needs grant it thee, and the people will not believe the goodness that I work in thee for them.

77b   'Nevertheless, daughter, there shall come a time when they shall be right fain to believe the grace that I have given thee for them; and I shall say to them, when they have passed out of this world: —

' "Lo! I ordained her to weep for her sins, and ye had her in great despite, but her charity would never cease for you."

'And therefore, daughter, they that are passed out of this world, good souls, shall highly thank Me for the grace and goodness that I have given thee; and they that are wicked shall grutch and have great pain, to suffer the grace that I shew to thee. And therefore I shall chastise them, as it were, for Myself.'

She prayed: — 'Nay, dearworthy Lord Jesus, chastise no creature for me. Thou knowest well, Lord, that I desire no vengeance, but I ask mercy and grace for all men if it be Thy will to grant it. Nevertheless, Lord, rather than they should be parted from Thee without end, chastise them, as Thou wilt Thyself.

'It seemeth, Lord, in my soul, that Thou art full of charity, for Thou sayest Thou wilt not the death of a sinful man. And Thou sayest also, Thou wilt that all men be saved. Then Lord, since Thou wouldst that all men should be saved, I must will the same; and Thou sayest Thyself that I must love my fellow Christian as mine own self. And, Lord, Thou knowest that I have wept and sorrowed many years, because I would be saved; and so must I do for my fellow Christian.'

APPENDIX

CHAPTER 65

Our Lord Jesus Christ said unto the said creature: —

'Daughter, thou shalt well see when thou art in Heaven with Me, that there is no man damned, but that he is well worthy to be damned, and thou shalt hold thyself well pleased with all My works. And, therefore, daughter, thank Me highly for this great charity that I work in thy heart, for it is Myself, Almighty God, that maketh thee to weep every day for thine own sins, for the great compassion that I give thee for My bitter Passion, and for the sorrows that My Mother had here on earth, for the anguish that she suffered, and the tears that she wept. Also, daughter, for the holy martyrs in Heaven; when thou hearest of them, thou givest Me thanks with crying and weeping for the grace that I have shewn to them. And when thou see-est any lepers, thou hast great compassion on them yielding Me thanks and praisings that I am more favourable to thee than I am to them. And also daughter, for the great sorrow that thou hast for all this world, that thou mightst help them as thou wouldst help thyself, both ghostly and bodily; and furthermore, or the sorrows that thou hast for the souls in Purgatory, that thou wouldst so gladly that they were out of their pain, that they might praise Me without end.

'And all this is Mine own goodness that I give to thee, wherefore thou art much bounden to thank Me. And, nevertheless, yet I thank thee for the great love thou hast for Me, and because thou hast such great will and such great desire that all men and women should love Me right well; for, as thou thinkest, all the world, holy and unholy, all of them would have money to live with, as is lawful to them, but all will not busy themselves to love Me, as they do to get themselves temporal goods. Also, daughter, I thank thee because thou thinkest that thou art so long out of My Blessed Presence. Furthermore, I thank thee specially, because thou canst suffer no man to break My commandments, nor to swear by Me, without it being a great pain to thee, and because thou art always ready to reprove them of their swearing for My love. And therefore thou hast suffered many a shrewd word and many a reproof, and thou shalt therefore have many a joy in Heaven.

'Daughter, I sent once Saint Paul unto thee, to strengthen thee and comfort thee, so that thou shouldst boldly speak in My Name from that day forward. And Saint Paul said unto thee that thou hadst suffered much tribulation because of his writings, and he promised thee that thou shouldst have as much grace thereagainst, for his love, as ever thou hadst shame and reproof for his love. He told thee also of many joys of Heaven, and of the great love that I had for thee.

'And, daughter, I have oftentimes said to thee that there is no saint in Heaven, but, if thou wilt speak with him, he is ready to comfort thee and speak with thee in My Name. My angels are ready to offer thy holy thoughts and thy prayers to Me, and the tears of thine eyes; also because thy tears are angels' drink, and are very wine and honey to them.

Therefore, My dearworthy daughter, be not irked of Me on earth, to sit alone

78b by thyself and think of My love, for I am not irked of thee and My merciful eye is ever upon thee.

'Daughter, thou mayest boldly say to Me: — "Jesus est amor meus"; that is to say, "Jesus is my love".

'Therefore, daughter, let Me be all thy love and all the joy of thy heart.

'Daughter, if thou wilt be-think thee well, thou hast right good cause to love Me above all things, for the great gifts I have given thee beforetime. And yet thou hast another great cause to love Me, for thou hast thy will of chastity as if thou wert a widow, thy husband living in good health.

'Daughter, I have drawn the love of thy heart from all men's hearts into My heart. At one time, daughter, thou thoughtest it had been in a manner impossible to be so, and at that time sufferedest thou full great pain in thy heart with fleshly affections. And then couldst thou well cry to Me, saying:—"Lord, for all Thy wounds' smart, draw all the love of my heart into Thy heart."

'Daughter, for all these causes, and many other causes and benefits which I have shewn for thee on this half the sea, and on yon half the sea, thou hast great cause to love Me.'

CHAPTER 66

'Now daughter, I will that thou eat flesh again, as thou wert wont to do, and that thou be obedient and ready to My will and to My bidding, and leave thine own will, and bid thy ghostly fathers that they let thee do after My will; and thou shalt have never the less grace, but so much the more, for thou shalt have the same reward in Heaven as though thou fastest still after thine own will. Daughter, I bade thee first that thou shouldst leave flesh meat and not eat it, and thou hast obeyed My will many years, and abstained after My counsel. Therefore I bid thee that thou resort again to flesh meat.'

The said creature, with reverent dread, said: —

'Ah! Blissful Lord, the people that hath known of my abstinence so many years and see-eth me now returning and eating flesh meat, will have great marvel, and, as I suppose, despise me and scorn me therefor.'

Our Lord said to her again: —

'Thou shalt no heed take of their scorn, but let every man say what he will.'

Then went she to her ghostly fathers and told them what Our Lord had said unto her. When her ghostly fathers knew the will of God, they charged her by 79a virtue of obedience to eat flesh meat as she had done many years before.

Then had she many a scorn and much reproof because she ate flesh again.

Also she had made a vow to fast one day in the week, for the worship of Our Lady, whilst she lived, which vow she kept many years.

Our Lady, appearing to her soul, bade her go to her confessor and say that she would have her discharged of her vow, so that she should be mighty to bear her ghostly labours, for without bodily strength, they might not be endured.

Then her confessor, seeing by the eye of discretion it was expedient to do so, commanded her by virtue of obedience to eat as other creatures did, measurably, where God would that she had her food.

And her grace was not decreased, but rather increased, for she would rather have fasted than have eaten, if it had been the will of God.

Furthermore, Our Lady said to her: —

'Daughter, thou art weak enough from weeping and crying, for both make thee weak and feeble enough. And I can thank thee more for eating thy meat for my love, than for fasting, that thou mayest endure thy perfection of weeping.'

CHAPTER 77

When the said creature had first her wonderful cries and, on a time, was in ghostly dalliance with her Sovereign Lord Christ Jesus, she said: —

'Lord, why wilt Thou give me such crying that people wonder at me therefor? And they say that I am in great peril, for, as they say, I am the cause that many men sin over me; and Thou knowest, Lord, that I would give no man cause or occasion for sin if I could help it, for I had rather, Lord, be in a prison ten fathoms deep, there to cry and weep for my sin, and for all men's sins, and specially   88b for Thy love, all my life time, than I should give the people occasion to sin over me wilfully.

'Lord, the world may not suffer me to do Thy will, or to follow after Thy stirring, and therefore I pray Thee, if it be Thy will, take these cryings from me at the time of sermons, so that I cry not at Thine holy preaching, and let me have them by myself alone, so that I be not put from hearing Thy holy preaching and Thy holy words; for greater pain may I not suffer in this world than being put from hearing Thy holy word. And if I were in prison, my greatest pain would be the loss of Thy holy words and of Thy holy sermons.

'And, Good Lord, if Thou wilt in any case, that I cry, I pray Thee, give it me alone in my chamber, as much as ever Thou wilt, and spare me amongst the people, if it please Thee.'

Our Merciful Lord Jesus, answering to her mind, said: —

'Daughter, pray not therefor; thou shalt not have thy desire in this, though My Mother and all the saints in Heaven pray for thee, for I shall make thee obedient to My will, so that thou shalt cry when I will, and where I will, both loudly and silently; for I tell thee, daughter, thou art Mine and I am thine, and so shalt thou be without end.

'Daughter, thou see-est how the planets are obedient to My will; that sometimes there come great thunder-cracks, and make the people full sore afraid. And some-times, daughter, thou see-est how I send great lightnings that burn churches and houses. Also sometimes thou see-est that I send great winds that blow down steeples, houses, and trees out of the earth and do much harm in many places, and yet may not the wind be seen, but it may well be felt.

'And right so, daughter, I fare with the might of My Godhead; it may not be seen with man's eye and yet it may well be felt in a simple soul where Me-liketh to work grace, as I do in thy soul. And as suddenly as the lightning cometh from Heaven, so suddenly come I into thy soul, and illuminate it with the light of grace and of understanding, and set it all on fire with love, and make the fire of love to burn there-in, and purge it full clean from all earthly filth. And some-times, daughter, I make earthquakes to frighten the people, so that they should dread Me.

'And so, daughter, ghostly have I done with thee, and with other chosen souls that shall be saved, for I turn the earth of their hearts upside down and make them sore afraid, so that they dread vengeance should fall on them for their sins.

'And so didst thou, daughter, when thou turnedst first to Me, and it is needful that young beginners do so; but now, daughter, thou hast great cause to love Me well, for the perfect charity that I give thee putteth away all dread from thee. And, though other men set little by thee, I set but the more praise by thee.

'As sure as thou art of the sun, when thou see-est it shining brightly, right so sure art thou of the love of God at all times.

'Also, daughter, thou knowest well that I send sometimes many great rains and sharp showers, and sometimes but small and soft drops. And right so I fare with thee, daughter, when it pleaseth Me to speak in thy soul. I give thee sometimes small weepings and soft tears, for a token that I love thee, and sometimes I give thee great cries and roarings, to make the people afraid with the grace that I put into thee, in token that I will that My Mother's sorrow be known by thee, that men and women might have the more compassion for her sorrow that she suffered for Me.

'And the third token is this, daughter, that whatever creatures will have as much sorrow for My Passion as thou hast done many a time, and will cease from their sins, then they shall have the bliss of Heaven without end.

'The fourth token is this; that any creature on earth, though he be ever so horrible a sinner, he need never fall into despair if he will take example of thy living and work somewhat there-after, as he may do.

'Also, daughter, the fifth token is; that I will that thou knowest in thyself, by the great pain that thou feelest in thy heart when thou criest so sore for My love, that it shall be the cause why thou shalt no pain feel when thou art come out of this world, and also that thou shalt have the less pain in thy dying. As thou hast such great compassion for My flesh, I must needs have compassion on thy flesh.

'And therefore, daughter, suffer the people to say what they will of thy crying, for thou art no cause of their sin. Daughter, the people sinned over Me, yet was I no cause of their sin.'

360

Then she said: — 'Ah! Lord, blessed may Thou be, for methinketh, Thou dost Thyself all that Thou biddest me do. In Holy Writ, Lord, Thou biddest me love mine enemies, and I wot well that, in all this world, there was never so great an enemy to me, as I have been to Thee. Therefore, Lord, though I were slain a hundred times a day, if it were possible, for Thy love, yet could I never yield Thee the goodness that Thou hast shewn to me.'

89b

Then answered Our Lord to her and said: —

'I pray thee, daughter, give Me nothing but love. Thou mayest never please Me better than to have Me ever in thy love, nor shalt thou ever, in any penance that thou mayest do on earth, please Me so much as by loving Me. And, daughter, if thou wilt be high in Heaven with Me, keep Me always in thy mind as much as thou mayest, and forget Me not at thy meat, but think always that I sit in thy heart and know every thought that is there-in, both good and ill, and that I perceive the least thinking and twinkling of thine eye. '

She said again to Our Lord: —

'Now truly, Lord, I would I could love Thee as much as Thou mightest make me love Thee. If it were possible, I would love Thee as well as all the saints in Heaven love Thee, and as well as all the creatures on earth might love Thee.

'And I would, Lord, for Thy love, be laid naked on a hurdle, all men to wonder on me for Thy love — so that it were no peril to their souls — and they to cast mud and mire on me, and to be drawn from town to town every day of my lifetime, if Thou wert pleased there-by, and no man's soul hindered. Thy will must be fulfilled and not mine.'

CHAPTER 84

.　　　　.　　　　.　　　　.　　　　.

Then Our Lord made a manner of thanking her forasmuch as she, in contemplation and in meditation, had been His Mother's maiden, and helped to keep Him in His childhood and so forth unto the time of His death, and said to her: —

'Daughter, thou shalt have as great meed and as great reward with Me in Heaven for thy good service, and the good deeds that thou hast done in thy mind and meditation, as if thou hadst done those same deeds with thy bodily senses outwardly. And also, daughter, when thou dost any service to thyself and to thy husband in meat or drink or any other thing that is needful to you, to thy ghostly fathers, or to any other that thou receivest in My Name, thou shalt have the same reward in Heaven as if thou didst it to Mine Own Person or to My Blessed Mother, and I shall thank thee therefor.

'Daughter, thou sayest that it is to Me a good name to be called "All Good" and thou shalt find that name is all good to thee. And daughter, thou sayest that it is well worthy that I be called "All Love", and thou shalt find that I am all love to thee, for I know every thought of thy heart.

'And I know well, daughter, that thou hast many times thought, if thou hadst many churches full of nobles, thou wouldst have given them away in My Name.

'And also thou hast thought that thou wouldst, if thou hadst had money enough, have made many abbeys, for My love, for religious men and women to dwell in, and given each of them a hundred pounds a year to be My servants.

99a 'And thou hast also, in thy mind, desired to have many priests in the town of Lynne, who might sing and read, night and day, to serve Me, worship Me, and praise and thank Me for the goodness that I have done to thee on earth.

'And therefore, daughter, I promised thee, thou shalt have the same meed and reward in Heaven for this goodwill and these good desires, as if thou hadst done them in deed. Daughter, I know all the thoughts of thy heart that thou hast to all manner of men and women, to all lepers, to all prisoners, and how much money thou wouldst give them a year, to serve Me with. I take it as if it were done in deed.

'And, daughter, I thank thee for all the charity that thou hast to all lecherous men and women, for thou prayest for them and weepest many a tear for them, desiring that I should deliver them out of sin, and be as gracious to them as I was to Mary Magdalene, and that they might have as great love to Me as Mary Magdalene had. And, with this condition, thou wouldst that every one of them should have twenty pounds a year to love Me and praise Me.

'And, daughter, this great charity, that thou hast in thy prayer for them, pleaseth Me right well; and also, daughter, I thank thee for the charity that thou hast in thy prayer.

'When thou prayest for all Jews and Saracens and all heathen people, that they should come to the Christian Faith, that My Name might be magnified in them, and for the holy tears and weepings that thou hast wept for them, praying and desiring that, if any prayer might bring them to grace or to Christendom, I should hear thy prayer for them, if it were My will.

'Furthermore, daughter, I thank thee for the general charity that thou hast to all the people that are now in this world alive, and to all those that are to come, unto this world's end, and because thou wouldst be hacked as small as flesh for the pot for their love, if I would, by thy death, save them all from damnation if it pleased Me. For thou sayest often in thy thought that there are enough in Hell, and thou wouldst that no more men should ever deserve to come there-in.

'And therefore, daughter, for all these good wishes and desires, thou shalt have full high meed and reward in Heaven. Believe it right well, and doubt it never a deal, for all these graces are My graces, and I work them in thee Myself, so that
99b thou shouldst have the more reward in Heaven. And I tell thee truly, daughter, every good thought and every good desire that thou hast in thy soul is the speech of God, even if it be that thou hearest Me not speaking to thee sometimes, as I do sometimes to thy clear understanding.

'And therefore, daughter, I am as a hidden God in thy soul, and I withdraw sometimes thy tears and thy devotion, so that thou shouldst think in thyself that thou hast no goodness of thyself, but all goodness cometh from Me; and also thou shouldst verily know what pain it is to do without Me, and what sweetness it is to feel Me, so that thou shouldst be the more busy to seek Me again; also daughter, so that thou shouldst know what pain other men have, who would feel Me, and may not. For there is many a man on earth who, if he had but one day in all his lifetime such as thou hast many days, he would ever love Me the better, and thank Me for that one day. And thou mayest not, daughter, do without Me one day without great pain. Therefore, daughter, thou hast great cause to love Me right well, for it is for no wrath, daughter, that I withdraw sometimes from thee the feeling of grace and the fervour of devotion, but so that thou shouldst know right well that thou mayest be no hypocrite for any weeping, for any crying, for any sweetness, for any devotion, for any remembrance of My Passion, or for any other ghostly grace that I give or send to thee.

'For these are not the devil's gifts, but they are My graces and My gifts; and these are Mine Own special gifts that I give to Mine Own chosen souls, whom I knew, from the beginning, should come to grace and dwell with Me without end.

'For in all other things, thou mayest be a hypocrite if thou wilt, that is to say, in understanding, in many beads bidding, in great fasting, in great penance-doing outwardly, so that men may see it, or in great alms deeds-doing with thy hands, or in good words-speaking with thy mouth. In all these, daughter, thou mayest be a hypocrite if thou wilt, and thou mayest also do them well and holily if thou wilt thyself.

'Lo, daughter, I have given thee such a love so that thou shalt no hypocrite be there-in. And daughter, thou shalt never lose time while thou art occupied there-in, for whosoever thinketh well, he may not sin for the time. And the devil knoweth not the holy thoughts that I give thee, nor any man on earth knoweth how well and holily thou art occupied with Me, nor even thyself can tell the great grace and goodness that thou feelest in Me. 100a

'And therefore, daughter, thou beguilest both the devil and the world with thy holy thoughts, and it is right great folly for the people of the world to judge thy heart, which no man may know, but God alone.

'And therefore, daughter, I tell thee truly that thou hast as great cause to rejoice and be merry in thy soul, as any lady or maiden in this world. My love is so much to thee, that I may not withdraw it from thee, for, daughter, no heart may think, nor tongue tell the great love that I have for thee, and to that I take witness of My Blessed Mother, of My holy angels, and of all the saints in Heaven, for they all worship Me, for thy love in Heaven.

'And so shall I be worshipped on earth for thy love, daughter, for I will have the grace that I have shewn to thee on earth, known to the world, so that people may wonder at My goodness and marvel at My great goodness that I have shewn to thee who hast been sinful, and because I have been so gracious and merciful to thee.

'They that are in the world shall not despair, be they ever so sinful, for they may have mercy and grace if they will, themselves.'

CHAPTER 86

O N a time, Our Lord spoke to the said creature, when it pleased Him, saying to her ghostly understanding: —

'Daughter, for as many times as thou hast received the Blessed Sacrament of the Altar with many holy thoughts, more than thou canst repeat, for so many times shalt thou be rewarded in Heaven with new joys and new comforts. And daughter, in Heaven shall it be known to thee how many days thou hast had of high contemplation, through My gift, on earth, and although it be so, that they are My gifts and My graces that I have given thee, yet shalt thou have the same grace and reward in Heaven, as if they were of thine own merits, for freely have I given them unto thee.

'But highly I thank thee, daughter, that thou hast suffered Me to work My will in thee, and that thou wouldst let Me be so homely with thee; for in anything, daughter, that thou mightst do on earth, thou mightst no better please Me than to suffer Me to speak in thy soul, for then thou understandest My will, and I understand thy will.

'And also, daughter, thou callest My Mother to come into thy soul, and take Me in her arms, and lay Me to her breasts and give Me suck.

'Also, daughter, I know the holy thoughts and the good desires that thou hast when thou receivest Me, and the good charity that thou hast to Me, at the time that thou receivest My Precious Body into thy soul; and also, how thou callest Mary Magdalene into thy soul to welcome Me, for daughter, I know well enough what thou thinkest. Thou thinkest that she is the worthiest, in thy soul, and thou trustest most to her prayers, next to My Mother, and so thou mayest, right well, daughter, for she is a right great mediator to Me for thee in the bliss of Heaven. And sometimes, daughter, thou thinkest thy soul so large and so wide that thou callest all the Court of Heaven into thy soul to welcome Me. I know right well, daughter, what thou sayest: — "Come all ye twelve Apostles that were so well beloved of God on earth, and receive your Lord in my soul."

'Also thou prayest Katherine, Margaret and all holy virgins to welcome Me in thy soul. And then thou prayest My Blessed Mother, Mary Magdalene, all apostles, martyrs, confessors, Katherine, Margaret, and all holy virgins, so that they should array the chamber of thy soul with many fair flowers, and with many sweet spices, that I may rest there-in. Furthermore, thou thinkest sometimes, daughter, as though thou hadst a cushion of gold, another of red velvet, a third of white silk in thy soul. And thou thinkest that My Father sitteth on the cushion of gold, for to Him is appropriated might and power. And thou thinkest that I, the Second Person, thy love and thy joy, sit on the red cushion of velvet, for on Me is all thy thought, because I bought thee so dearly, and thou thinkest that thou canst never requite Me the love that I have shewn thee, though thou wert slain a thousand times a day, if it were possible, for My love.

'Thus thou thinkest, daughter, in thy soul, that I am worthy to sit on a red cushion, in remembrance of the red blood that I shed for thee.

'Moreover, thou thinkest that the Holy Ghost sitteth on a white cushion, for thou thinkest that He is full of love and purity, and therefore it beseemeth Him to sit on a white cushion, for He is the giver of all holy thoughts and chastity.

'And yet I wot well enough, daughter, that thou thinkest thou mayest not worship the Father, unless thou worship the Son, and that thou mayest not worship the Son unless thou worship the Holy Ghost. And also thou thinkest sometimes, daughter, that the Father is Almighty and All-knowing, and all grace and goodness. And thou thinkest the same of the Son, that He is Almighty and All-knowing and all grace and goodness. And thou thinkest that the Holy Ghost hath the same properties, equal with the Father and the Son, proceeding from 102b Them both.

Also thou thinkest that each of the Three Persons in the Trinity hath what the other hath, in Their Godhead; and so thou believest verily, daughter, in thy soul that there be three divers Persons and one God in substance, and that each knoweth what the others knoweth, and each may do what the others may do, and each wills what the others will. And, daughter, this is a very faith and a right faith, and this faith hast thou only of My gift.

'And therefore, daughter, if thou wilt bethink thee well, thou hast great cause to love Me right well, and to give Me all wholly thy heart, that I may fully rest there-in, as I will Myself. For, if thou sufferest Me, daughter, to rest in thy soul on earth, believe it right well that thou shalt rest with Me in Heaven without end.

'And therefore, daughter, have thou no wonder, though thou weep sore when thou art houselled, and receivest My Blessed Body in the form of bread, for thou prayest to Me before ever thou art houselled, saying to Me in thy mind: —

' "As truly, Lord, as Thou lovest me, make me clean from all sin, and give me grace to receive Thy Precious Body worthily, with all manner of worship and reverence."

'And, daughter, wot thee well, I hear thy prayer, for a better word mayest thou not say to My liking than "As truly as I love Thee", for then I fulfil My grace in thee, and give thee many a holy thought. It is impossible to tell thee them all.

'And by the great homeliness that I shew to thee at that time, thou art much the bolder to ask Me grace for thyself, for thy husband, and for thy children, and thou makest every Christian man and woman thy child in thy soul for the time, and wouldst have as much grace for them, as for thine own children.

'Also thou askest mercy for thy husband, and thou thinkest that thou art beholden to Me, that I have given thee such a man as would suffer thee to live chaste, he being in life and in good health of body. Forsooth, daughter, thou thinkest full true, and therefore hast thou great cause to love Me right well.

'Daughter, if thou knewest how many wives there are in this world, that would love Me and serve Me right well and duly, if they might be as free from their husbands as thou art from thine, thou wouldst see that thou wert right much 103a beholden unto Me. And yet are they put from their will and suffer full great pain, and therefore shall they have right great reward in Heaven, for I receive every good will as for deed.

'Sometimes, daughter, I make thee to have great sorrow for thy ghostly father's sins especially, so that he should have as full forgiveness of his sins as thou wouldst have of thine. And sometimes, when thou receivest the Precious Sacrament, I make thee to pray for thy ghostly father in this wise — that as many men and women might be turned by his preaching, as thou wouldst were turned by the tears of thine eyes, and that My holy words might settle as sore in their hearts, as thou wouldst they should settle in thy heart.

'And also, thou askest the same grace for all good men that preach My word on earth, that they might profit all reasonable creatures.

'And oftentimes, on that day that thou receivest My Precious Body, thou askest grace and mercy for all thy friends, and for all thine enemies that ever did thee shame or reproof, either scorned thee or japed thee for the grace that I work in thee; and for all this world, both young and old, with many tears, sore weeping, and sobbing, thou hast suffered much shame and much reproof, and therefore shalt thou have full much bliss in Heaven.

'Daughter, be not ashamed to receive My grace when I will give it thee, for I shall not be ashamed of thee, so that thou shalt be received into the bliss of Heaven, there to be rewarded for every good thought, for every good word, for every good deed, and for every day of contemplation, and for all good desires that thou hast had here in this world, with Me everlastingly as My dearworthy darling, as My blessed spouse and as My holy wife.

'Therefore, dread thee not, daughter, though people wonder why thou weepest so sore when thou receivest Me, for, if they knew what grace I put into thee at that time, they would rather wonder that thy heart burst not asunder. And so it would be, if I measured not that grace Myself; but thou see-est well, daughter, thyself, that when thou hast received Me into thy soul, thou art in peace and in quiet, and sobbest no longer.

103b 'And thereof the people hath great wonder, but there need be no wonder in thee, for thou knowest well that I fare like a husband who should wed a wife. At the time he wedded her, he thinketh that he is secure enough of her, and that no man shall part them asunder, for then, daughter, may they go to bed together without any shame or dread of the people, and sleep in rest and peace, if they will.

'And thus, daughter, it fareth betwixt thee and Me, for thou hast every week, especially on the Sunday, great fear and dread in thy soul, how thou mayest best be sure of My love, and with great reverence and holy dread how thou mayest best receive Me to the salvation of thy soul with all manner of meekness, lowliness, and charity, as any lady in this world is busy to receive her husband, when he cometh home and hath been long from her.

'My dearworthy daughter, I thank thee highly for all men that thou hast kept, when sick, in My Name, and for all the kindness and service that thou hast done to them in any degree, for thou shalt have the same reward with Me in Heaven, as though thou hadst kept Mine Own Self, while I was here on earth.

'Also daughter, I thank thee for as many times as thou hast bathed Me, in thy soul, at home in thy chamber, as if I had been there present in My manhood, for I know well, daughter, all the holy thoughts that thou hast shewn to Me in thy mind.

'And also, daughter, I thank thee for all the times that thou hast harboured Me and My blessed Mother in thy bed.

'For these, and for all other good thoughts and good deeds that thou hast thought in My Name, and wrought for My love, thou shalt have, with Me and with My Mother, with My holy angels, with Mine apostles, with My martyrs, confessors and virgins, and with all My holy saints, all manner of joy and bliss, lasting without end.'

CHAPTER 87

THE said creature lay full still in the church, hearing and understanding this sweet dalliance in her soul as clearly as one friend would speak to another. And when she heard the great promises that Our Lord Jesus Christ made to her, then she thanked Him with great weepings and sobbings, and with many holy and reverent thoughts saying in her mind:— 104a

'Lord Jesus, blessed may Thou be, for this deserved I never of Thee, but I would I were in that place where I should never displease Thee from this time forward.'

With such manner of thoughts, and many more than I could ever write, she worshipped and magnified Our Lord Jesus Christ for His holy visitation and His comfort.

And in such manner of visitations and holy contemplations as are before written, much more subtle and more high without comparison than be written, the said creature had continued her life, through the preserving of Our Lord Christ Jesus, more than twenty-five years, when this treatise was written, week by week, and day by day, unless she were occupied with sick folk, or else were prevented by other needful occupations as were necessary unto her, or to her fellow Christians. Then it was withdrawn sometimes, for it can be had but in great quiet of soul through long exercise.

By this manner of speech and dalliance, she was made mighty and strong in the love of Our Lord, and greatly stabilized in her faith and increased in meekness and charity with other good virtues. And she firmly and steadfastly believed that it was God that spake in her soul, and no evil spirit, for in His speech she had most strength and most comfort and the most increase of virtue, blessed be God.

Divers times, when the creature was so sick that she expected to die, and other folk thought the same, it was answered in her soul that she would not die, but she would live and fare well. And so she did.

Sometimes Our Lady spake to her and comforted her in her sickness. Sometimes Saint Peter, or Saint Paul, sometimes Saint Mary Magdalene, Saint Katherine, Saint Margaret or whatever saint in Heaven that she could think of, through the will and sufferance of God. They spoke to the understanding of her

104b soul, and informed her how she should love God, and how she should best please Him, and answered to what she would ask of them, and she could understand by their manner of dalliance which of them it was that spake unto her and comforted her.

Our Lord of His high mercy visited her so much and so plenteously with His holy speeches and His holy dalliance, that she knew not, many times, how the day went. She supposed, for a time of five hours or six, that it had not been the space of one hour. It was so sweet and so devout that it fared as if she had been in a heaven. She thought never long there-of, nor was she ever irked there-of. The time went away, she knew not how. She would rather have served God, if she might have lived so long, a hundred years in this manner of life, than one day as she began first.

And oftentimes she said to Our Lord Jesus: — 'Ah! Lord Jesus, since it is so sweet to weep for Thy love on earth, I wot well it shall be right joyful to be with Thee in Heaven. Therefore, Lord, I pray Thee, let me never have other joy on earth but mourning and weeping for Thy love. For methinketh, Lord, though I were in Hell, if I might weep there and mourn for Thy love as I do here, Hell would not annoy me, but it would be a manner of Heaven, for Thy love putteth away all manner of dread of our ghostly enemy, for I had rather be there, as long as Thou wouldst, and please Thee, than be in this world and displease Thee.

'Therefore, Lord, as Thou wilt, so may it be.'

CHAPTER 88

WHEN this book was first in writing, the said creature was more at home in her chamber with her writer, and said fewer beads for speed of writing than she had done years before. And when she came to church and would hear Mass, purposing to say her Matins and such other devotions as she had used afore-time, her heart was drawn away from the saying and set much on meditation.

She being afraid of the displeasure of Our Lord, He said unto her soul: —

'Dread thee not, daughter; as many beads as thou wouldst say, I accept them as though thou saidest them, and thy study that thou studiest to have written by the grace I have shewed to thee, pleaseth Me right much, and he that writeth also. For, though ye were in the church and wept both together as well as ever thou didst, yet would ye not please Me more than ye do with your writing, for, **105a** daughter, by this book, many a man shall be turned to Me and believe there-in.

'Daughter, where is a better prayer by thine own reason, than to pray to Me with thy heart or thy thought. Daughter, when thou prayest by thought, thou understandest thyself what thou asketh of Me, but thou understandest also what I say to thee, and thou understandest what I promised thee, to thee and to thine and to all thy ghostly fathers.

'And, as for Master Robert, thy confessor, I have granted thee what thou hast desired, that he should have half thy tears and half the good works that I have wrought in thee. Therefore he shall truly be rewarded for thy weeping, as though he had wept himself.

'And believe well, daughter, that ye shall be full merry in Heaven together at the last, and shall bless the time that ever one of you knew the other.

'And daughter, thou shalt bless Me without end that ever I gave thee so true a ghostly father, for, though he hath been sharp to thee sometimes, it hath been greatly to thy profit, for thou wouldst else have had too great affection to his person. And, when he was sharp to thee, then thou ran with all thy mind to Me saying: — "Lord, there is no trust but in thee alone." And thou criedest to Me with all thy heart: — "Lord, for Thy wounds' smart, draw all my love into Thine heart."

'And, daughter, so have I done. Thou thinkest oftentimes that I have done right much for thee, and thou thinkest that it is a great miracle that I have drawn all thine affection to Myself, for sometimes thou wert so affected to some particular person, that thou thoughtest, that time, it had been in a manner impossible to have withdrawn thine affection from him. And later, thou hast desired, if it had pleased Me, that the same person should have forsaken thee for My love, for, if he had not supported thee, few men would have set any price by thee, as it seemed. And thou thoughtst, if he had have forsaken thee, it had been the greatest reproof that ever came to thee, as opposed to the people; and therefore, thou wouldst have suffered that reproof with good will, if it had pleased Me.

'And thus, with such doleful thoughts thou increased thy love Me-ward, and therefore, daughter, I receive thy desires as if they were done in deed. And I know right well that thou hast true love to that same person, and I have often said to thee that he should be right fain to love thee, and he should believe that it is God that speaketh in thee, and no devil. Also, daughter, that person hath pleased Me right well, for he hath often in his sermons excused thy weeping and thy crying, and so hath Master Aleyn done also, and therefore they shall have full great reward in Heaven, daughter. I have told thee many times that I should uphold thy weeping and thy crying by sermons and preaching. 105b

'Also, daughter, I tell thee that Master Robert, thy ghostly father, pleaseth Me full much when he biddeth thee believe that I love thee, and I know well that thou hast great faith in his words, and so thou mayest, right well, for he will not flatter thee; and also daughter, I am highly pleased with him, for he biddeth thee that thou shouldst sit still and give thy heart to meditation and think such holy thoughts as God will put into thy mind.

'And oftentimes I have bidden thee so Myself, and yet thou wilt not do thereafter but with much grutching; and yet am I not displeased with thee, for, daughter, I have often said unto thee that, whether thou prayest with thy mouth, or thinkest with thy heart, whether thou readest or hearest reading, I will be pleased with thee. And yet, daughter, I tell thee, if thou wouldst believe Me, that thinking is the best for thee and most shall increase thy love to Me; and the more homely that thou sufferest Me to be in thy soul on earth, it is worthy and rightful that I be the more homely with thy soul in Heaven.

'And therefore, daughter, if thou wilt not do after My counsel, do after the counsel of thy ghostly father, for he biddeth thee do the same as I bid thee do.

'Daughter, when thy ghostly father sayeth to thee, that thou displeasest God, thou believest him right well, and then takest thou much sorrow and great grief, and weepest full fast till thou hast gotten grace again. And then I came oftentimes to thee Myself and comfort thee, for, daughter, I may not suffer thee to have pain any while, but I must give remedy. And therefore, daughter, I come to thee, and make thee sure of My love, and tell thee with Mine own mouth that thou art as sure of My love as God is God and that nothing is so secure to thee on earth that thou mayest see with thy bodily eye. And therefore, blessed daughter, love him that loveth thee and forget Me not, daughter, for I forget 106a not thee, for My merciful eye is ever upon thee. And that knew My merciful Mother full well, daughter, for she hath oftentimes told thee so, and many other saints also.

'And therefore, daughter, thou hast great cause to love Me right well, and to give Me all thy whole heart with all thine affections, for that I desire, and nothing else, of thee; and I shall give thee there-again all My heart. And if thou wilt be obedient to My will, I shall be obedient to thy will, daughter. Believe it right well.'

HER METHOD OF PRAYER

120b THIS creature, of whom is treated before, used, for many years, to begin her prayers in this manner:—

First, when she came to church, kneeling before the Sacrament, in the worship of the Blessed Trinity (Father, Son, and Holy Ghost, One God and Three Persons), of that Glorious Queen of Mercy Our Lady, Saint Mary, and of the twelve Apostles, she said this holy hymn, 'Veni Creator Spiritus', with all the verses belonging thereto, that God should illuminate her soul, as He did His Apostles on Pentecost Day, and indue her with the gifts of the Holy Ghost, that she might have grace to understand His will, and perform it in working, and that she might have grace to withstand the temptations of her ghostly enemies, and eschew all manner of sin and wickedness.

When she had said 'Veni Creator Spiritus', with the verses, she said on in this manner: — 'The Holy Ghost I take to witness, Our Lady, Saint Mary, the Mother of God, all the holy Court of Heaven, and all my ghostly fathers here on earth, that, though it were possible that I might have knowledge and understanding of the secrets of God by the telling of any devil in hell, I would not.

'And as surely, as I would not know, here, see, feel or understand in my soul in this life, more than is the will of God that I should know, so surely God may

370

help me in all my works, in all my thoughts and in all my speech, eating and drinking, sleeping and waking.

'As surely as it is not my will nor my intent to worship any false devil for my God, nor any false faith, nor to have any false belief, so surely I defy the devil and all his false counsel, and all that I have ever done, said, or thought after the counsel of the devil thinking it had been the counsel of God and the inspiration of the Holy Ghost.

'If it hath not been so, God, Who hath insight and knowledge of the secrets of all men's hearts, have mercy on me therefor, and grant me in this life, a well of tears springing plenteously, with which I may wash away my sins through Thy mercy and Thy goodness.

'And, Lord, for Thy high mercy, all the tears that may increase my love, and 121a make more my merit in Heaven, and help and profit my fellow Christian souls, alive or dead, visit me with, here on earth.

'Good Lord, spare no more the eyes in my head than Thou didst the blood in Thy Body which Thou sheddest plenteously for sinful men's souls, and grant me so much pain and sorrow in this world that I be not delayed from Thy bliss, and the beholding of Thy glorious Face when I shall pass hence.

'As for my crying, my sobbing, and my weeping, Lord God Almighty, as surely as Thou knowest what scorn, what shame, what despite, and what reproof I have had therefor, and, as surely as it is not in my power to weep either aloud or in quiet, for any devotion or for any sweetness, but only by the gift of the Holy Ghost, so surely, Lord, excuse me against all this world to know and trow that it is Thy work and Thy gift for magnifying Thy Name and for increasing other men's love to Thee, Jesus.

'And I pray Thee, Sovereign Lord Christ Jesus, that as many men may be turned by my crying and my weeping, as have scorned me therefor, or shall scorn me to the world's end. And many more if it be Your will. And in respect of any earthly man's love, as surely as I would have no love but God, to love above all things and all other creatures, love for God and in God, so surely quench in me all fleshly lust, and in all those that I have beheld Thy Blissful Body in. And give us Thy holy dread in our hearts, for thy Wounds' smart.

'Lord, make my ghostly fathers to dread Thee in me, and to love Thee in me, and make all the world to have more sorrow for their own sins, for the sorrow Thou hast given me for other men's sins. Good Jesus, make my will Thy will, and Thy will, my will, so that I may have no will but Thy will only.

'Now, good Lord Christ Jesus, I cry You mercy for all states that be in Holy Church, for the Pope and all his cardinals, for all archbishops and bishops, and for all the order of priesthood, for all men and women of religion, and especially 121b for them that are busy to save and defend the Faith of Holy Church. Lord, for Thy mercy, bless them and grant them the victory over all their enemies, and speed them in all that they go about in Thy worship; for all that are in grace, at this time, God send them perseverance unto their lives' end, and make me worthy to be partaker of their prayers, and them of mine, and each of us of others.

'I cry Thee mercy, Blissful Lord, for the King of England and for all Christian kings, and for all lords and ladies that are in this world. God set them in such behaviour that they may most please Thee, and be lords and ladies in Heaven without end.

'I cry Thee mercy, Lord, for the rich men in this world, who have Thy goods in possession; give them grace to spend them to Thy pleasing.

'I cry Thee mercy, Lord, for Jews and Saracens and all heathen people.

'Good Lord, have mind that there is many a saint in Heaven, who sometime was heathen on earth, and so Thou hast spread Thy mercy to them that are on earth.

'Lord, Thou sayest Thyself that no man shall come to Thee without Thee nor any man be drawn unless Thou drawest him. And therefore, Lord, if there be any man undrawn, I pray Thee, draw him after Thee.

'Me Thou hast drawn, Lord, and I deserved never to have been drawn, but after Thy great mercy, Thou hast drawn me. If all this world knew all my wickedness as Thou dost, they would marvel and wonder at the great goodness that Thou hast shewn me. I would that all this world were worthy to thank Thee for me, and as Thou hast made of unworthy creatures, worthy ones, so make all this world worthy to thank Thee and praise Thee.

'I cry Thee mercy, Lord, for all false heretics, and for all mis-believers, for all false tithepayers, thieves, adulterers, and all common women, and for all mischievous livers. Lord, for Thy mercy, have mercy upon them, if it be Thy will, and bring them out of their misbehaviour the sooner for my prayers.

'I cry thee mercy, Lord, for all those that are tempted and vexed by their ghostly enemies, that Thou, of Thy mercy, will give them grace to withstand their temptations, and deliver them there-of, when it most pleaseth Thee.

'I cry Thee mercy, Lord, for all my ghostly fathers, that Thou vouchsafe to spread as much grace in their souls as I would that Thou didst in mine.

'I cry Thee mercy, Lord, for all my children, ghostly and bodily, and for all the people in this world, that Thou make their sins to me by true contrition, as it were my own sins, and forgive them as I would that Thou forgive me.

'I cry Thee mercy, Lord, for all my friends and all mine enemies, for all that are sick, especially for all lepers, for all bedridden men and women, for all that are in prison, and for all creatures that, in this world, have spoken of me either good or ill, or shall do so unto the world's end.

'Have mercy upon them, and be as gracious to their souls as I would that Thou wert to mine.

'And they that have said an evil of me, for Thy mercy, forgive it them; and they that have said well, I pray Thee, Lord, reward them, for that is through their charity and not through my merits, for, though Thou sufferedest all this world to avenge Thee on me and to hate me, because I have displeased Thee, Thou didst me no wrong.

'I cry Thee mercy, Lord, for all the souls that are in the pains of Purgatory, there abiding Thy mercy and the prayers of Holy Church as surely, Lord, as they are Thine own chosen souls. Be as gracious to them as I would Thou wert to mine if it were in the same pain as they are in.

'Lord Christ Jesus, I thank Thee for all health and all wealth, for all riches and all poverty, for sickness and all scorns, for all spites and all wrongs and for all divers tribulations that have fallen or shall fall to me as long as I live. Highly I thank Thee if Thou wouldst let me suffer any pain in this world in remission of my sins and increase of my merit in Heaven.

'As surely as I have great cause to thank Thee, hear my prayers, for though I had as many hearts and souls enclosed in my soul as God knew from the beginning how many should dwell in Heaven without end, and as there are drops of water, fresh and salt, chips of gravel, stones small and great, grasses growing in all the 122b earth, kernels of corn, fishes, fowls, beasts, and leaves on trees, when most plenty is, feather of fowl, or hair of man or beast, seeds that grow in the earth, or in weeds, in flowers, in land or in water when most grow, and as many creatures as on earth have been and are, or shall be, or might be by Thy might, and as there are stars and angels in Thy sight, or other kinds of things that groweth upon earth, and each were a soul as holy as ever was Our Lady Saint Mary who bore Jesus Our Saviour, and if it were possible that each could think or speak as great a reverence and worship as ever did Our Lady Saint Mary here on earth, and now doth in Heaven and shall do without end, I may right well think in my heart and speak it with my mouth at this time in worship of the Trinity and of all the Court of Heaven, to the great shame and disgrace of Satan who fell from God's face, and of all his wicked spirits, so that all these hearts and souls could never thank God nor fully praise Him, fully bless Him, or fully worship Him, fully love Him, or fully give laudation praise and reverence to Him as He were worthy to have, for the great mercy that He hath shewn to me on earth. That I cannot do nor may do.

'I pray my Lady, who is the only Mother of God, the well of grace, flower and fairest of all women that ever God wrought on earth, the most worthy in His sight, the most beloved, dear and dearworthy unto Him, bestworthy to be heard of God and the highest that hath deserved it in this life, benign Lady, meek Lady, charitable Lady, with all the reverence that is in Heaven, and with all your holy saints, I pray you, Lady, offer ye thanks and praise to the Blissful Trinity for love of me, asking mercy and grace for me and for all my ghostly fathers, and perseverance unto our lives' ends in that life we may most please God in.

'I bless my God in my soul and all you that are in Heaven.

'Blessed may God be in you all, and ye all in God.

'Blessed be Thou, Lord, for all Thy mercies that Thou hast shewn to all that are in Heaven and on earth.

'And especially I bless Thee, Lord, for Mary Magdalene, Mary of Egypt, for 123a Saint Paul, and for Saint Austin.

'And as Thou hast shewn Thy mercy to them, so shew Thy mercy to me and to all that ask Thee mercy of heart.

'The peace and the rest that Thou hast bequeathed to Thy disciples and Thy lovers, may Thou bequeath to me on earth and in Heaven without end.

'Have mind, Lord, of the woman that was taken in adultery and brought before Thee, and as Thou drove away all her enemies from her, and she stood alone by Thee, so verily may Thou drive away all mine enemies from me, both bodily and ghostly that I may stand alone by Thee, and make my soul dead to all the joys of this world, and quick and greedy to high contemplation in God.

'Have mind, Lord, of Lazarus that lay four days dead in his grave, and as I have been in that holy place, where Thy Body was quick and dead and crucified for men's sins and where Lazarus was raised from death to life, as surely Lord, if any man or woman be dead at this hour through deadly sin, if any prayer may help them, hear my prayers for them and make them live without end.

'Gramercy, Lord, for all those sins Thou hast kept me from, which I have not done, and gramercy, Lord, for all the sorrow that Thou hast given me for those I have done.

'For these graces, and for all other graces which are needful to me and to all the creatures on earth, and for all those that have faith and trust, or shall have faith and trust, in my prayers unto the world's end, such grace as they desire, ghostly or bodily, to the profit of their souls, I pray Thee, Lord, grant them, for the multitude of Thy mercy. Amen.'

NOTES

A short description of the Abbeys and Churches mentioned by Margery Kempe is given for those who may be unable to visit them personally. Many are in ruins, some have disappeared and the remainder are lacking their old stained glass and ornaments; but enough remains for lovers of architectural beauty to imagine the glory that is gone.

A. MOUNT GRACE PRIORY NEAR NORTHALLERTON. Now a ruin. Before the Reformation it belonged to the Carthusian monks. The note on the fly-leaf of the MS. shews that the book was at one time in their possession, and there are marginal notes and sketches by them on most of its pages.

B. PENTENEY ABBEY. The Augustinian Priory near Swaffham in Norfolk. It was founded in the reign of Henry II and is now a ruin.

C. DENNY ABBEY. A convent near Cambridge, founded by Mary of Valence in the reign of Edward III on the site of the Benedictine cell. The remains of the chapel are now used as a barn.

D. HAYLES ABBEY. The Cistercian Abbey near Winchcombe, a daughter house of Beaulieu in Hampshire, which it closely resembled. It is now a ruin, but has recently been cleared and laid out so that what is left can be seen and the ground plan traced. The relic of the Holy Blood was brought from Germany to Hayles by Edmund, second Earl of Cornwall.

E. ST. MARGARET'S, KING'S LYNN. The parish church. It was built in the thirteenth and fourteenth centuries, but in 1741 the spire of the south-west tower fell in a gale and crushed the roof of the nave. After this the nave and aisles were entirely rebuilt. The side chapels, which Margery Kempe refers to as the Prior's Chapel, the Jesyne and St. John's Chapel have disappeared. The lantern on the roof, through which she saw the sparks falling when the Guildhall was on fire, has been removed. The stained glass has gone. St. Margaret's was attached to the Benedictine Priory.

F. ST. NICHOLAS' CHAPEL, KING'S LYNN. This was one of the two chapels of ease, described in Chapter 25 as 'annexed' to St. Margaret's Church. The present chapel is a lovely piece of Perpendicular architecture built in 1410, with the tower of the old chapel, built in 1200. The stained glass has gone, as have the sedilia, the three carved stone canopied seats in the sanctuary, on which the priest and deacons sat. Only a portion of the canopy remains, enough to recall the beauty of it. The remainder has been roughly hacked away. The ten Miserere seats, of carved wood, were removed from the choir in 1852, and are now in the Victoria and Albert Museum, where they are at least safe from vandalism. As regards the dispute over the font and other privileges, two attempts were made to obtain these. The first was in 1378 when John Peye, a local chaplain, petitioned Pope Urban VI to grant them, which he did, provided they were not inimical to the interests of the

375

parish church of St. Margaret. But on that ground the grant was successfully opposed by many influential burgesses of the town, including John Brunham, Margery's father, and John Kempe, her father-in-law. Later, in 1432, after the present edifice had been built, the mayor, aldermen, burgesses and commons of Lynn made application to Robert Brunham, Prior of Norwich, the ecclesiastical superior of the Prior of St. Margaret's, again asking for the privileges to be granted. The matter was laid before Bishop Alnwick of Norwich who, as Margery says, eventually decided against it. Margery's family were again in opposition and no font was approved until after the Reformation, when the chapel had passed into other hands. The details are preserved in the archives of King's Lynn.

G. ST. JAMES' CHAPEL, KING'S LYNN. This was the other of the two chapels of ease 'annexed' to St. Margaret's Church. All that remains is a window and a buttress now included in a modern building.

H. THE GUILD HALL, KING'S LYNN. The present Guild Hall was built in 1423 to replace the one burnt in 1421, as described by Margery in Chapter 67, and contains many treasures, including the Cup traditionally bestowed on the town by King John after one of his visits.

I. THE GREY FRIARS MONASTERY, KING'S LYNN. All that remains of the Monastery of the Grey Friars (or Franciscans) is the tower, with its lantern. The Franciscans are also known as Friars Minor.

J. THE WHITE FRIARS MONASTERY, KING'S LYNN. The Gateway alone shews where the Monastery of the White Friars (or Carmelites) stood.

K. THE AUSTIN FRIARS were begging hermits of the order of St. Augustine. Their habits were black but differed somewhat from the Dominicans.

L. THE PREACHING FRIARS. These are the Dominicans, called from their dress, Black Friars. They had a monastery in King's Lynn, but the last remnant of its walls was demolished in 1845.

M. CAWOOD. 10 miles from York. In Saxon times the manor of Cawood was given by Athelstan to the fifteenth Archbishop of York. Cawood Castle, now a ruin, was the Archiepiscopal residence.

N. LEICESTER. The Abbey of Leicester was one of the abbeys of the Austin, or Black, Canons. There is little left of it, but the ruins have been cleared away, so that the layout can be traced by the foundations.

O. LEICESTER. All Hallows Church, now known as All Saints, the same edifice in which Margery was tried, is in High Cross Street, which was then the principal street in Leicester. It has a fine Norman doorway and a famous Early English font. The Church itself is in the Early Decorated style, but the chancel is modern.

P. WALSINGHAM. The Shrine of Our Lady of Walsingham was erected in 1061 by the Lady Richeldis at Our Lady's request. It was a replica of the Holy House at Nazareth and remained one of the most famous places of pilgrimage in Europe until it was destroyed at the Reformation. It has recently been rebuilt on its old site, and as nearly as possible in its old form.

NOTES

Q. ST. STEPHEN'S CHURCH, NORWICH. A fine example of late Perpendicular architecture. The chancel and nave were rebuilt between 1530 and 1550. The Trinity to which Margery refers as making offerings was an altar in the south aisle. Richard of Caistor, the 'Good Vicar', was at St. Stephen's Church from 1402 to 1420.

R. RAFNYS. No place of this name has been found near Jerusalem. Margery Kempe gives little information regarding her route in the Holy Land. It was, however, customary for pilgrims to land at Jaffa and, after visiting Jerusalem, to travel northwards towards Damascus and then to re-embark at Tyre or Beyrout. This journey is the one taken and described by Bertrandon de la Brocquière in 1432, and by Sir John Maundeville in 1322. The latter mentions the 'City of Raphane' as being between Damascus and the sea and this may be the 'Rafnys' of Margery.

CHRONOLOGY

MARGERY KEMPE gives no dates beyond those of the writing of the MS. It is therefore only possible to arrive at an approximate chronology by comparing such clues as she gives with known historical events and by reference to the archives of King's Lynn.

She was born about 1373 and married in 1393 to John Kempe who had been made a burgess that year. He may have been about twenty-seven then.

In 1414 she started on pilgrimage to the Holy Land and was in Rome for the celebrations over the confirmation of St. Bridget's canonization. This confirmation took place in 1415, and later in the same year, that of Agincourt, she returned via Middelburg to England. Two years later, about 1417, she repaid Richard what she had borrowed from him in Rome, before she started from Bristol for St. James in Spain. This was only a short absence, before and after which she was persecuted for Lollardism. There was great activity against the Lollards at that time, their leader, Sir John Oldcastle (Lord Cobham) having, in 1417, emerged from hiding, been apprehended and executed.

She was present at the burning of the Guildhall at Lynn in 1421. The accident to her husband seems to have happened about 1425 and his death and that of her son about 1432. This dates her journey with her daughter-in-law to Germany about 1434. Though she mentions in Chapter 5 Second Book, that whilst in Germany, there was 'open war between the English and those peoples', there was in fact no declared state of war in those parts then, and it must be presumed that she was referring to the continuous piracy and acts of confiscation that went on at that time, with consequent reprisals, between the English and German merchants. The possibility that she was referring to the Duke of Gloucester's incursion into Hainault in 1424, which would have been more or less on her intended route, is not consistent with other inferences. If she had been sixty then, she must have been over fifty at the time of her pilgrimage to the Holy Land, and it seems evident that she was considerably younger than that. Her first work, so ill written and illspelt as to have been almost unintelligible, was finished by 1432, and four years later she began to re-write it.

WYNKYN DE WORDE'S EXTRACTS

T HESE extracts are given in the order in which they occur in Wynkyn de Worde's book, but are not word for word the same as in Margery Kempe's MS.

Page	Lines	First and Last Words of Extract
349	10—13	I thank . . . slay thee.
349	17—20	I swear . . . without end.
83	2— 8	Daughter . . . My goodness.
354	10—14	Daughter . . . thy soul.
354	16—25	To bid . . . many beads.
355	27—28	Daughter . . . all thy heart.
361	10—13	Daughter . . . good and ill.
275	24—25	Daughter . . . full dear.
368	15—21	Lord, I pray Thee . . . so may it be.
295	13—29	She had . . . without end.
108	1— 6	When she saw . . . or the beast.
253	4—12	The more she . . . of the creature.
125	28—32	In anything . . . of thee.
259	24—13 on p. 260	Our merciful Lord . . . prosperity.
362	7—12	Thou hast also . . . done in deed.
361	27—30	Daughter . . . outwardly.
362	15—37	And daughter . . . never a deal.
361	19—23	I would, Lord . . . not mine.
117	7—11	Daughter . . . give it to.
257	26— 5 on p. 258	The same pardon . . . at Rafnys.
179	2— 5	That day . . . suffered tribulation.
181	9	Patience . . . miracle working.
197	8—11	Daughter . . . seven years.
206	25—26	Lord . . . my little pain.
235	5—10	Daughter . . . My Passion.
356	14—20	Ah! My dearworthy Lord . . . love God.

INDEX

INDEX

INDEX

Gold, 101, 136, 144, 214
Greystoke, Lady, 200
Guildhall, Lynn, fire at, 237, *note H*

Habergeon, 48
Haburion, 354
Hair-cloth, 32, 48, 348, 354
Hampol, Richard, 231
Hayles, 163, *note D*
Hessle, 193, 194
Hevyngham, Dom Thomas, 209
Hospital of St. Thomas, Rome, 123, 124, 140
Host, 80
Hull, 193
Humber, 193, 202, 203
Husband, 24, 30, 44, 47, 59, 96, 97, 155, 183, 204, 264, 307
Hylton, 69, 215

Image in chest, 119
Ipswich, 309, 310
Ireland, 118

Jelyan, Dame, 72
Jerusalem, 58, 78, 106, 111, 117
Jesyne, 233, 247, *note E*
Jews, 156, 187, 211, 274 *et seq.*, 362, 372
Jordan, 115

Kendale, Sir John, 181
Kerchief, Our Lady's, 122
King Henry V, 158, 251, 372

Lambeth, 64
Legate, Pope's, 100
Leicester, 164
—— Abbey of, 174, *note N*
—— Mayor of, 164 *et seq.*
—— Steward of, 167 *et seq.*
Lepers, 259, 260, 302
Lincoln, Bishop of, 60, 172
Lollard, 55, 165, 186, 194, 203
London, 64, 65, 204, 335
—— Man of, 203
—— Woman of, 326, 328, 332
Lynn, Prior of, 209, 250

Madness, Margery's, 24
—— Woman's, 262
Maiden, Margery's, 59, 74, 98, 101, 104, 140
Mantle, 61
Marcelle, 138
Marchale, Thomas, 159, 164, 168, 175
Marks, 157, 160
Marriage, 23

Married life, 30, 44, 47, 264
Mass-penny, 85
Master, 153
Melton Mowbray, 175
Middelburg, 149
Money, 58, 63, 85, 94, 98, 101, 117, 119, 135, 136, 151, 154, 156, 157, 160, 194, 292, 362
Monk, the wicked, 51
Moses' Rod, 175
Mount Grace Priory, *note A*

N., Master, 42
Newcastle, man of, 159
Nobles, 94, 98, 154, 214, 362
Norway, 315
Norwich, 67, 94, 96, 152, 221, 310
—— Bishop of, 94, 245

Oldcastle, Sir John, 198

Pafnys, 258
Palmer, 190
Passion of Christ, 271 *et seq.*
Patrick, 174 *et seq.*
Penteney Abbey, 92, *note B*
Pestilence, 292
Pilgrimages, 46, 58, 96, 162
Plenary Remission, 112, 122
Prophecies, 85
Proverb, 126
Prussia, 303
—— officials of, 317

Quarentyne, Mount of, 115

Rafnys, 117, *note R*
Removing, time of, 209
Repingdon, Bishop Philip, 60
Reynald, 340
Rhodes, Knights of, 123
Richard, 118, 123, 124, 135, 157
Ring, 61, 121
Robert, Master, 96, 204, 209, 247, 369
Rome, 58, 117, 118, 123, 147

Saints:
    Anne, 38
    Bonaventure, 215, 231
    Bridget, 69, 80, 139, 215
    Elizabeth, 39
    Elizabeth of Hungary, 231
    James, 58, 113, 156
    Jerome, 73, 147
    John the Baptist, 39

INDEX